SPLINTERED

**CRITICAL
RACE THEORY**

**AND THE
PROGRESSIVE
WAR ON TRUTH**

SPLINTERED

CRITICAL RACE THEORY

AND THE PROGRESSIVE WAR ON TRUTH

JONATHAN BUTCHER

BOMBARDIER
BOOKS

Published by Bombardier Books
An Imprint of Post Hill Press
ISBN: 978-1-63758-266-4
ISBN (eBook): 978-1-63758-267-1

Splintered:
Critical Race Theory and the Progressive War on Truth
© 2022 by Jonathan Butcher
All Rights Reserved

Cover Design by Matt Margolis

Post Hill Press
New York • Nashville
posthillpress.com

Published in the United States of America
2 3 4 5 6 7 8 9 10

DEDICATION

To Pearce, Elijah, Ruth, and Jack—
that we may always pursue the truth together.

TABLE OF CONTENTS

INTRODUCTION

When Nancy Andersen saw her son's homework assignment just before Thanksgiving in 2019, she "started getting really, really scared." Her son, who was attending a private K–8 school near Durham, North Carolina, brought home an essay his teacher had given the fourth-grade class, which stated that the first Thanksgiving celebration in the New World resulted in "genocide, environmental devastation, poverty, world wars, [and] racism."[1] The "Pilgrim heart" was one of "bigotry, hatred, greed, and self-righteousness."

Nancy was shocked. "This was scary and caught me by surprise," Nancy said. In fourth grade, children are as impressionable as they will ever be. School is a carnival of friends, the woody smell of pencils, and a fascination with the crisp edges of textbooks. At that age, the faces of American presidents and seventeenth-century explorers, Martin Luther King, Jr., and Sally Ride still evoke in children the same feelings of awe as pictures of movie stars and athletes. Children have a vague understanding that these people really did exist (or that some still do). To a child behind a desk, a baseball player's feats and those of an astronaut are much the same. A multidimensional picture showing that even heroic people are flawed, and the

---

1   Interview with Nancy Andersen, April 20, 2021, and Jacqueline Keeler, "Thanksgiving: A Native American View," available at Learning for Justice, "Thanksgiving Mourning," *https://www.learningforjustice.org/classroom-resources/lessons/thanksgiving-mourning*.

recognition that these flaws rarely make someone's entire life worth condemning, are important lessons—but lessons that are years away from fourth grade.

Nancy learned that her son's school was using material created by Learning for Justice, a group that creates K–12 lesson plans based on the idea that "race and racism are embedded in institutions and everyday life." School officials were also using lessons from Montessori for Social Justice, an organization trying to "dismantle systems of oppression" under the assumption that America is systemically oppressive. Montessori for Social Justice leaders released this statement in June 2020: "The United States was founded on the oppression, rape, murder, and enslavement of Black people."[2]

We can all agree that some Americans of prior generations failed to live up to the national promise of freedom and opportunity for everyone, regardless of skin color. Slavery, the reconstruction era after the Civil War, and Jim Crow laws all conflicted with the inalienable rights inscribed in the Declaration of Independence and the U.S. Constitution. But to say that America was founded on the oppression, rape, murder, and enslavement of black people and not the pursuit of religious freedom, economic opportunity, discovery, and any number of other reasons people came to the U.S. is a very cynical view of this country.

Furthermore, so much has changed in America over the past sixty years. In *The Disuniting of America,* first published in 1991, Arthur Schlesinger, historian and one-time advisor to John F. Kennedy, said, "There are few better arguments for the Bill of

---

2   Learning for Justice, "Color Blindness," *https://www.learningforjustice.org/professional-development/color-blindness,* Montessori for Social Justice, "Black Lives Matter: Statement from the Board," June 3, 2020, *https://montessoriforsocialjustice.org/black-lives-matter-montessori-for-social-justice/,* and Montessori Community School, "Diversity and Equity," *https://mcsdurham.org/about-mcs/diversity-and-equity.*

Rights than the revolution in race relations over the last half century."[3] Former civil rights activist and award-winning author Shelby Steele explains that there is a difference between individual acts of racism, which are a sad fact of human life, and believing that an entire nation is irredeemably racist or dedicated to preserving racism. Steele says, "Certainly there is still racial discrimination in America, but I believe that the unconscious replaying of our [black people's] oppression is now the greatest barrier to our full equality."[4]

Steele is right. And surveys find that most parents feel the same as Nancy when she says that she does not want her child being taught that America is "evil" or that it was founded by bigots.[5]

Nancy's experience, though, is becoming common around the country. Her son's school was using instructional materials based on critical race theory, a branch of the Marxist philosophy called Critical Theory, which has been spreading within and among colleges and universities for decades. Now, even teachers are teaching critical race theory in public and private schools, as will be described in the pages of this book.

As critical race theorist Angela Harris writes in *Critical Race Theory: An Introduction,* "Critical race theory not only dares to treat race as central to the law and policy of the United States, it dares to look beyond the popular belief that getting rid of racism means simply getting rid of ignorance, or encouraging everyone

---

3   Arthur Schlesinger, *The Disuniting of America: Reflections on a Multicultural Society* (New York: W.W. Norton & Company, 1998), p. 161.

4   Shelby Steele, *The Content of Our Character: A New Vision of Race in America* (New York: Harper Collins, 1998), p. 49.

5   See, for example, Parents Defending Education, "Parents Defending Education National Poll: Americans Overwhelmingly Reject 'Woke' Race and Gender Policies in K–12 Education," May 10, 2021, *https://www.defendinged.org/commentaries/parents-defending-education-national-poll-americans-overwhelmingly-reject-woke-race-and-gender-policies-in-K–12-education.*

to 'get along.'"[6] As I explain here, critical race theorists have little need to "get along" with others; they demand action, resistance to existing authorities, specifically. The critical worldview "questions the very foundations of the liberal order, including equality theory, legal reasoning, Enlightenment rationalism, and neutral principles of constitutional law."[7]

Translation: critical race theorists, and the critical theorists on which critical race theorists based their ideas, are attacking the basic ideas that make up Americans' national identity, represented by the pictures of their Founding Fathers, and the first female astronaut, and so many others who line the walls of any elementary school classroom. Critical theory is a gadfly, as historian Martin Jay once described the worldview, creating doubt in Americans' minds about their country's promises of liberty and opportunity.[8] Critical race theorists added to the original critical theory by saying society's goal is not equality for everyone under the law, but instead is power, including the power to force others to say that they are guilty of harming other people just because of the color of their skin.

"This is not innocence," Nancy says. "This is not fostering curiosity in a child."

Fed up with the response from school officials when she complained about these lessons in her son's class, Nancy moved her children to a new school. "I couldn't trust these people with my kids," Nancy says.

---

6   Angela Harris, "Foreword," in Richard Delgado and Jean Stefancic, eds., *Critical Race Theory: An Introduction*, (New York: New York University Press, 2001), p. xx.

7   Delgado and Stefancic, *Critical Race Theory: An Introduction*, p. 3.

8   Martin Jay, *The Dialectical Imagination: A History of the Frankfurt School and the Institute of Social Research* (Berkeley: University of California Press, 1996), p. 41.

OOO

Critical race theory is closer to your child's desk than you may realize. Lawmakers in Washington, DC, are making sure of that. On January 20, 2021, Inauguration Day, President Joe Biden signed seventeen executive orders—more on his first day on the job than the three previous presidents combined. Most of the orders overturned decisions that outgoing President Donald Trump had enacted, but one of these orders, in particular, demonstrates the stark differences between how Americans on the Right and Left sides of the partisan divide today think about the country that is their home.[9]

In an executive order titled "Advancing Racial Equity and Support for Underserved Communities through the Federal Government," President Biden's administration claimed ownership of American history, telling teachers and other educators to focus on racist acts and systems in America's *past*.[10] Since he who owns the past owns the future, as George Orwell recognized in *1984*, the new president's order has profound implications for this and future generations of Americans. The Oval Office is two states and hundreds of miles away from Nancy Andersen's son's former school, with its smell of pencils and classrooms full of bright-eyed children, but both sites were battlegrounds where adults of this generation were deciding how to explain their country's heritage to the next.

---

9   "2021 Joe Biden Executive Orders," *Federal Register, https://www.federalregister. gov/presidential-documents/executive-orders/joe-biden/2021*, and Amanda Shendruk, "Biden Signed More Executive Actions on Day One than Trump, Obama, and Bush Combined," Quartz, January 20, 2021, *https://qz.com/1960296/ what-executive-orders-did-joe-biden-sign-on-his-first-day/*.

10   The White House, "Executive Order on Advancing Racial Equity and Support for Underserved Communities Through the Federal Government," Presidential Actions, January 20, 2021, *https://www.whitehouse.gov/briefing-room/presidential-ac-tions/2021/01/20/executive-order-advancing-racial-equity-and-support-for-under-served-communities-through-the-federal-government/*.

In the "Advancing Racial Equity" order, President Biden revoked a commission that President Trump had created in the waning months of his presidency. In September 2020, President Trump had called for the creation of a 1776 Commission, a group of scholars whom President Trump would later task with promoting "patriotic education."[11] President Trump said that the commission was to "enable a rising generation to understand the history and principles of the founding of the United States in 1776 and to strive to form a more perfect union."

Just twenty years ago, the commission's directive would have been unremarkable—hardly worthy of censure. But President Biden's order on his first day in office rescinded the commission, and the new administration removed the 1776 Commission's report, which the commission had released just days earlier, from the White House website.

With the stroke of a pen, a new president of the United States deemed the principles of America's founding so controversial that a report describing them had to be removed.

Yet what were the details of the commission's story that President Biden so roundly rejected? Released on the observance of Martin Luther King, Jr.'s birthday in January 2021, the commission's report amounted to a forty-five-page summary of American history with facts and ideas that, until recently, were taught to American schoolchildren as a matter of basic education.[12] Led by Hillsdale College president Larry Arnn and former Vanderbilt University professor Carol Swain, "The 1776 Report" cited contributions from the Founding Fathers and Abraham Lincoln, and, in a welcome

---

11 Nicole Guadiano, "Trump Creates 1776 Commission to Promote 'Patriotic Education,'" *Politico*, November 2, 2020, *https://www.politico.com/news/2020/11/02/trump-1776-commission-education-433885*.

12 The President's Advisory 1776 Commission, "The 1776 Report," January 2021, *https://thf_media.s3.amazonaws.com/2021/The-Presidents-Advisory-1776-Commission.pdf*.

display of national modesty, the report also pointed to ways in which America failed to live up to its promise of equality for all under the law.

The commissioners wrote that, "neither America nor any other nation has perfected living up to the universal truths of equality, liberty, justice, and government by consent." Later, the commissioners acknowledged that Americans are constantly trying to help the nation live up to its ideals, saying that,

> [I]t is important to note that by design there is room in the Constitution for significant change and reform. Indeed, great reforms—like abolition, women's suffrage, anti-Communism, the Civil Rights Movement, and the Pro-Life Movement— have often come forward that improve our dedication to the principles of the Declaration of Independence under the Constitution.[13]

These admissions lend credibility to the commission's other statements about why "love for our country" is still important, beginning in our schools:

> A wholesome education also passes on the stories of great Americans from the past who have contributed their genius, sacrifices, and lives to build and preserve this nation. They strengthen the bond that a vast and diverse people can point to as that which makes us one community, fostered by civil political conversation and a shared and grateful memory.[14]

Despite this recognition of our Founders' mistakes and our need to improve the ways in which we apply our founding documents, members of the mainstream media called the report "racist." Critics accused the commissioners of warping the history

---

13   Ibid.
14   Ibid.

of slavery.[15] Some of these critics were quick to point out implications that they believed these ideas would have on schoolchildren. As the executive director of the American Historical Association, James Grossman, claimed, "The nonsense that's in this report will be used to legitimate similar nonsense."[16]

Praising America's ideals, while admitting Americans' failure to always live up to those ideals, is nonsense?

Upon closer inspection, Americans will find that President Biden's executive order and the "woke" critics of the 1776 Commission were simply following a trend sweeping K–12 schools around the U.S. This trend has dominated colleges' curricula for decades. Social justice warriors marching under the banner of critical race theory are now driving local elementary, middle, and high schools' lessons in the opposite direction of striving toward a "more perfect union."

Consider: California Department of Education officials created an ethnic studies curriculum that suggests that students create a "land acknowledgement poster" to recognize that "colonization is an ongoing process."[17] Students will finish pledging allegiance to the flag one morning only to open a lesson instructing them that they are living on "occupied/unceded/ seized territory." As explained in Chapter 2, the model curriculum also assigns students the late Howard Zinn's discredited *A People's History of the United States*, an erroneous retelling of U.S.

---

15 Derrick Clifton, "How the Trump Administration's '1776 Report' Warps the History of Racism and Slavery," NBC News, January 20, 2021, *https://www.nbcnews.com/news/ nbcblk/how-trump-administration-s-1776-report-warps-history-racism-slavery-n1254926*, and Maegan Vazquez, "Trump Administration Issues Racist School Curriculum Report on MLK Day," CNN.com, January 18, 2021, *https://www.cnn.com/2021/01/18/ politics/1776-commission-report-donald-trump/index.html*.

16 Collin Brinkley, "Joe Biden Revokes Donald Trump's '1776 Commission' Report Promoting 'Patriotic Education,'" *Philadelphia Inquirer*, January 21, 2021, *https:// www.inquirer.com/education/biden-revokes-trump-report-promoting-patriotic-educa- tion-20210121.html*.

17 California Department of Education, "Ethnic Studies Model Curriculum: Chapter 4: Sample Lessons and Topics," p. 330, *https://www.cde.ca.gov/ci/cr/cf/esmc.asp*.

history from Columbus to the late twentieth century.[18] While we must be honest about the stains of racism and discrimination on America's record, Zinn's penchant for finding oppression around every corner in his revisionist tale of U.S. history is enough to make even Marx blush.

State-level education officials in Michigan, Illinois, Ohio, and other states are promoting school materials similar to California's new ethnic studies curriculum. The teaching focuses on power structures in society and ethnic differences between groups instead of equality for everyone under the law. The authors of these new self-described "diversity and equity" programs and multicultural curricula strip ideas out of civics and history lessons that honor America's Founding Fathers, and even twentieth-century heroes who fought for civil rights for black Americans. From magazines and newspapers to social media and mainstream news outlets, and now K–12 school textbooks, critical race theorists are spreading their divisive ideas across American culture and delivering a message that America—today—is plagued by "systemic racism."

By trying to change students' perspectives on this country for the worse, these radical activists will have long-lasting effects on our culture. History is complicated. No textbook that is honest about history, civics, and social studies can drape superhero capes on the Founding Fathers and call the issue settled. Yet critical race theorists today are not designing coursework that considers America a land of opportunity while acknowledging failures to live up to this promise in the past. Instead, the woke new instructional materials that educators are beginning to use—textbooks, worksheets, online presentations, and more—to teach civics and history and even math

---

18   Howard Zinn, *A People's History of the United States,* reissue (New York: Harper Perennial Modern Classics, 2015). The first edition was published in 1980.

are inundated with ideas such as that "white supremacy shapes all of our lives and work," and, as California's new curriculum describes, that we should not see ourselves as Americans, but as members of different tribes competing for power over others' lives.[19]

◯◯◯

The first critical theorists were German Marxists. These radicals wanted to revise Karl Marx's ideas for public consumption after the German working class's failure to gain control of the country in the early twentieth century. This group of writers and teachers, which would become known as the Frankfurt School (so named because the first critical theory research institute was housed at the University of Frankfurt), was frustrated that the German revolutionaries had failed during the same period that the Bolsheviks took power in Russia and formed the Soviet Union. But these neo-Marxists understood that their ideas could change German culture as well as Germans' working conditions.

The Frankfurt School combined Marx's idea that the world is divided between oppressors and the oppressed with the postmodern belief that there is no authentic truth. The Frankfurt School preached that people from different backgrounds, ethnicities, and genders are engaged in a constant struggle for control over public and private institutions, such as schools and businesses. The writers and activists whom the Frankfurt School would inspire in America and around the world went on to argue in academic journals and across college classrooms that people should be skeptical of represen-

---

19 Clarice Brazas and Charlie McGeehan, "What White Colleagues Need to Understand," *Teaching Tolerance*, Issue 64 (Spring 2020), *https://www.learningforjustice.org/magazine/spring-2020/what-white-colleagues-need-to-understand.*

tative government and the rule of law—key characteristics of America's identity.

Parents and policymakers, and any American concerned for this country, must recognize, then, that if critical race theory becomes a staple of schools in the U.S., educators—whether knowingly or unwittingly—are planting the seeds of division. As Chapter 3 explains, the violent riots on college campuses in recent years are fueled by years of critical instruction on campuses. If you want to know what life looks like under critical race theory, look no further than the cancel culture dominating the ivory tower—as well as everyday life. It is only a few small steps from college campuses—where our future employees, neighbors, and schoolteachers are trained—to schools, workplaces, churches, and any other part of our communities.

Americans do not need an ideology that will drive them further apart. Today, conversations between Americans from different parts of the country, or even from similar locales but from different social, economic, and ethnic backgrounds, can resemble exchanges between people from different countries.

Americans recognize this divide. If you ask two people to explain the outcomes of the presidential elections of 2016 and 2020, you are likely to get two opposite answers. Likewise, different people have different explanations for why rioters stormed cities across the country during the COVID-19 pandemic in 2020. Or why violent activists stormed the U.S. Capitol on January 6, 2021. All may agree that a divide, a cultural "splintering" even, exists. After the attack on the Capitol, 74 percent of voters said that "democracy in the U.S. is under threat" in a Quinnipiac University poll.[20] As Americans watched protestors paint "Black Lives Matter" on

---

20 Quinnipiac University, "74% of Voters Say Democracy in the U.S. Is Under Threat, Quinnipiac University National Poll Finds; 52% Say President Trump Should Be Removed from Office," January 11, 2021, *https://poll.qu.edu/poll-release?releaseid=3733.*

busy streets during the summer of 2020, mainstream pundits breathlessly tried to explain how the rioters' destruction of black-, Latino-, immigrant-, and white-owned businesses in cities around the country did not conflict with the Black Lives Matter movement's claimed message of justice. While teachers unions called for defunding police during the riotous summer, a Gallup poll found that 81 percent of black Americans wanted the same levels of police presence, or more, than they currently had in their area.[21]

Increasingly, Americans find themselves talking past each other. Or not listening at all. Critical race theory is making things far worse. This worldview does not unite people from different backgrounds or with different opinions. As Derrick Bell, one of critical race theory's leading thinkers, put it, this worldview supports "wide-scale resistance."[22] Resistance to what? To America's creed of freedom, opportunity, and equality under the law for everyone.

Unfortunately, America is vulnerable to such resistance because of Americans' increasing lack of historical knowledge and civic understanding. The absence of this shared knowledge creates an intellectual vacuum—which is being filled by critical race theory—and demonstrates the lack of a common cultural understanding of important features of American life.

According to the Annenberg Public Policy Center at the University of Pennsylvania, which releases a survey of Americans' civic knowledge every Constitution Day (September 17), slightly more than half (51 percent) of this nationally representative sample of Americans could name all three branches of govern-

---

21   Lydia Saad, "Black Americans Want Police to Retain Local Presence," Gallup, August 5, 2020, *https://news.gallup.com/poll/316571/black-americans-police-retain-local-presence.aspx*.

22   Derrick A. Bell, "David C. Baum Memorial Lecture: Who's Afraid of Critical Race Theory?" *University of Illinois Law Review* (1995), p. 900, *http://publish.illinois.edu/lawreview/archives/volume-1995/*.

ment in 2020.[23] This was the highest percentage since the survey began in 2006, and a dramatic improvement from 2019, when just 39 percent of respondents could name all three branches.

That was the good news. The bad news is that nearly one in four respondents could not name *any* of the three branches. Also, 37 percent of respondents could not name a single First Amendment freedom, almost double the figure from the last time that question was asked on the survey in 2017.

Nearly one-quarter of the population being unable to understand even the most rudimentary aspects of how their government works is a frightening prospect. For only half to know all three branches of government is hardly consoling. So, when they are presented with an alternative, false, and misleading narrative about America and the vital issue of racial discrimination in its past, far too many Americans lack the knowledge to recognize and reject such revisionist history. As critical race theorists push their worldview into K–12 classrooms, there are few who can articulate responses.

OOO

To understand why the divisive ideas of critical theory and its offshoots, such as critical race theory, should concern each of us, not just those on college campuses or parents with school-age children, we should pause to consider what it is that creates a culture. University of Virginia scholar James Davison Hunter, who coined the term "culture war" in 1991, describes culture as the "sum total of attitudes, values, and opinions of the individuals making up a society."[24] These attitudes and opinions pro-

23   Annenberg Public Policy Center, "Annenberg Civics Knowledge Survey," University of Pennsylvania, September 17, 2020, *https://www.annenbergpublicpolicycenter.org/political-communication/civics-knowledge-survey/*.

24   James Davison Hunter, "The Enduring Culture War," in Hunter et al., eds., *Is There a Culture War? A Dialogue on Values and American Public Life* (Washington, DC: Brookings Institution Press, 2006), pp. 10–40.

vide a means for people in the same culture to communicate with each other. People from different cultures often struggle to agree on the basic assumptions about correct and incorrect behavior, as they have different traditions and ways of measuring right and wrong, happiness, and success in life.

The experience of an American anthropologist studying a northern African tribe illustrates this point. In 1966, Laura Bohannan was studying the Tiv people living in the then newly formed country of Nigeria.[25] She visited a Tiv community that had settled near the Benue River, a day's drive from what is now Nigeria's capital city of Abuja. These Tiv were farmers, primarily, but as Bohannan explains, the Tiv also brewed beer, the production and consumption of which helped pass the time during the Benue's flood season.

Before her second visit to the field, Bohannan spoke with a colleague at Oxford, the university at which she was based in England, who told her that Americans struggle to understand Shakespeare because the Bard was "a very English poet, and one can easily misinterpret the universal by misunderstanding the particular." Bohannan disagreed and argued that "human nature is pretty much the same the whole world over." They sparred over this idea without reaching agreement and parted ways with Bohannan's friend offering her a copy of *Hamlet* to take with her on her next expedition, to test its universality.

After she arrived in Nigeria, the rainy season set in, and Bohannan sat with a group of Tiv, drinking beer and sharing stories. Bohannan thought a retelling of *Hamlet* would be a good way to contribute to the conversation, and to test her theory of human nature. Bohannan writes that "here was my chance to prove *Hamlet* universally intelligible."

---

25   Laura Bohannan, "Shakespeare in the Bush," *Natural History* (August–September 1966), *http://people.morrisville.edu/~reymers/readings/ANTH101/Shakespeare_in_the_Bush-Bohannan.pdf.*

She immediately ran into trouble and discovered that people, in fact, do need to share foundational ideas, otherwise communication, never mind agreement, is impossible.

To start, Bohannan's companions could not understand the concept of Hamlet's father's ghost, because the closest thing the Tiv had to the idea of a "soul" was an omen or message from a witch. Eventually, they settled on the idea of a zombie, but Bohannan was still frustrated because she had to explain that the characters couldn't touch the ghost. As Bohannan described the encounter:

"No, a 'ghost' is someone who is dead but who walks around and can talk, and people can hear him and see him but not touch him."

They objected. "One can touch zombies."

"No, no! It was not a dead body the witches had animated to sacrifice and eat. No one else made Hamlet's dead father walk. He did it himself."

"Dead men can't walk," protested my audience as one man.

I was quite willing to compromise.

"A 'ghost' is the dead man's shadow."

But again they objected. "Dead men cast no shadows."

"They do in my country," I snapped.

Imagine Bohannan's difficulty explaining the trouble with Hamlet's uncle marrying his father's wife when the Tiv told her that they expected a dead man's brother to marry his wife and take care of his children and farmland.

Bohannan writes, "'In our country also,' [one of the Tiv elders] added to me, 'the younger brother marries the elder brother's widow and becomes the father of his children.'"

Another of the group assembled around the fire asked Bohannan if Hamlet's father and uncle "have one mother," to which Bohannan writes, "His question barely penetrated my mind; I was too upset and thrown too far off-balance by having one of the most important elements of *Hamlet* (that Claudius, Hamlet's uncle, married Gertrude, his mother) knocked straight out of the picture."

Bohannan pressed on with the play, but after arguments from the Tiv that Gertrude should not have waited to remarry and confusion over whether Hamlet's father's ghost could talk, eventually she says, "*Hamlet* was clearly out of my hands." She had to concede a wide variety of concepts regarding familial authority and social customs to the Tiv's interpretations.

Despite her best efforts, and after attempting to adhere to the general plot of the story, Bohannan's audience arrived at different conclusions about the characters' motivations and the moral lessons to be gleaned from Shakespeare's masterwork. For example, after Hamlet kills Polonius behind the curtain, thinking it was Claudius, a Tiv elder reasoned, "But if his father's brother has indeed been wicked enough to bewitch Hamlet and make him mad that would be a good story indeed, for it would be his fault that Hamlet, being mad, no longer had any sense and thus was ready to kill his father's brother."

Bohannan then says, "Hamlet was again a good story to them, but it no longer seemed quite the same story to me."

Bohannan's struggles demonstrate why cultural "habitus," a concept explained more in Chapter 4, is important. Habitus is the "continuity and stability of culture, especially as it frames the parameters of our experience," explains Hunter.[26] When President Biden's administration rescinded the 1776 Commission and the commission's report, the president decided that the story of America's promise of liberty for all, an idea that shapes our habitus, was no longer the same story that Americans had shared for ages.

OOO

The recent failures to find common ground in the midst of these complicated episodes is a festering sore on our civic life. Those holding out hope that the Civil War and the civil rights movement taught us that violence is the worst way to settle our differences, should be disappointed by the riots of summer 2020 and the storming of the U.S. Capitol building in January 2021. We do not have to agree on everything. But we find ourselves today unable to even conduct a conversation on our problems and their causes from the same starting point. This makes consensus on issues of law and policy rare occurrences. And, the problem is more than an inability to agree on issues of policy: A cultural chasm is developing between Americans over the basic understanding of their history.

In 2006, Hunter explained the cultural divide this way, connecting it to the key institutions of K–12 schools:

> [U]nderneath the myriad political controversies over so-called cultural issues, there were yet deeper crises over the very meaning and purpose of the core institutions of American civilization...Beyond the politics of educational curriculum, the quarrels over textbooks in public schools constituted a more serious

---

26 Hunter, *The Death of Character: Moral Education in an Age Without Good or Evil* (New York: Basic Books, 2000), p. 291.

disagreement over the national ideals Americans pass on to the next generation.... Cumulatively, these debates concerning the wide range of social institutions amounted to a struggle over the meaning of America.[27]

The 1776 Commission's saga—the necessity for its creation, as well as its demolition—did not start in Washington. It began in the general culture, among writers and thinkers in universities delivering critical race theory's message of oppression. Critical race theorists have moved to K–12 schools, bringing that message into American homes, as parents are learning how proponents of the dogma are teaching their children to treat people based on the color of their skin—a nightmarish notion that should have been left to rust after the civil rights movement.

Most American policymakers, taxpayers, and families have quite literally lost influence over this crucial platform for the preservation of ideas of personal character and national identity. The instructional content in schools is largely a mystery to parents or anyone who is not involved with a school board—until objectional material comes home in a child's backpack.

For example, in 2020, Texas Governor Greg Abbott made headlines when he said that a teacher who instructed middle school students to write about a cartoon comparing modern-day police officers to members of the KKK should be fired.[28] But Abbott wasn't the only one shocked by the course content. Once they saw the assignment, many parents were furious. "Don't indoctrinate our children to think this way,"

---

27   Hunter, "The Enduring Culture War," in *Is There a Culture War?* pp. 10–40.
28   Brian Lopez, "Gov. Abbott Wants Wylie ISD Teacher Fired for Using Cartoon Comparing Police with KKK," *Fort Worth Star-Telegram*, August 24, 2020, *https://www. star-telegram.com/news/local/education/article245201370.html.*

one parent told the *Fort Worth Star-Telegram*.[29] Parents should be asking how the lesson made its way into the classroom in the first place without them, or another parent of a child in the class or policymakers, knowing.

Since politics is located downstream from culture, it was only a matter of time before critical race theory spread from colleges and K–12 schools to Washington. Critical race theorists have found a welcoming administration in President Biden's team, and federal policymakers are attempting to enshrine the ideas in federal law. In April 2021, President Biden proposed that the U.S. Department of Education award federal spending to public school teachers who commit to applying critical race theory in civics and history instruction.[30] If approved, the rule would have been part of the largest federal law governing Washington's oversight of K–12 schools (more on the fate of what became of this proposed rule in the epilogue to this book). Critical race theory will have traveled from culture (homes and schools) to politics (government)—and will then be funneled back to culture in an ever more destructive cycle.

Because not everyone was treated equally under the law at the time of the Constitution's adoption, critical theorists, specifically critical race theorists, consider America's creed itself to be at fault, when it is the failure of some people in American history to live up to this creed. Gunnar Myrdal's classic book *An American Dilemma*, which helped to set the stage among intellectuals in the 1940s for the 1960s civil rights movement, argued

---

29   Ibid.
30   U.S. Department of Education, Office of Elementary and Secondary Education, "Proposed Priorities—American History and Civics Education," *Federal Register*, Vol. 86, No. 73 (April 19, 2021), p. 20348, *https://www.federalregister.gov/documents/2021/04/19/2021-08068/proposed-priorities-american-history-and-civics-education#footnote-2-p20349*.

that America could not be a nation based on liberty and equality while discriminating against people based on their race.

Something would have to give. Either the American creed needed to change, or America's discriminatory and racial policies would have to go. "Americans of all national origins, classes, regions, creeds, and colors, have something in common: a social ethos, a political creed. It is difficult to avoid the judgment that this 'American Creed' is the cement in the structure of this great and disparate nation," Myrdal wrote.[31] Modern-day critical race theorists, such as Ibram X. Kendi, dismiss Myrdal's work while failing to explain Myrdal's central ideas (note that Kendi says he is "inspired" by critical race theorists and that the theory is "foundational" to his work[32]). We will consider the significance of Myrdal's ideas in Chapter 4.

Fortunately for all Americans, the civil rights movement resulted in policymakers' erasing racial prejudice from American law. Critical race theorists' insistence today that people are guilty of oppression because of their skin color, not their character or their actions, is an affront to the sacrifices of those who so bravely took part in this movement. No single law or Supreme Court decision, such as *Brown v. Board of Education*, can magically erase racism in America. But these policy changes do correctly prohibit official racism and begin to change cultural assumptions—our habitus—so that discrimination is rejected at every turn.

President Trump created the 1776 Commission in response to journalists' attempts to rewrite American history based on the idea that the American story is only about racial oppres-

31   Gunnar Myrdal, *An American Dilemma: The Negro Problem and Modern Democracy*, Vol. I (London: Routledge, 2017), p. 3. Originally published by Harper & Row in 1944.

32   Jason Johnson, "Critical Race Theory Is a Convenient Target for Conservatives," Slate.com, June 12, 2021, *https://slate.com/news-and-politics/2021/06/critical-race-theory-ibram-kendi-racism-racists.html*.

sion. Editorial essays from the *New York Times Magazine*'s "1619 Project" released alongside K–12 lessons describing the project's essays in 2019, argued that every part of our nation's past should be explained with respect to the institution of slavery, claiming that the nation's ideals of liberty and equality were "false when they were written."[33] This 1619 Project curriculum, now in some four thousand five hundred schools, is but one example of K–12 materials that claim that the U.S. is irredeemably racist.[34]

The high-profile 1619 Project also made inaccurate claims about early Americans' motivations for fighting the Revolutionary War, such as the idea that one of colonists' primary motivations was to protect slavery, and incorrectly placed the roots of capitalism squarely on pre-Civil War plantations. Pulitzer Prize-winning historians and scholars of economic history have refuted these two false claims and other factual inaccuracies. Still, the mainstream media, which have become a staunch ally of the woke agenda, are betting that many in the general public will not notice the falsehoods—another sign of the sad state of history and civics knowledge in America today.[35]

The 1619 Project has reached a wide audience thanks to the *Times* and the Pulitzer Center's (separate from the center that awards Pulitzer Prizes) support. These outlets are recasting the nation's entire history as racist. Remarkably, given the project's condemnation of American ideals and

33 Nikole Hannah Jones, "Our Democracy's Founding Ideals Were False When They Were Written. Black Americans Have Fought to Make Them True," *New York Times Magazine*, August 14, 2019, *https://www.nytimes.com/interactive/2019/08/14/magazine/black-history-american-democracy.html.*

34 Jeff Barrus, "Nikole Hannah-Jones Wins Pulitzer Prize for 1619 Project," Pulitzer Center, May 4, 2020, *https://pulitzercenter.org/blog/nikole-hannah-jones-wins-pulitzer-prize-1619-project.*

35 Lindsey M. Burke, Jonathan Butcher, Mike Gonzalez, and Emilie Kao, "The Culture of American K-12 Education: A National Survey of Parents and School Board Members," Heritage Foundation *Special Report* No. 241, January 11, 2021, p. 19, *https://www.heritage.org/sites/default/files/2021-01/SR241.pdf.*

its factual inaccuracies and false claims, President Biden's administration has cited the 1619 Project as an example of civics and history content that K–12 educators should use in schools.[36] The 1619 Project, like the ethnic studies programs described earlier, are aligned with critical race theory's pernicious perspective that tries to weaken Americans' allegiance to their nation.

Parents want educators and students to wrestle with issues of race and virtue and freedom—we cannot, nor should we, avoid these issues. Fifty-nine percent of parents who responded to a nationally representative survey in April and May 2020 want educators to teach students that "the birth of the nation is 1776, the year the colonists declared independence," not 1619, when English settlers brought slaves to what would become the Virginia colony.[37] Seventy percent of respondents to this survey said that teachers should tell students that "slavery was a tragedy that harmed the nation, but our freedom and prosperity represent who we are as a nation, offering a beacon to those wanting to immigrate here." We have to reckon with this debate, understand the opposing sides, and then choose to live and raise the next generation in a culture in which we celebrate our differences while clinging to America's promises, along with historical facts in any retelling of the American story.

This book describes the sources of these pressing problems and offers solutions. Policymakers and educators can help us to preserve a culture in which American history gives us things to learn

---

36   U.S. Department of Education, Office of Elementary and Secondary Education, "Proposed Priorities—American History and Civics Education."

37   Burke, Butcher, Gonzalez, and Kao, "The Culture of American K-12 Education: A National Survey of Parents and School Board Members."

from, to mourn, and to celebrate. Chapter 1 introduces some of the critical content found in K–12 schools today and explains critical theory's Marxist origins. Once members of the Frankfurt School came to America, their ideas evolved into critical legal theory, which argues that American law is systemically racist, and later critical race theory, which incorporates all the ideas of critical theory and critical legal theory and adds an obsession with racial differences. Those designing "ethnic" or "multicultural" curricula, along with diversity training programs for students and teachers, are basing their materials on critical theory's intellectual foundation.

Chapter 2 offers examples of woke instructional material in K–12 schools that teaches students to judge others based on their skin color, and calls for educators to treat students differently based on race. These shocking examples of prejudice directly conflict with the civil rights movement's achievements and goals and contradict federal civil rights laws.

College campuses around the U.S. offer a glimpse of the intolerant, sometimes violent, societies that exist under the auspices of critical theory. It was on college campuses in the U.S. that critical theorists from Germany developed their philosophy, teachings that spread to law schools and colleges of education, where K–12 teachers are trained. Chapter 3 explains that at the shout-downs and riots on campuses over the past decade, students could be heard shouting words and phrases from critical theory's (and critical race theory's) lexicon—which should serve as a warning to everyone.

Chapter 4 explains Americans' general lack of civic and historical knowledge. Student achievement in K–12 schools serves as a clear example, but so, too, do the examples of school leaders who have lost sight of schools' civic mission to prepare children to be participating members of society.

In losing sight of this mission, school leaders have created a moral vacuum into which critical theorists are inserting their ideas of constant oppression and class- and race-based conflicts. This chapter then outlines three cultural assumptions—examples of habitus—that Americans need to share, and to teach their children, in order to restore a sense of national identity around America's creed. These three cultural assumptions form the basis of a "civil theory" we can use to reject critical race theory. Parents, policymakers, and educators should roundly reject critical race theory, and design content for classrooms, especially civics content, around these ideas:

First, while too many Americans failed to live up to their national creed in the past, this fact does not represent a shortcoming of the creed, but a failure by individuals and communities in prior generations to fulfill it. America's commitment to life, liberty, and the pursuit of happiness and of human equality before God and under the law, beliefs central to America's identity, are the ideas we need to apply today. These ideas can help us to overcome the divisive ideas of critical race theory and provide a sense of national identity we can all celebrate.

Second, black Americans' successes in building a culture and participating in the economy even under the terrible conditions that slavery and Jim Crow laws caused are extraordinary. We—all of us—should celebrate these accomplishments and teach the attitudes and behaviors that made these successes possible. These achievements are part of America's shared experience. This in no way minimizes the hardships and injustice that black Americans faced. Rather, this conversation would elevate their successes as an example of human accomplishment in the face of adversity.

Third, our society will be defined by our cultural disposition on how we treat those with whom we disagree. One of the most lasting, time-tested beliefs is that we should love our enemies. This attitude combines several virtues, including love, kindness, gratitude, and humility, on which the founders based our constitutional republic. Critical race theory stands in stark contrast to loving your neighbor (never mind loving your enemy) and is rooted in conflict and resistance and a perpetual search for enemies. No nation can long survive when adults teach these ideas to the next generation.

OOO

We should all be concerned about losing an appreciation for a civil society that allows everyone, regardless of ethnicity or background, to pursue the American dream.

This dream is being lost. To wit: in October 2020, the Falls Church City School Board in Virginia surveyed students, teachers, and community members and asked whether Thomas Jefferson Elementary School and George Mason High School should be renamed due to their namesakes owning slaves.[38] Both of these men were not only Founding Fathers (though Mason's refusal to sign the Constitution because, in part, he believed the members of the Constitutional Convention did not "deal more harshly with the institution of slavery" resulted in historians considering him the "forgotten founder"), but have special historical significance for Virginia.[39]

---

38 Falls Church City Public Schools, "School Board Finalizes School Renaming Process," October 7, 2020, *https://www.fccps.org/o/fccps/article/322150.*

39 George Mason University Antonin Scalia Law School, "George Mason, the Man," *https://www.law.gmu.edu/about/mason_man.*

Though a simple majority those surveyed—including parents and staff members—wanted to keep the names, the board "canceled," to use a word common in woke parlance, both Jefferson and Mason. Yet Mason was the author of the Virginia Declaration of Rights, which predated even the Declaration of Independence. Mason's Declaration had imitators across the U.S., and even overseas following its introduction in Virginia.[40] The first and second-to-last sections of the Virginia Declaration are especially relevant for Americans struggling to come to terms with critical race theory's ideas today:

> *That all men are by nature equally free and independent and have certain inherent rights, of which, when they enter into a state of society, they cannot, by any compact, deprive or divest their posterity; namely, the enjoyment of life and liberty, with the means of acquiring and possessing property, and pursuing and obtaining happiness and safety.*

And

> *That no free government, or the blessings of liberty, can be preserved to any people, but by a firm adherence to justice, moderation, temperance, frugality, and virtue; by frequent recurrence to fundamental principles; and by the recognition by all citizens that they have duties as well as rights...*[41]

If we want everyone to be able to pursue the "enjoyment of life and liberty" and to obtain "happiness and safety," we allow race-based discrimination in schools at our own peril. My hope is that, when the next generation looks back at this

---

40   Ibid.
41   Commonwealth of Virginia, "Virginia Law: Constitution of Virginia," *https://law.lis. virginia.gov/constitution/article1/section15/#:~:text=That%20no%20free%20government %2C%20nor,rights%2C%20and%20that%20such%20rights.*

one, it will find examples of Americans who made core values and beliefs about the nation's character inseparable from the teaching of civics and accurate history. The pursuit of these values and truths is essential for saving our culture—and our country.

CHAPTER 1

THE PROBLEM

In May 2021, a CNN writer described critical race theory as "a concept that's been around for decades and that seeks to understand and address inequality and racism in the U.S."[1] Sounds innocent enough. According to the American Bar Association, critical race theory is "a practice of integrating race and racism in society that emerged in the legal academy and spread into other fields of scholarship."[2]

True, critical race theorists base their philosophy on critical legal theory, expanding legal interpretations of government policy to include race. But critical race theory is decidedly not just trying to "address inequality" and "integrate" aspects of race into public and private life. Though the passage of the Civil Rights Act of 1964 made racial discrimination illegal, and the civil rights movement made racial bias culturally repugnant, critical race theorists designed a worldview that injects racial prejudice back into American life.

---

1   Faith Karimi, "What Critical Race Theory Is—and Isn't," CNN.com, May 6, 2021, *https://www.cnn.com/2020/10/01/us/critical-race-theory-explainer-trnd/index.html.*

2   Janel George, "A Lesson on Critical Race Theory," *Human Rights Magazine,* Vol. 46, No. 2 (January 2021), *https://www.americanbar.org/groups/crsj/publications/human_rights_magazine_home/civil-rights-reimagining-policing/a-lesson-on-critical-race-theory/.*

Critical race theory is an offshoot of critical theory, imported to the United States between the world wars by a group of German Marxists, whose ideology—that society consists of oppressors and victims—became known as the Frankfurt School. Critical race theory posits that American society consists of oppressors and victims as defined by skin color. Critical race theorists view America's laws, government, and society with disdain, and this disdain has infiltrated K–12 schools. Examples abound of education officials and teachers who are trying to train children to be activists and to be prepared to be disruptive, not to help children grow into adults who want to be part of a civil society.

In a *Los Angeles Magazine* interview from August 2021, Cecily Myart-Cruz, president of United Teachers Los Angeles (UTLA), the teachers union in the nation's second-largest school district, approvingly captured the essence of critical race theory in K–12 schools today. The Los Angeles Unified School District is one of many districts around the country that assigns classroom materials based on critical race theory. Myart-Cruz said that even though pandemic-related school closures in the 2020–2021 school year may have limited instructional time, students learned how to be rioters after watching the violence in summer 2020. Unbelievably, Myart-Cruz said, "There is no such thing as learning loss. Our kids didn't lose anything. It's OK that our babies may not have learned all their times tables…. They know the difference between a riot and a protest. They know the words *insurrection* and *coup*."[3]

Hardly an innocent theory.

---

3   Jason McGahan, "Exclusive: Cecily Myart-Cruz's Hostile Takeover of L.A.'s Public Schools," *Los Angeles Magazine*, August 26, 2021, *https://www.lamag.com/citythinkblog/cecily-myart-cruz-teachers-union/*.

And, if critical race theory is merely an attempt to understand inequality in America, why would informed parents fear that their children accept the theory's main ideas? Why would parents and teachers feel the need to speak anonymously about what critical race theory is teaching children, and why are parents and teachers terrified of what will happen if those pushing the theory in schools find out?

Megan, a teacher and parent living near Los Alamitos, California, did not want her real name to be used. She thought she would get fired for speaking out against the things happening in the district where she teaches and the neighboring district where her children go to school. Some of her discomfort grew out of the atmosphere of secrecy that school administrators developed.

She noticed that some essays her children were assigned to read were written by people claiming to be racist themselves— because of the color of their skin (hint: white), not because of any wrongs the essay's authors had committed. Then, at a district board meeting, Megan saw that district officials were adopting new standards that aligned with "social justice," a term that may sound admirable, but officials did not allow any time for public comments or questions about the new standards. "Something is going on here," Megan told me.

The district was adopting social justice standards created by Learning for Justice, an arm of the radical leftist Southern Poverty Law Center. (Nancy Andersen, our parent from the introduction, was also shocked by Learning for Justice's racially biased materials.)[4] The standards feel less like a lesson plan and

---

4   Hosam Elattar, "Los Alamitos School Board to Vote on Social Justice Standards; Anaheim District to Require Ethnic Studies," *Voice of OC*, May 11, 2021, *https://voiceofoc.org/2021/05/los-alamitos-school-board-to-vote-on-social-justice-standards-anaheim-district-to-require-ethnic-studies/*, and Learning for Justice, "Social Justice Standards," *https://www.learningforjustice.org/frameworks/social-justice-standards*.

more like a little red book; the introduction contains the phrase "collective action" three times in the same paragraph. Students are to "affirm and accurately describe their membership in multiple identity groups"—this latter phrase is explained below. The standards emphasize "respect" (since we are counting, the standards use "respect" twenty times), while repeated discussions of tribal identities are found throughout. "America" is used once, in the title of an assigned book.

The standards' emphasis on racial identities at the expense of a shared idea of being Americans was not lost on Megan, and intense community debates over critical race theory are becoming more common. In Rockwood, Missouri, a group of parents who wanted to remain anonymous exposed an email that an English teacher in their school district had sent to other school officials with ideas for ways to keep parents in the dark about what was happening in the classroom.[5] The email stated: "[L]et's face it, our parents [the parents of the students in this school district] are talking across buildings and grade levels, so knowing what these parents are honing in [sic] on can be helpful." The teacher explained that school leaders had received so many complaints from parents about lessons on "power imbalances" in society and "cultural identity" that the feedback could not be considered "isolated events."

The teacher's advice? *To hide* the new critical content from parents: "Right now, DON'T use the word privilege," the teacher advises (uppercase in original). Parents "believe that the word

5 Luke Rosiak, "School District Tells Principals to Create Fake Curriculum to Sent Parents After Complains of Indoctrination," *The Daily Wire*, April 28, 2021, *https://www.dailywire.com/news/rockwood-schools-fake-curriculum-parents-indoctrination*. See also Parents Defending Education, "Rockwood School District Teachers Receive Email Telling Them to Hide Lesson Materials, Assignments from Parents," *https://defendinged.org/incidents/rockwood-school-district-teachers-receive-email-telling-them-to-hide-lesson-materials-assignments-from-parents/*.

activists means to go out and spit in cops [sic] faces and protest by setting cars on fire (yes, this is a bit of leap, or maybe it isn't)," the email reads.

When parents express their concerns, the teacher says, "This doesn't mean throw out the lesson and find a new one. Just pull the resource off Canvas [a digital classroom program where teachers can share information with parents] so parents cannot see it." Later, the teacher says, "Keep teaching! Just don't make everything visible on Canvas."

Parent-led groups, such as No Left Turn in Education, exposed this correspondence.[6] When Parents Defending Education, a grassroots organization advocating for parents' rights in local schools, contacted Rockwood officials, district leaders said that the email does not reflect the district's values. Too late, of course. The internet has a difficult time forgetting.

○○○

Let's count the usage of a particular word once again: in his inaugural address, President Biden used the word "unity" nine times.[7] Just four months later, his administration encouraged teachers to follow a script that divides Americans into tribes according to race, sex, and other God-given characteristics in the proposed federal rule from April 2021[8] described in the introduction. Officials who drafted the rule claimed that America is "systemically racist," and cited *The New York Times*' 1619 Project as an example of the work on which teachers should rely for civics and history classes. Left unmentioned in the *Federal Register* were

---

6   Email correspondence with Elana Fishbein, July 31, 2021.
7   The White House, "Inaugural Address by President Joseph R. Biden, Jr.," January 20, 2021, *https://www.whitehouse.gov/briefing-room/speeches-remarks/2021/01/20/inaugural-address-by-president-joseph-r-biden-jr/.*
8   U.S. Department of Education, Office of Elementary and Secondary Education, "Proposed Priorities—American History and Civics Education."

the project's errors and the *Times*'s insistence that the year 1619 should replace 1776 as America's birthdate, an idea that surveys find is unpopular with parents.[9]

How can the president cry "unity" at one moment, while his administration shouts "divide" in the next?

Critical race theory's principles are heavy on division. Chapter 2 reviews lessons from schools around the country in depth, but just a small sample of teaching material based on critical race theory should be enough to trouble any parent hoping to raise children who will judge people by their character, not the color of their skin:

- In July 2020, officials at the Smithsonian Institution's National Museum of African American History and Culture apologized for and removed an educational infographic titled "Aspects & Assumptions of Whiteness & White Culture in the United States," stating that they had "erred." According to the infographic, the notions of "self-reliance," "the nuclear family," "hard work is the key to success," "work before play," having a "plan for the future," and "be polite" are all part of an oppressive white culture and evidence of systemic racism.[10] The museum, claiming that "Education is core to our mission," had intended that educators use this infographic in the classroom.

- In Michigan, Governor Gretchen Whitmer's Governor's Educator Advisory Council recommends that teachers revise their instructional practices by assigning articles,

9   Burke, Butcher, Gonzalez, and Kao, "The Culture of American K-12 Education: A National Survey of Parents and School Board Members."

10   Chacour Koop, "Smithsonian Museum Apologizes for Saying Hard Work, Rational Thought Is 'White Culture,'" *Miami Herald*, July 17, 2020, *https://www.miamiherald.com/news/nation-world/national/article244309587.html.*

such as "103 Things White People Can Do for Racial Justice," in which the author says that students should assume that every act is racist and always ask: "How much racism was in play?"[11]

- A group called Woke Kindergarten has created videos to teach kindergarteners—five- and six-year-olds—about transgender and racial minority political activists. Another video displays pictures of Black Lives Matter posters and police barricades while asking young children to find basic colors (for example, red, blue, and yellow) in the pictures.[12]

Such ideas divide communities by brainwashing children to always see people in terms of skin color and ethnicity, whether it is relevant or not. critical race theorists use race as a wedge to drive people apart, so that the focus of public life becomes not unity, but power. Boston University professor and author Ibram X. Kendi, who told the online magazine *Slate* that his "antiracist" ideas are based on critical race theory, writes, "The language of colorblindness—like the language of 'not racist'—is a mask to hide racism."[13] These lessons do not ask students to consider the effects of slavery or the harm of Jim Crow laws, but to believe that racism is all-pervasive in law, policymaking, and culture today. These are not lessons in diversity, but lessons in how to reject what should be our shared sense of civil behavior and right and wrong—such as

11   Corinne Shutack, "103 Things White People Can Do for Racial Justice," Medium, August 13, 2017, *https://medium.com/equality-includes-you/what-white-people-can-do-for-racial-justice-f2d18b0e0234*, and Michigan Governor's Educator Advisory Council, "Social Justice & Anti-Racist Educator Resources," *https://www.michigan.gov/documents/mde/GEAC_Resources_697529_7.pdf.*

12   Woke Kindergarten, "60-Second Texts," *https://www.wokekindergarten.org/60secondtexts.*

13   Ibram X. Kendi, *How to Be an Antiracist* (New York: One World, 2019), p. 10.

being polite, which the Smithsonian's infographic condemned as part of "white culture."

If critical race theory's elements sound like the opposite of the civil rights movement's lessons and provisions in the Civil Rights Act of 1964, it is because critical race theorists do not believe that equality under the law set the nation on a course to fulfilling its national ideals. Critical race theorist and law professor Angela Harris, who wrote the foreword to *Critical Race Theory: An Introduction*,[14] explained critical theory's general goals like so: "Challenging power relations, as critical theorists love to do, means provoking anger, disquiet, anxiety, and even fear in those with a settled understanding of who they are and where they belong."[15]

This chapter traces critical race theory's origins and explains the theory's Marxist roots. Once these roots are exposed, we can match critical race theory's principles with the lessons found in classrooms around the country. A teacher does not have to use the words "critical race theory" to capture the racially discriminatory ideas at the very center of this worldview. Once parents and policymakers know what ideas to look for when trying to identify critical ideas, they will recognize just how deeply embedded critical race theory has become in K–12 classrooms.

○○○

Critical race theorists' obsession with power and systemic racism did not originate in America. As historian Martin Jay explains, a group of German academics of Jewish descent developed critical theory in the early twentieth century. These writers and

---

14   Angela Harris, "Foreword," in Delgado and Stefancic, *Critical Race Theory: An Introduction*.

15   Angela Harris, "Compassion and Critique," *Columbia Journal of Race and Law*, Vol. 1, No. 3 (July 2012), p. 328, *http://blogs.law.columbia.edu/abolition1313/files/2020/08/Angela-Harris-Compassion-and-Critique-1.pdf*.

thinkers were searching for the "true" or "pure" Marxism.[16] These intellectuals, led by the independently wealthy Marxist Felix Weil, were frustrated that the German working class had failed to stage a revolution and turn Germany into a socialist state around the same time as the Bolsheviks transformed Russia into the Soviet Union after World War I. Critical theorist Herbert Marcuse, one of the original members of the Frankfurt School, later wrote that in the Frankfurt School's early days, he wanted to know "just why, at a time when authentic conditions for revolution were present, the revolution [in Germany] had collapsed or been defeated."[17]

In 1923, Weil called together like-minded intellectuals for a First Marxist Work Week (*Erste Marxistische Arbeitswoche*), where a small gathering of these frustrated socialists conceived the idea for an independent research center. The "goal of [this] revolutionary activity was understood as the unifying of theory and praxis, which would be in direct contrast to the situation prevailing under capitalism."[18] The First Marxist Work Week participants believed that people who succeeded in businesses operating in free market economies were oppressing the working class, and that Marxists should *act* (engage in "praxis") to disrupt capitalism. Weil's group wanted its revolutionary ideas to be applied. The members felt that the working class as a whole was not revolutionary enough in Germany to take power even during the turbulent years that followed the war. Critical theorists, however, would later argue that anyone who feels oppressed, including ethnic minorities everywhere, should live

---

16   Martin Jay, *The Dialectical Imagination: A History of the Frankfurt School and the Institute of Social Research* (Berkeley: University of California Press, 1996).

17   Stuart Jeffries, *Grand Hotel Abyss: The Lives of the Frankfurt School* (New York: Verso, 2016).

18   Jay, *The Dialectical Imagination*, p. 4.

out Critical Theory's commitment to resisting the authorities in government and society.[19]

Other Marxists from that period, including Max Horkheimer and Theodor Adorno, joined Weil's group, and they formed their institution housed at the University of Frankfurt. The group considered naming the new department the Institute for Marxism, but, Jay says, "abandoned [the name] as too provocative." Eventually, however, the school did earn the nickname Café Marx.[20]

By 1933, the Nazis held power in Germany and forced the members of the Frankfurt School to flee, first to Geneva and eventually to America, where Columbia University officials invited them to relocate. Jay, who was sympathetic to the critical theorists' goals, recognized the irony in the Frankfurt School's move to America: "And so the International Institute for Social Research, as revolutionary and Marxist as it had appeared in Frankfurt in the twenties, came to settle in the center of the capitalist world, New York City."[21]

This irony is one of many surrounding the Frankfurt School, some darker than others: these Jewish intellectuals established their Institute for Social Research in Frankfurt, the city where chemical and pharmaceutical conglomerate IG Farben manufactured the infamous Zyklon B used in Auschwitz gas chambers.[22] These devoted Marxists, such as Leo Löwenthal and Horkheimer, came from wealthy families whose parents and relatives had made their fortunes in capitalist business. Today, of course, Frankfurt is home to the largest of Germany's seven

---

19   David North, "Lenin, Trotsky and the Marxism of the October Revolution," World Socialist Website, March 19, 2018, *https://www.wsws.org/en/articles/2018/03/19/leip-m19.html.*

20   Jeffries, *Grand Hotel Abyss*, p. 77.

21   Jay, *The Dialectical Imagination*, p. 39.

22   Jeffries, *Grand Hotel Abyss*, p. 67, and Gerhard Schneibel, "Stock of Former Nazi Chemicals Giant to Be Delisted," Deutsche Welle, August 19, 2011, *https://www.dw.com/en/stock-of-former-nazi-chemicals-giant-to-be-delisted/a-15327052.*

stock exchanges, hardly a legacy of which Marxists would be proud.[23] Yet it was in America that Frankfurt School members would continue to develop the critical philosophy, relying on Marxism and class struggles as their intellectual foundation, though Frankfurt School writers were careful to erase the "M word from [their] research papers so as not to affront [their] American hosts and potential sponsors."[24] In the example above of K–12 teachers hiding their teaching of critical ideas from parents, educators were continuing this tradition of subterfuge. There are more examples to come.

"Critical" aptly describes the worldview because the philosophy, "a gadfly of other systems," is meant to criticize the traditional uses of language and reason to describe the world around us ("traditional theory").[25] Horkheimer writes that "critical theory stands in opposition to other theories."[26] Critical theorists believe that reason—logical thinking based on reality as we understand it—should be rejected.

When he became director of the Frankfurt School, Horkheimer described critical theory's main ideas and goals in his inaugural essay "Traditional and Critical Theory." He said that the Frankfurt School's version of Marxism would not be limited to economics or class-consciousness, but should extend to culture. Critical theorists wanted to change all existing beliefs and morals in society. Horkheimer said that the Frankfurt School must answer the:

---

23 Börse Frankfurt, *https://www.boerse-frankfurt.de/en.*

24 Jeffries, *Grand Hotel Abyss*, p. 9.

25 Jay, *The Dialectical Imagination*, p. 41.

26 Max Horkheimer, "Traditional and Critical Theory," in *Critical Theory: Selected Essays* (London: Continuum International Publishing Group, 1975) *https://www. google.com/url?sa=t&rct=j&q=&esrc=s&source=web&cd=&ved=2ahUKEwiZ_Yvv1I_vAh-VCRTABHQHPA9gQFjAPegQIIhAD&url=https%3A%2F%2Fwww.sfu.ca%2F~andrew-f%2Fhork.doc&usg=AOvVaw2H6B7dqA9VKF-FkPoPTvKL.*

...question of the connection between the economic life of society, the psychological development of individuals and challenges in the realm of culture in the narrower sense (to which belong not only the so-called intellectual elements such as science, art, and religion, but also law, customs, fashion, public opinion, sports, leisure activities, lifestyle, etc.).

Critical theorists in America studying law, racial issues, and education have heeded this call to integrate critical ideas into law and culture.[27]

Critical theorists still want their philosophy to inspire action in the form of resistance to capitalism, but also resistance to traditional liberal ideas, such as a constitutional republic, specifically. As Jay explains, "[t]he first critical theorists had lived at a time when a new 'negative' (that is, revolutionary) force in society—the proletariat—was stirring, a force that could be seen as the agency that would fulfill their philosophy."[28]

Though Horkheimer, Marcuse, and others would lose faith in members of the working class's ability to engage in a revolution, the Frankfurt School's "ambitious project" was action, "the ultimate unity of critical theory and revolutionary practice."[29] We will see the subsequent use of this applied revolutionary element of critical theory through "action civics" and in the writings of Paulo Freire and others described later in this chapter.

Critical theory has one more central idea that is worth describing before turning to its application: a postmodern belief that there is no authentic truth in the world, only

---

27   Horkheimer, "Traditional and Critical Theory," and "The Present Situation of Social Philosophy and the Tasks of an Institute for Social Research," in *Between Philosophy and Social Science: Selected Early Writings* (Cambridge, MA: MIT Press, 1993).

28   Jay, *The Dialectical Imagination*, p. 43.

29   Jay, *The Dialectical Imagination*, p. 253.

observations and experience.[30] Horkheimer explains, cloudy as this concept may be, that "perceived fact is therefore co-determined by human ideas and concepts, even before its conscious theoretical elaboration by the knowing individual."[31] Stated simply, Horkheimer claims that what people consider truth is created by the wealthy—the bourgeois class—and that facts are subjective.[32]

Horkheimer wrote later that "bourgeois philosophy has been a single attempt to make knowledge serve the dominant means of production."[33] What we learn in school and from books is really information meant to control those from lower economic classes. Kendi says that "intelligence is as subjective as beauty," and that the "achievement gap" between test scores of children from different races is the "linchpin of behavioral racism."[34] True, SAT scores do not determine the worth, or necessarily the intelligence, of an individual. Educators, though, cannot prepare students for life after school without some standard measure of what children have learned. How can parents and teachers know which students need more help without some indicator of their skill level?

According to critical theory, since circumstances are always changing, there are no truths that people can apply to their lives, because every new situation requires decisions based on new truths. This postmodern relativism rejects religious faith and perennial virtues, such as honesty and courage, and all other character traits on which Americans have always

---

30 Internet Encyclopedia of Philosophy, "The Frankfurt School and Critical Theory," *https://iep.utm.edu/frankfur/*.
31 Horkheimer, "Traditional and Critical Theory."
32 Martin Jay says that the Frankfurt School eventually decided that truth is created by "domination" in general, not just class warfare. See Jay, *The Dialectical Imagination*, p. 256, and Horkheimer, "Traditional and Critical Theory."
33 Jay, *The Dialectical Imagination*, p. 258.
34 Kendi, *How to Be an Antiracist*, pp. 4, 101.

relied to sustain their families, raise their children, and build strong communities.

OOO

The Frankfurt School's ideas inspired critical legal theory, feminist movements, gender studies, and critical race theory, to name a few philosophical schools that emerged throughout the twentieth century.[35] Critical legal theory is the application of critical theory, with all its Marxist components, to American law. In critical legal theory, America's laws are systemically oppressive and designed to keep ethnic minorities in the underclass. Derrick Bell, one of the founders of critical race theory, says that

> *even those whites who lack wealth and power are sustained in their sense of racial superiority and thus rendered more willing to accept their lesser share by an unspoken but no less certain property right in their "whiteness."* **This right is recognized and upheld by courts and society like all property rights under a government created and sustained primarily for that purpose.**[36] *(Emphasis added.)*

Another summary of critical legal theory explains that liberal ideals, such as "the notion that individuals possess 'inherent' or fundamental rights...particularly come under strenuous attack by crits [an abbreviation for critical theorists generally, but referring here to critical legal theorists]."[37] Critical legal theorists argue that "liberalism's unresolved contradictions thus undermine the notion that its regime of legal

---

35   Delgado and Stefancic, *Critical Race Theory: An Introduction.*

36   Delgado and Stefancic, *The Derrick Bell Reader* (New York: New York University Press, 2005), p. 28.

37   Robert A. Williams, Jr., "Taking Rights Aggressively: The Perils and Promise of Critical Legal Theory for Peoples of Color," Minnesota Journal of Law & Inequality, Vol. 5, No. 1 (March 1987), p. 117.

rights can ultimately transform 'the oppressive character of our social relations.'"[38]

Critical legal theorists often use the idea of "deconstruction" to criticize the American legal system. Under deconstruction, clear words, specifically, have alternate meanings. For the purposes of critical theorists, everyone should seek out the examples of oppression ostensibly built into language. Jacques Derrida is one of the foundational thinkers behind language deconstruction, and though he mostly applied deconstruction to literary interpretation—reviewing novels and stories—critical legal theorists (and as we will see, critical pedagogues, too) use his approach to argue for dismantling America's justice system.[39]

Critical race theorists followed critical legal theorists and applied the critical perspective to race. Though the Frankfurt School tried to move beyond Marx's focus on economics as the philosophy evolved over time, critical race theorists have not lost touch with Marx's main ideas: "Marx's dazzling analysis of capitalism and his conviction that the laws of historical materialism would bring on the revolution of the proletariat as inevitably as the sun rises are still riveting to contemporary theorists," wrote Angela Harris.[40] Ibram Kendi wrote, "Antiracist policies cannot eliminate class racism without anticapitalist policies."[41]

At its center, critical race theory rejects the very ideas that define America, ideas that Americans should share in order to sustain a civil society. Derrick Bell writes that, "We use a number of different voices, but all recognize that the American social

---

38   Ibid.
39   J. M. Balkin, "Deconstructive Practice and Legal Theory," *The Yale Law Journal*, Vol. 96, No. 743 (1987).
40   Harris, "Compassion and Critique," and Jay, *The Dialectical Imagination.*
41   Kendi, *How to Be an Antiracist*, p. 159.

order is maintained and perpetuated by racial subordination."[42] Racism, according to Bell, is permanent.[43] Critical race theorists regularly use the term "systemic racism" today, expanding on critical legal theory's main ideas. Note, too, Bell's insistence on replacing cultural assimilation with cultural resistance, which would destabilize, well, everything.

The racial component that critical race theory adds to the critical philosophy is that the world should be seen through the lens of race always and at all times. As Angela Harris wrote in 2001—as if it were 1850 or 1950—critical race theory "dares to treat race as central to the law and policy of the United States" because "racism is part of the structure of legal institutions."[44] critical race theorists go beyond the law to intangibles that are, by definition, impossible to measure, such as the presence of racism in people's subconscious emotions.

Critical race theorists, in their own descriptions of their theory, say that they are not attempting to resolve differences between different people or groups, nor to create a more compassionate public square. Nary a notion of civil discourse or shared ideals and experiences in sight. Harris says that it's not enough to feel compassion or to "care" about subordinated people, though she argues that both of these emotions should be part of critical race theorists' work. Rather than using compassion to mend relationships, however, Harris writes, "caring must be connected to moral outrage to produce a commitment to action."[45]

Black men and women in the U.S. suffered greatly under slavery and in the Jim Crow era, and members of minority eth-

---

42   Bell, "David C. Baum Memorial Lecture: Who's Afraid of Critical Race Theory?"

43   Bell, *Faces at the Bottom of the Well: The Permanence of Racism* (New York: Basic Books, 1992), and Angela Harris, "Compassion and Critique."

44   Angela Harris, "Foreword," in Delgado and Stefancic, *Critical Race Theory: An Introduction.*

45   Angela Harris, "Compassion and Critique."

nicities face individual cases of racial discrimination today (as do whites). There is no explaining away the racism in America's past, but there is simply no evidence to support the outrageous claims that America is an irredeemably racist nation or that our laws are inherently biased against individuals from certain ethnic backgrounds—in fact, federal civil rights law expressly forbids bias in the workplace and in courts of law. As we will see in the examples of critical race theory in K–12 curricula, these theorists spend a notable amount of time and energy trying to inject the racially discriminatory elements of the theory into math, as well as history and civics.

To critical race theorists today, federal civil rights laws are neither necessary nor sufficient to accomplish critical ends. In 2017, Kendi wrote that the Civil Rights Act of 1964 was "intended to dismantle racism" but "also spurred *racist* progress."[46] (Emphasis in original). Kendi's reasoning contains conflicting positions, though. He says that the 1964 law should have focused on "guaranteeing equal opportunity" instead of merely "dismantling Jim Crow," but he does not ask whether black Americans have the same *opportunities* as white Americans. Instead, he argues that everyone should have the same *outcomes* in life.

He cites "health disparities" and different rates of unemployment and incarceration among Americans who are white and those who are black, but those are outcomes, not public policy inputs. Kendi criticizes the Civil Rights Act because it did not create equal outcomes, an impossible task for any single law, or government as a whole for that matter. The critical approach to manufacturing artificial student outcomes has seeped into schools, too. A California school district

---

46   Kendi, "The Civil Rights Act Was a Victory Against Racism. But Racists Also Won," *The Washington Post*, July 2, 2017, *https://www.washingtonpost.com/news/made-by-history/wp/2017/07/02/the-civil-rights-act-was-a-victory-against-racism-but-racists-also-won/*.

adopted a "Racial Equity" (not equality) policy that says that the district "seeks to ensure that policies and practices produce equitable outcomes for students who identify as Black, Indigenous, People of Color (BIPOC)."[47] That individual achievement and behavior should not determine individual outcomes, but a government body, in this case a school, is a terrifying notion. Government cannot create identical outcomes for everyone without coercion—forcing some people to have less of what they earn while others are bestowed more than they earned.

Still, Kendi is right in one respect: America has not defeated the existence of racism, at least in the form of individual racist acts. No nation could possibly do so. Yet Americans rejected government-sponsored discrimination and racism and that is consistent with the national creed. As many black former civil rights activists and leaders recognize today, this official rejection of racism is an essential feature of American life.

Critical legal theorists and critical race theorists are not trying to align their ideas with virtues, such as personal responsibility, that were so important to civil rights activists in the 1950s and 1960s. In fact, historian Arthur Schlesinger says that in America's history, "The American Creed...meant even more to blacks than to whites, since it was the great means of claiming their unfulfilled rights." Quoting Gunnar Myrdal, Schlesinger says, "Blacks, new immigrants, Jews, and other disadvantaged groups [from the early to mid-twentieth century] 'could not

---

47   Piedmont Unified School District, "Racial Equity," Board Policy No. 0415.1, *http://www.piedmont.k12.ca.us/wp-content/uploads/2020/09/BP-AR-0415.1-Racial-Equity.pdf.*

possibly have invented a system of political ideals which better corresponded to their interests.'"[48]

Robert Woodson, founder of the Woodson Center, an organization dedicated to improving the lives of minorities through violence reduction and entrepreneurship programs, and Georgetown University professor Joshua Mitchell write that the civil rights movement "helped deliver America from the historic sins of slavery and Jim Crow by forcing the nation to confront the full humanity of its black citizens."[49]

Woodson and Mitchell write that America has a "redemptive promise" and that "oppression wasn't destiny," the exact opposite of critical race theory's established positions. They continue: "Like all Americans, blacks have triumphed over their circumstances only when they have adopted bourgeois virtues such as hard work, respect for learning, self-discipline, faith and personal responsibility."

Former civil rights activist and author Shelby Steele says that individual initiative is "the only thing that finally delivers *anyone* from poverty"—yet the necessity of individual initiative is a notion that critical race theorists commonly use as evidence of systemic racism in America, given their belief that individual initiative only works for white people. "With our eyes on innocence we see racism everywhere and miss opportunity even as we stumble over it," Steele says.[50]

In sum, the main features of critical race theory are that America is systemically racist toward anyone who is not white; the world is separated between victims and their victimizers; facts

---

48   Arthur Schlesinger, *The Disuniting of America* (New York: W.W. Norton & Company, 1998), p. 45.

49   Robert Woodson and Joshua Mitchell, "How the Left Hijacked Civil Rights," *The Wall Street Journal*, January 15, 2021, *https://www.wsj.com/articles/how-the-left-hijacked-civil-rights-11610748711.*

50   Steele, *The Content of Our Character*, p. 16.

depend on experiences; and minority individuals are the only ones who can speak with authority on issues relating to their ethnicity—all of which are applications of ideas that originated in the Frankfurt School.

CRITICAL PEDAGOGY

In a review of the academic literature on critical race theory and education in 2015, María Ledesma and Dolores Calderón waste no time in explaining approvingly that critical race theory has saturated K–12 instruction. As the authors wrote in 2015, "Within the span of the last two decades, critical race theory (CRT) has become an increasingly permanent fixture in the toolkit of education researchers seeking to critically examine educational opportunities, school climate, representation, and pedagogy, to name a few."[51]

This process of saturation started in colleges of education, where K–12 teachers are trained before they enter the classroom. In a 2019 study that surveyed the syllabi of colleges of education[52] at the University of Wisconsin (home to *U.S. News & World Report*'s second-highest-ranked teachers college), the University of Michigan (fourteenth), and the University of North Carolina (UNC, thirtieth), researchers found that the author tied for the highest number of syllabi appearances in UNC's courses was Gloria Ladson-Billings. Ladson-Billings is the author of seminal works on critical race theory, such as "Just What Is Critical Race Theory and What's

---

51 María C. Ledesma and Dolores Calderón, "Critical Race Theory in Education: A Review of Past Literature and a Look into the Future," *Qualitative Inquiry*, Vol. 21, No. 3 (March 2015), *https://journals.sagepub.com/toc/qixa/21/3*.

52 Jay Schalin, "The Politicization of University Schools of Education: The Long March through the Education Schools," The James G. Martin Center, February 2019, *https://www.jamesgmartin.center/wp-content/uploads/2019/02/The-Politicization-of-University-Schools-of-Education.pdf*.

It Doing in a *Nice* Field Like Education?"[53] Ladson-Billings stands alone at the top in the review of the University of Wisconsin's teacher college content.

Around the country, though, arguably the most widely cited and frequently assigned book in U.S. colleges of education is by Paulo Freire, a Brazilian Marxist active in the 1960s and 1970s. While Freire wrote *Pedagogy of the Oppressed* well before Derrick Bell and Kimberlé Crenshaw and others conceived critical race theory, Freire's ideas align closely with the worldview of critical race theorists and critical theorists.[54] For decades, professors in colleges of education have included Freire in what is considered critical pedagogy, the application of critical theory to teaching.[55]

A 2009 review of teacher college syllabi released found that Freire's book was one of the texts most often required at competitive institutions.[56] Book sales increased 60 percent from 2018 to 2019, at the time of *Pedagogy*'s fiftieth anniversary.[57] Thus Freire's ideas and their applications matter to parents and policymakers today if they are to understand the woke philosophy.

The Zinn Foundation, an institute based on the writings and work of revisionist historian Howard Zinn (a professor

---

53 Gloria Ladson-Billings, "Just What Is Critical Race Theory and What's It Doing in a Nice Field Like Education?" *International Journal of Qualitative Studies in Education*, Vol. 11, No. 1 (January 1998), pp. 7–24, Linda Darling-Hammond, Jennifer French, and Sílvía Paloma Garcia-Lopez, eds., *Learning to Teach for Social Justice* (New York: Teachers College Press, 2002), and Schalin, "The Politicization of University Schools of Education: The Long March through the Education Schools."

54 See, for example, Ladson-Billings, "Liberatory Consequences of Literacy: A Case of Culturally Relevant Instruction for African American Students," *The Journal of Negro Education* Vol. 61, No. 3 (Summer 1992), pp. 378–391.

55 Paulo Freire, *Pedagogy of the Oppressed*, 30th Anniversary Edition (New York: Continuum, 2005).

56 David Steiner, "Skewed Perspective," *Education Next*, Vol. 5, No. 1, October 20, 2009, *https://www.educationnext.org/skewedperspective/*.

57 Liza Featherstone, "Paulo Freire's *Pedagogy of the Oppressed* at Fifty," JSTOR Daily, September 30, 2020, *https://daily.jstor.org/paulo-freires-pedagogy-of-the-oppressed-at-fifty/*.

and writer whom the FBI watched closely in the 1950s due to his ties with the Communist Party USA), calls Freire's book "one of the foundational texts in the field of critical pedagogy, which attempts to help students question and challenge domination, and the beliefs and practices that dominate."[58] One observer reckons that *Pedagogy* has achieved more global fame than any other book translated from Portuguese."[59]

Freire, born in 1921 and the son of a police officer, wrote his work as a philosophical treatise on how to become a revolutionary.[60] Freire lived during a period of upheaval in Brazil. Active in government, he spent time in prison after a military coup in 1964, then fled the country after his release. During his time in exile, he wrote *Pedagogy*, drawing on his experiences teaching people in poor communities in Brazil to read. He used this experience to argue that those who are highly educated should teach those from lower economic classes how to free themselves from oppression.

Given the accolades from K–12 educators in America, we should be surprised to learn that Freire's book is not actually about K–12 education. Freire's book discusses the idea of teachers and students merely symbolically. *Pedagogy* is a guide explaining how the world is divided according to economic classes. Members of lower economic classes should strive for liberation from their oppressors.

Freire's "school" is not a traditional K–12 classroom, but the world. His book is a revolutionary text of the Marxist tradition that divides the world into oppressors and the oppressed; he calls those who want to liberate people from their oppression the "teachers," and the peasants who need to be liber-

---

58   Zinn Foundation, "Pedagogy of the Oppressed," Teaching Materials, *https://www.zinnedproject.org/materials/pedagogy-of-the-oppressed/*, and Mary Grabar, *Debunking Howard Zinn: Exposing the Fake History That Turned a Generation against America* (Washington, DC: Regnery History, 2019), p. 65.
59   Featherstone, "Paulo Freire's *Pedagogy of the Oppressed* at Fifty."
60   Ibid.

ated the "students." Thus, the text uses symbolic language about schools to make its point about the need for oppressed groups to rebel.

An admirer of Che Guevara and Mao Zedong, as well as Marx, Freire's class-consciousness and obsession with victimization comes directly from the annals of Critical Theory. He writes,

> *More and more, the oppressors are using science and technology as unquestionably powerful instruments for their purpose: the maintenance of the oppressive order through manipulation and repression. The oppressed, as objects, as "things," have no purpose except those their oppressors prescribe for them.*[61]

For Freire, the duty of the unoppressed is to prepare the poor for revolution. Yet those who are not oppressed are simply self-serving and vile, even if they try to help the victimized by providing an education. Freire writes, "The generosity of the oppressors is nourished by an unjust order, which must be maintained in order to justify that generosity."[62] This is similar to Bell's position, now held by Kendi, that white Americans allowed civil rights to progress only because it was in their own interest.

Educators today use Freire's ideas to advance two main instructional ideas: the criticism of facts, and the teaching of students to be activists. Freire derides the teaching of objective facts as the "banking" approach to education. He writes, "Those who use the banking approach, knowingly or unknowingly (for there are innumerable well-intentioned bank-clerk teachers who do not realize that they are serving only to dehumanize), fail to perceive that the deposits themselves contain contradictions about reality." Freire

---

61 Freire, *Pedagogy of the Oppressed*, p. 60.
62 Ibid., p. 60.

explains that he is opposed both to the teaching of facts and the facts themselves.

But students need facts so that they can use them later to evaluate ideas and learn from the mistakes and achievements of others. Students need a base level of knowledge to have discussions with each other and their teachers.

Consider the *Stanford Encyclopedia of Philosophy*'s definition of "civics," the subject that, along with history, is at the center of the federal debate over America's past: "All the processes that affect people's beliefs, commitments, capabilities and actions as members or prospective members of communities."[63] Teachers and students need some set of shared facts, otherwise conversations would be meaningless. Cultural anthropologist Laura Bohannan's experience with the Tiv people, described in the introduction, applies here—her attempts to communicate with the Tiv were sorely hampered by the lack of common ideas, shared experiences, and shared cultural mores.

But Freire will have none of it. He writes, "The more students work at storing the deposits entrusted to them, the less they develop the critical consciousness which would result from their intervention in the world as transformers of that world." And here is the second important application of Freire's ideas: that students must be activists, engaged in changing and even disrupting the world around them. "Reality," Freire explains, "is really a process, undergoing constant transformation."

We can all agree that change is the only constant in life, but without some knowledge of how other people have responded to challenges similar to those we are facing, we are left with little more than gut reactions to make decisions. To that end, Freire says, "Liberation is a praxis: the action and reflection of men

---

63   *Stanford Encyclopedia of Philosophy*, "Civic Education," August 31, 2018, *https://plato. stanford.edu/entries/civic-education/*.

and women upon their world in order to transform it." This idea underpins the growing movement in favor of "action civics," which replaces traditional instruction with, as the name suggests, student activism. (See Chapter 2.)

Freire's teachings align with Richard Delgado and Jean Stefancic's description of critical race theory: "Unlike some academic disciplines, critical race theory contains an activist dimension," seeking not just to "understand our social situations, but to change it."[64] This teaching and the worldview inspiring it are not trying to help America to fulfill its promise that current and future generations will have the same opportunities regardless of race, sex, nation of origin, or any other immutable characteristic. Instead, Freire, Delgado, Stefancic, and others want us to always be looking for reasons to consider ourselves or others as victims or victimizers and trying to disrupt the government and social institutions that are making us so.

Educators' use of Freire's ideas in classrooms, especially in the West, creates incongruities between the content and most students' lives. One reviewer from the socialist *Jacobin* magazine, Liza Featherstone, says: "While Freire viewed the purpose of education as the liberation of the oppressed, in elite classrooms...the challenges for a liberatory pedagogy is to teach empathy and solidarity with the oppressed—who, in many cases, are not in the room."[65]

OOO

Freire's sharply skewed perspective and the critical ideas consistent with it are wreaking havoc on schools today. Teachers unions are among the groups advocating Freire's critical pedagogy and instructional materials based on critical race

---

64   Delgado and Stefancic, *Critical Race Theory: An Introduction.*
65   Featherstone, "Paulo Freire's *Pedagogy of the Oppressed* at Fifty."

theory. For example, at the July 2021 National Education Association (NEA) annual meeting, the nation's largest teachers union adopted a statement that says that it will support and lead in activities that "result in increasing the implementation" of "culturally responsive education" and "critical race theory."[66] (Just three days after the conference ended, though, the statement disappeared from the NEA's website, along with the entire archive of NEA agenda items from other annual conferences.)

In 2020, the United Federation of Teachers (UFT), the union representing teachers in New York City, also adopted a resolution that aligns with critical theorists' principles. The resolution states that there are "systemic problems" in law and policy that oppress ethnic minorities; "anti-Black police violence continues to take place in the United States without accountability"; and "the UFT supports culturally responsive educational practices, including but not limited to…the expansion of Black studies as well as Asian, Latinx, and Native American studies programs and LGTBQ history in our P–12 classrooms."[67] Educators who use critical race theory in schools today frequently use the term "culturally responsive" to describe instruction that teaches students that they are members of different tribes, oppressed by their government.

The UFT resolved to support a Black Lives Matter resolution that states that union members will "proactively encourage its members to invest in critical reflection…[on] racial injustice." The resolution called on teachers to use curricular

---

66 National Education Association 2021 Annual Meeting, New Business Item A, archived at *https://archive.is/Dkozm*, and news release, "NEA Delegates Approve Measure to Ensure Safe and Just Schools for All Students," National Education Association, July 1, 2021, *https://ra.nea.org/2021/07/01/nea-delegates-approve-measure-to-ensure-safe-and-just-schools-for-all-students/*.

67 More Caucus New York, "Wed. 11/18 Vote YES on the Black Lives Matter at Schools Resolution at the UFT Delegates Assembly," November 16, 2020, *https://morecaucusnyc.wordpress.com/2020/11/16/wed-11-18-vote-yes-on-the-black-lives-matter-at-schools-resolution-at-the-uft-delegates-assembly/*.

material from the Culturally Responsive Sustaining-Education Framework. New York State Department of Education officials created this framework to help educators to "affirm racial, linguistic, and cultural identities" and "empower students as agents of social change," again, training students to be activists.[68] The framework says that a "complex system of biases and structural inequities is at play [in schools], deeply rooted in our nation's history, culture, and institutions."[69] Critical race theorists believe that Americans cannot separate racism from their national identity, which makes America's failures of the past the defining feature of America's present.

The UFT said that it is "committed to disrupting the Western-prescribed nuclear family structure requirement by supporting each other as extended families and 'villages' that collectively care for one another, and especially 'our' children to the degree that mothers, parents, and children are comfortable."[70] This "disrupting" of students' perception of the family runs directly counter to the resolution's other guiding principles of "respecting and celebrating differences and commonalities" and being "committed to embodying and practicing justice, liberation and peace in our engagements with one another." We are to respect and celebrate differences unless some is part of a nuclear family.

This statement is one of the many examples of the contradictions inherent in critical theory, where the ideas simultaneously call for tolerance of others while specifically listing the character traits and relationships that it opposes—character traits and relationships that have, in fact, been important to individuals and communities for millennia around the world.

---

68 New York State Department of Education, "Culturally Responsive-Sustaining Education Framework," *http://www.nysed.gov/curriculum-instruction/culturally-responsive-sustaining-education-framework.*

69 Ibid.

70 United Federation of Teachers, "Resolution in Support of Black Lives Matter at School," November 18, 2020, *https://www.uft.org/news/union-resolutions/resolution-support-black-lives-matter-school.*

Some critical pedagogues have extended their ideas even further to another revision of critical theory, called critical race pedagogy, which one writer calls "an analysis of racial, ethnic and gender subordination in education that relies mostly upon the perceptions, experiences and counter-hegemonic practices of educators of color…" But this definition is hardly distinguishable from Freire's ideas, critical race theory, and the foundational critical concepts that the Frankfurt School developed.[71] Again, these studies focus on teaching teachers and students to discover their victimization, whether it exists or not. We are to assume animus in society, government, and from people who are different from us, and disrupt systems of power—as well as the lives of people with whom we disagree.

DECOLONIZATION

Critical assumptions that the oppressors control school culture and curricula require critical pedagogues to challenge existing curricula, leading to another critical concept, that of "decolonization." As the name suggests, decolonization refers to efforts to remove or displace groups that occupy territory belonging to others. As the idea's founders and their successors explain, though, the territory can be intangible—including ideas, traditions, and teaching materials.

Frantz Fanon was one of the first to describe the necessary ingredients of decolonization. Born in Martinique in 1925, he spent much of his life practicing psychiatry in Europe and Africa (Algeria, specifically).[72] Fanon does not mince words in his final book, *The Wretched of the Earth*:

---

71   Marvin Lynn, "Inserting the 'Race' into Critical Pedagogy: An Analysis of 'Race-Based Epistemologies,'" *Educational Philosophy and Theory*, Vol. 36, No. 2 (2004).

72   Helen Pluckrose and James Lindsay, *Cynical Theories* (Durham, NC: Pitchstone Publishing, 2020), and *Stanford Encyclopedia of Philosophy*, "Frantz Fanon," March 14, 2019, *https://plato.stanford.edu/entries/frantz-fanon/*.

National liberation, national renaissance, the restoration of nationhood to the people, commonwealth: whatever may be the headings used or the new formulas introduced, decolonization is always a violent phenomenon. At whatever level we study it— relationships between individuals, new names for sports clubs, the human admixture at cocktail parties, in the police, on the directing boards of national or private banks—decolonization is quite simply the replacing of a certain "species" of men by another "species" of men.[73]

While some may argue that Fanon did not advocate violence in all situations, Fanon does in fact call for violent revolution so often that it is impossible to consider him to be divided on the use of physical conflict in revolution to achieve socialist goals.[74] In *A Dying Colonialism*, he does say, "In a war of liberation, the colonized people must win, but they must do so cleanly, without barbarity."[75] But he also wrote in the same book: "The armed struggle breaks up the old routine life of the countryside and villages, excites, exalts, and opens wide the doors of the future."[76] So when he says in *The Wretched of the Earth*, "To tell the truth, the proof of success lies in a whole social structure being changed from the bottom up," how can this call for change be considered anything but violent?[77] Fanon's ideal process for change is a "program of complete disorder," he says.

Just as Freire's experiences with the poor in Brazil influenced *Pedagogy of the Oppressed*, Fanon's writings were influenced by his experiences during the Algerian revolution. Education, for one, was part of the cultural system that was an "expression of respect for the established order" and served to create around

---

73 Frantz Fanon, *The Wretched of the Earth* (New York: Grove Press, 1963).
74 Dennis Forsythe, "Frantz Fanon—the Marx of the Third World," *Phylon*, Vol. 34, No. 2 (1973), pp. 160–170.
75 Fanon, *A Dying Colonialism* (New York: Grove Press, 1965), p. 24.
76 Ibid., pp. 1–2.
77 Fanon, *The Wretched of the Earth*.

the "exploited person an atmosphere of submission and of inhibition." He writes, "Use all means to turn the scale, including, of course, that of violence."[78]

So when educators use the term "decolonization" today in reference to books or curricula, we must remember the origins of the concept and its founder's preferred methods. Take, for example, a 2020 article on the website of PBS—the former home of "Sesame Street"—titled "Decolonizing Our Classrooms Starts with Us."[79] The author, a middle school teacher, writes that, "Educators have a special role in the revolution, they always have," and in order to be "anti-racist," teachers must "analyze how dominant ideology and white supremacy have shaped our individual beliefs and behaviors."

Fanon, like Freire, published his ideas before academics developed critical race theory, but the Marxist, violent ideas of how to analyze oppression are consistent with, and frequently found as part of, critical race theory's application in classrooms.

OOO

Noted critical race theorist and critical pedagogue Gloria Ladson-Billings writes that multicultural curricula have "challenged old perceptions of America as a 'White' country," though even Ladson-Billings admits in her article from 2003 that school curricula are far more diverse than they used to be: "Today it is almost impossible to walk into an elementary school in the United States and not find representation of 'multicultural America.'"[80]

---

78 Ibid.
79 Terry Kawi, "Decolonizing Our Classrooms Starts with Us," PBS, August 3, 2020, *https://www.pbs.org/education/blog/decolonizing-our-classrooms-starts-with-us.*
80 Ladson-Billings, "New Directions in Multicultural Education: Complexities, Boundaries, and Critical Race Theory," Semantic Scholar, 2010, pp. 50–65, *https://www.semanticscholar.org/paper/New-Directions-in-Multicultural-Education-%2C-%2C-and-Ladson-Billings/83f46d93e3b83d0d698842d785a9185f363f42df#paper-header.*

But Ladson-Billings is not satisfied with the idea that "we are all multiculturalists now." There is still work to be done to revolutionize American schools and change the material that teachers use to teach students. Critical pedagogues, such as bell hooks (née Gloria Jean Watkins), associate Freire's "banking" system of teaching and learning with colonization, or domination, of education by groups of people, namely white people.

In *Teaching to Transgress*, hooks demonstrates that decolonization remains central to the critical perspective. She says that when she was in graduate school, there was "the assumption that memorizing information and regurgitating it represented gaining knowledge that could be deposited, stored, and used at a later date."[81] This familiar description of learning is not evidence of oppression, though from the critical perspective, such instruction creates victims. hooks says that the "colonizing forces are so powerful in this white supremacist capitalist patriarchy, it seems that black people are always having to renew a commitment to a decolonizing political process that should be fundamental to our lives and is not."

More recently, the National Council for the Social Studies (NCSS) has endorsed the "decolonization," or "dismantling," of the teaching of history and social studies.[82] In a 2020 article in *Social Education*, the NCSS's flagship journal, LaGarrett King writes, "These ideas of power, oppression, and racism have to be understood as systemic and institutional, not individual or cosmetic." Power and oppression "are created and sustained throughout society."

---

81 bell hooks, *Teaching to Transgress: Education as the Practice of Freedom* (New York: Routledge, 1994), p. 5, *https://academictrap.files.wordpress.com/2015/03/bell-hooks-teaching-to-transgress.pdf.* (bell hooks lowercases her name on purpose.)
82 LaGarrett J. King, "Black History Is Not American History: Toward a Framework of Black Historical Consciousness," *Social Education*, Vol. 84, No. 6 (November/December 2020), pp. 335–341, *https://www.socialstudies.org/sites/default/files/view-article-2020-12/se8406335.pdf.*

Individual success and the importance of civil society are the targets of critical theory's ever-present pursuit of dismantling systems of power. As hooks writes, "our lives must be a living example of our politics."[83]

OOO

Observers can easily find examples of curricula and textbooks pushing the idea that truth and facts are obstacles to resistance, or that facts are merely illusions. Again, according to critical theory, facts are only as true as those experiencing them allow them to be, all based on personal interpretations. Educators are even applying critical theory to elementary and middle-school *math.*

Educators from the University of California system, and school district officials from Sacramento, Los Angeles, Monterrey, and San Diego, along with still more researchers from private foundations supported financially by the Bill and Melinda Gates Foundation, created a curriculum called "Equitable Math." In Equitable Math, critical pedagogues have changed the focus of math from "getting the right answer" to "dismantling white supremacy."[84] Shouldn't the goal of math instruction be to teach students to find the right answer?

But mathematical accuracy is not critical race theorists' objective. San Mateo school district officials released a statement on Equitable Math saying that educators need to "address gaps in student outcomes with activities for uncovering bias and strategies for infusing antiracist pedagogy."[85] According to district officials, racism—not an individual's efforts—is the reason that some students do not perform as well as others.

---

83 hooks, *Teaching to Transgress.*
84 Equitable Math, "A Pathway to Equitable Math Instruction," pp. 1 and 6, *https:// equitablemath.org/wp-content/uploads/sites/2/2020/11/1_STRIDE1.pdf.*
85 San Mateo County Office of Education, "San Mateo County Partners to Support Equity in Math Education," *https://www.smcoe.org/about/county-office-of-education/ news/san-mateo-county-partners-to-support-equity-in-math-education.html.*

The curricular guides call on teachers to tell students to build biases against others who do not look like them, saying that teachers should "engage with the ways that white supremacy culture shows up in math classrooms." The curriculum then turns to ethnic identities and the use of language:

> *The systems that uphold these white supremacist practices are most clearly seen in policies that devalue students' home languages and cultures, and instead force assimilation through English-only initiatives and the abundant shower of white-only literature and learning materials.*

Equitable Math's guidebooks include a recommendation to teach minority students about the job possibilities in STEM fields (science, technology, engineering, and math), but this recommendation is inserted between diatribes about systemic racism and explicit instruction to teach students that who gets the credit for success in life matters more than one's contributions to that success.

Racism in numeracy is not the only target of Equitable Math—capitalism is a target, too. The instructional materials tell teachers to "identify and challenge the ways that math is used to uphold capitalist, imperialist, and racist views," obviously pointing directly at civic and historical concepts and critical theory's Marxist origins and away from efforts to give students the skills they will need for adult life and the workplace.

In the midst of all this, parents should be asking whether students will also learn to add, subtract, multiply, and divide.

The curriculum designers explicitly call on teachers to turn students into activists—in math class: "Expose students to examples of people who have used math as resistance. Provide learning opportunities that use math as resistance."[86]

---

86 Equitable Math, "A Pathway to Equitable Math Instruction," p. 9.

The Equitable Math curriculum is not an isolated example of critical race theorists' impacts on mathematics. Gloria Ladson-Billings was the keynote speaker at the 2019 National Council of Teachers of Mathematics annual event.[87] The Black Lives Matter movement has created a set of recommended materials for K–12 schools, one of which is an essay titled "Open Secrets in First-Grade Math: Teaching about White Supremacy on American Currency."[88] Counting correct change is an afterthought: "For many of my students, the very thing they're promised will give them a better life—money—reflects the story of American imperialism and oppression: The dime is a reminder of Japanese internment, the quarter a reminder of slavery, the $20 bill a reminder of Native genocide."

Like the White House debate about the interpretation of American history and what it means for "equity" and "diversity," these math examples demonstrate the ideas and beliefs that educators see as the important concepts to pass on to children. Thus the White House debate over how to teach history and the controversy involving the 1619 Project and the 1776 Commission are not just struggles happening in the media and in Washington, but are part of a cultural shift that is taking place in classrooms—and hence the population—around the country.

Equitable Math replaces numbers with calls for revolution, attempting to turn students into anti-American activists and, ideally, revolutionaries.

---

87   National Council of Teachers of Mathematics, "NCTM San Diego Annual Conference Program & Presentation," 2019, *https://www.nctm.org/Conferences-and-Professional-Development/Annual-Meeting-and-Exposition/Program-and-Presentation/*.

88   Bret Turner, "Open Secrets in First Grade Math: Teaching about White Supremacy on American Currency," Learning for Justice, January 2, 2019, *https://www.learningfor-justice.org/magazine/open-secrets-in-firstgrade-math-teaching-about-white-supremacy-on-american-currency*.

OOO

The critical approach to teaching the soft sciences (such as literature and history) also reveals a conscious decision to question the existence of correct answers. Derrick Bell was an early practitioner of a method of using fictional stories or narratives—as opposed to nonfiction writing—to describe systems of oppression. His fictional stories were his interpretations of a world mired in racism. Critical pedagogues call such stories "alternative epistemologies."[89] For critical writers, these stories are more useful than facts, as they argue that truth is determined by the circumstances in which someone encounters his individual truth.

"Challenging old classics is the literary equivalent of replacing statues of racist figures," explained the *School Library Journal* in June 2020, as rioters were, in fact, tearing down statues of America's historical figures (soon to include, mind-bogglingly, Abraham Lincoln) after the death of George Floyd at the hands of a police officer in Minneapolis.[90] And, like the toppling of statues, this call to reject "old classics" is, in fact, more like the unthinking destruction of monuments than it is about thinking deeply on different reading materials in school.

This new perspective on teaching even has its own hashtag, #DisruptTexts, and rejects authors whom activists declare not committed to "anti-racist/anti-bias teaching pedagogy and practices."[91] For example, the #DisruptTexts website believes that "if you must teach [Shakespeare] due to school policies and lack of autonomy...the only way to do so is by disrupting his

---

89   Ledesma and Calderón, "Critical Race Theory in Education: A Review of Past Literature and a Look into the Future," pp. 206–222.

90   Padma Venkatraman, "Weeding Out Racism's Invisible Roots: Rethinking Children's Classics," *School Library Journal*, June 19, 2020, *https://www.slj.com/?detailStory=weeding-out-racisms-invisible-roots-rethinking-childrens-classics-libraries-diverse-books.*

91   #DisruptTexts, "What Is #DisruptTexts?" *https://disrupttexts.org/lets-get-to-work/.*

plays."[92] The activists explain that, "The more we learn alongside teachers who are disrupting texts, the more we move away from continuing to give space to these voices; the more we want to decenter the male white voices completely."[93]

They conclude: "This is about white supremacy and colonization." One Michigan educator's comments on the #DisruptTexts' website said that classics "plague our curriculum" and does not plan to "even return to teaching" Shakespeare.[94] Shakespeare is not alone in being tossed aside, of course. A *Wall Street Journal* headline from December 2020 on #DisruptTexts read: "Even Homer Gets Mobbed," and the author, Meghan Cox Gurdon, explains that the "ethos" of this trend is that "children shouldn't have to read stories written in anything other than their present-day vernacular."[95]

But the problem is more than just abandoning books your parents read for more current tomes, explains Gurdon: "If there is harm in classic literature, it comes from *not* teaching it," and students who are not taught such classics "will suffer a poverty of language and cultural reference." (The racial overtones, cultural and character-based implications, and specific state examples of the implementation of ideas like those from Equitable Math and #DisruptTexts are discussed in Chapter 2.)

With the rush to displace classic works of literature, the literary rioters are refusing to teach important facts and cultural knowledge contained in books such as *To Kill a Mockingbird*, another target of the #DisruptTexts group. The profound sig-

---

92   #DisruptTexts, "Disrupting Shakespeare," *https://disrupttexts.org/2018/10/25/5-disrupting-shakespeare/*.

93   Ibid.

94   Lorena German, "#DisruptTexts in Michigan," #DisruptTexts.org, May 25, 2020, *https://disrupttexts.org/2020/05/25/disrupttexts-in-michigan/*.

95   Meghan Cox Gurdon, "Even Homer Gets Mobbed," *The Wall Street Journal*, December 27, 2020, *https://www.wsj.com/articles/even-homer-gets-mobbed-11609095872*.

nificance of a white lawyer, Atticus Finch, defending a falsely accused black man, all contained in a fictional book published in the midst of the civil rights era, is lost in favor of "interrogating our own biases."[96]

There is great risk in rejecting the past in this way. Not least of which is that the memory of the real-life people who fought for freedom, as well as their ideas and achievements, will be casualties.

In one of the many racially charged riots in 2020, a group of rioters in Wisconsin tore down a statue of Hans Christian Heg, a Civil War-era *abolitionist* who led Union soldiers against the Confederacy and was active in rehabilitating convicted criminals and returning them to public life.[97] Heg and his family had immigrated from Norway, and he developed a reputation for welcoming other immigrants: "Heg's barn was open to all, and every summer saw it thronged with large parties of new comers who made it their home during the first days and weeks after their long journey."[98]

Assimilation was on Heg's mind when he wrote in a newspaper in 1861 that the officers of his Union regiment "will be men who speak the Scandinavian languages. Thus an opportunity to enter the service is afforded those Scandinavians who do not yet speak English."[99] Furthermore, "Slavery was abhorrent to him, and the sincerity of his views was later to

---

96 #DisruptTexts, "Core Principles," *https://disrupttexts.org/core-principles/*.

97 Wisconsin Historical Society, "Heg, Col. Hans Christian (1829–1863): Wisconsin Civil War Officer, Politician," Historical Essay, *https://www.wisconsinhistory.org/Records/Article/CS2545*, and Lawrence Andrea, "Hans Christian Heg Was an Abolitionist Who Died Trying to End Slavery. What to Know About the Man Whose Statue Was Toppled in Madison," *Milwaukee Journal-Sentinel*, June 24, 2020, *https://www.jsonline.com/story/news/local/wisconsin/2020/06/24/hans-christian-hegs-abolitionist-statue-toppled-madison-what-know/3248692001/*.

98 Theodore C. Blegen, "Colonel Hans Christian Heg," *The Wisconsin Magazine of History*, Vol. 4, No. 2 (December 1990), p. 142, *https://www.jstor.org/stable/pdf/4630294.pdf*.

99 National Park Service, "Hans Heg," *https://www.nps.gov/people/hans-heg.htm*.

be proved by the supreme sacrifice," wrote one historian in *The Wisconsin Magazine of History*.[100] Heg would later reform the Wisconsin prison system to focus on vocational training of prisoners instead of punishment. ("Nothing will arouse the virtuous aspirations of a fallen man so powerfully as the conviction that it still lies in his power to regain the rights he has forfeited, and that he yet can be respected by society as a fellow-man," Heg wrote in the *Annual Report of the State Prison Commissioner* in 1861.)[101]

Today's rioters destroyed a statue of a man representing many of the same ideals that self-proclaimed social justice advocates claim to support. Such actions tear at the fabric of communities and our shared customs and traditions, and are signals of a dramatic displacement of cultural mores taking place right before our eyes.

CONCLUSION

Surveys demonstrate that teachers are now less confident in the use of facts to communicate knowledge to students. Researchers at RAND asked teachers about their confidence in twelve different concepts related to social studies, history, and civics—and "to know facts" was ranked last. In "Truth Decay: Social Studies Teachers' Perspectives on Key Civic Outcomes in 2010 and 2019," the authors write that "individual teachers typically have some degree of autonomy over what happens in the classroom" and this "may be especially true in the field of social studies."[102] Just 32 percent of teachers said that "to know

---

100 Blegen, "Colonel Hans Christian Heg."
101 Ibid., and Hans Heg, *Annual Report of the State Prison Commissioner, for the Year Ending September 30, 1861*, p. 2.
102 Laura S. Hamilton, Julia H. Kaufman, and Lynn Hu, "Truth Decay: Social Studies Teachers' Perspectives on Key Civic Outcomes in 2010 and 2019," RAND, 2020, *https://www.rand.org/pubs/research_reports/RRA112-4.html*.

facts (e.g., the location of the fifty states) and dates (e.g., Pearl Harbor)" was "absolutely essential."

The most important item? "To be tolerant of people and groups who are different from themselves" was called "absolutely essential" by 80 percent of the respondents. As we will see in other examples of critical race theory material for K–12 schools, some education officials are quick to talk about the need for racial reconciliation using critical materials, but once those materials become public these officials prove less confident in their chosen solution. Smithsonian officials' removal of the "whiteness" infographic in the summer of 2020 is one example. Ohio state school board officials' resolution on systemic racism is another—officials were less confident about critical ideas once state residents had the opportunity to react to the material. In July 2020, board members adopted a resolution decrying systemic racism and asked the state department of education to recommend reading material to schools. But after department staff made the recommendations public, taxpayer and parent complaints pushed state education leaders to remove the list from the state agency's website, shortly after it had been posted. (More details are provided in Chapter 2.)

Readers should note that though the Smithsonian's infographic included the claim that the nuclear family is an example of oppressive white culture, U.S. Department of Education data find that 45 percent of black children living with only their mother, and 36 living with only their father, live in poverty, while just 12 percent of black children from two-parent families live in poverty.[103] Furthermore, as American Enterprise Institute scholar Ian Rowe points out, the percentage of

---

103 Ian Rowe, "The Power of the Two-Parent Home Is Not a Myth," American Enterprise Institute, January 8, 2020, *https://www.aei.org/articles/the-power-of-the-two-parent-home-is-not-a-myth/*.

births to unmarried white women has risen faster in the past thirty years than the percentage of births to unmarried black women—which Rowe says means that "the decline in family structure is an existential challenge facing communities of all backgrounds and one that all should tackle together."[104] Such data challenge the idea that the nuclear family is bad for children—in need of disruption—and that the nuclear family is somehow only for white Americans.

OOO

Maintaining a record of how education officials are using critical race theory in K–12 schools is important for parents and policymakers because education special interest groups are sending mixed messages. During the same week that the NEA committed its members to pushing critical ideas in classrooms, American Federation of Teachers president Randi Weingarten announced that, "Critical Race Theory is not taught in elementary schools or high schools."[105] One glance at the Equitable Math curriculum described above, along with the #DisruptTexts movement, reveals that Weingarten's claim is false. Yet, Weingarten says those opposed to critical race theory—again, with all its discriminatory elements described here—are "bullying teachers and trying to stop us from teaching students accurate history."

Ledesma and Calderón conclude their literature review saying, "CRT has evolved into a type of revolutionary project... we owe it to ourselves, and others, to help safeguard CRT," a

104 Ibid., and Elizabeth Wildsmith, Jennifer Manlove, and Elizabeth Cook, "Dramatic Increase in the Proportion of Births Outside of Marriage in the United States from 1990 to 2016," ChildTrends, August 8, 2018, *https://www.childtrends.org/publications/dramatic-increase-in-percentage-of-births-outside-marriage-among-whites-hispanics-and-women-with-higher-education-levels.*

105 Brittany Bernstein, "Teachers'-Union Head Claims CRT Is Only Taught at Colleges," *National Review Online,* July 6, 2021, *https://www.nationalreview.com/news/teachers-union-head-claims-crt-is-only-taught-at-colleges/.*

crusade the nation's largest teacher union continued with its announcement at the July 2021 conference described earlier (an announcement that the union later hid from public view). Ledesma and Calderón write that critical race theorists should, "whenever possible…recouple CRT to *all* of its historical roots"[106] (emphasis in original), roots that reach back to German Marxists from the early twentieth century. Chapter 2 provides specific examples of how critical race theory and critical pedagogy are being used in K–12 classrooms, and demonstrate just how widely accepted these ideas have become.

---

106 Ledesma and Calderón, "Critical Race Theory in Education," p. 218.

CHAPTER 2

K-12 EDUCATION UNDER ATTACK

"It sounded more like a recruitment seminar than an educational experience." In March 2021, Garren Bratcher, the father of a San Juan High School freshman, asked his daughter Ella's teacher for a different lesson after his daughter was required to study the Black Lives Matter (BLM) movement. He argued that the lessons tried to convince his daughter to agree with BLM's ideals, including such ideas as that transgender people should "lead" in classrooms and that the "nuclear family structure" should be "disrupted"—the same set of guiding principles that the leading New York City teachers union adopted, as explained in Chapter 1.[1] According to the BLM documents, public schools in America "[honor] the pervasive system of racism from which our country gains its roots" and must be changed.[2] School officials refused to provide a different lesson plan.

---

1 Marissa Perlman, "North Highlands Dad Angry His Daughter Is Being Taught about Black Lives Matter," CBS 13 Sacramento, March 18, 2021, *https://sacramento.cbslocal.com/2021/03/18/garren-bratcher-black-lives-matter-lesson-san-juan-high-school/*, and Black Lives Matter at School, "13 Guiding Principles," *https://www.blacklivesmatteratschool.com/13-guiding-principles.html.*
2 Black Lives Matter at School, "The Demands," *https://www.blacklivesmatteratschool.com/the-demands.html.*

"It made me really uncomfortable in class," Ella Bratcher told a local news station. San Juan's lesson is part of an ethnic studies program that California Department of Education officials created. Officials relied on content created by groups such as Learning for Justice, a branch of the radical leftist Southern Poverty Law Center, cited already in the introduction and Chapter 1 of this book and whose instructional material is based on critical race theory's central ideas.

California's ethnic studies lesson on the Black Lives Matter movement, specifically, uses Learning for Justice's course content, content that says that teachers should "encourage [students] to see themselves as activists."[3] According to the Learning for Justice lesson, "Guiding high schoolers to identify how dominant historical narratives silence stories of resistance can help them make connections between the past and the present."

Learning for Justice's lesson also says that public policies that promote "desegregation"—not segregation—are "symptoms of the systemic racism that has plagued the United States" and are similar to "state-sanctioned violence."[4]

This is how educators are applying critical race theory in classrooms. Racism is everywhere, America leaders intentionally designed laws and policies to oppress ethnic minorities, and students must be activists against the country they call home. There is no American dream, only one long nightmare.

---

3   Jamilah Pitts, "Bringing Black Lives Matter into the Classroom, Part II," *Teaching Tolerance,* Issue 56 (Summer 2017), *https://www.learningforjustice.org/magazine/summer-2017/bringing-black-lives-matter-into-the-classroom-part-ii,* and California Department of Education, "Ethnic Studies Model Curriculum: Chapter 4: Sample Lessons and Topics," p. 74, *https://www.cde.ca.gov/ci/cr/cf/esmc.asp.*
4   Ibid.

OOO

One of the most important parts of a teacher's job, shared with parents and family and friends, should be to help children to identify prejudice so that it can be rejected. Critical race theorists, beholders of the new conventional thinking in schools, grind prejudice into students by teaching them that discrimination is all around them. Life becomes an exercise in finding examples of how we are oppressed.

California's new ethnic studies course is an example of the new conventional thinking in K–12 schools.

In October 2020, California Governor Gavin Newsom vetoed a bill that would have required all high school students to complete a course in ethnic studies before graduating.[5] For four years, the California Department of Education had been drafting academic standards and a model ethnic studies curriculum that the agency would distribute to teachers and students around the state. According to reports, the veto was a surprise to many. Just weeks before his veto, Newsom had signed a state law that made ethnic studies a graduation requirement for the state university system.[6]

As it turns out, Newsom would not need to make an ethnic studies course a requirement. By fall 2020, the Los Angeles, San Diego, and Fresno school districts were already planning to make the ethnic studies course a high school graduation requirement even without the state mandate. Thus Newsom's veto did not stop this ethnic studies program in its tracks—in fact, the state department of education released a final ver-

---

5   Office of the Governor of the State of California, Veto Letter for Assembly Bill 331, September 30, 2020, *https://www.gov.ca.gov/wp-content/uploads/2020/09/AB-331.pdf.*
6   John Fensterwald, "Gov. Newsome Vetoes Requirement for Ethnic Studies Course in High School," *EdSource,* October 1, 2020, *https://edsource.org/2020/gov-newsom-vetoes-requirement-for-ethnic-studies-course-in-high-school/640877.*

sion of the curriculum in March 2021.[7] Even without a state requirement, ethnic studies—which, as we will see, contains critical race theory's divisive ideals—will be taught in schools in the most populous state in the union.

"Ethnic studies" is too mild to describe California's new state-sponsored course materials. Though the model curriculum begins with the statement, "Ethnic studies is for all students," the curricular materials explain that some ethnicities are more important than others.[8] Capitalists, of course, are colonizers, the creators of systemic racism.[9] The four "foundational disciplines" in the model curriculum—(1) Identity, (2) History and Movement, (3) Systems of Power, and (4) Social Movements and Equity—read like one of Paulo Freire or Derrick Bell's essays. The curriculum says, "At its core, the field of ethnic studies is the interdisciplinary study of race, ethnicity, and Indigeneity, with an emphasis on the experiences of people of color in the United States." The materials will emphasize the "common experience of racism."

The introduction to the model curriculum wastes no time introducing intersectionality, one of the "guiding outcomes" for the course:

> *The field also addresses the concept of intersectionality, which recognizes that people have different overlapping identities, for example, a transgender Latina or a Jewish African American. These intersecting identities shape individuals' experiences of racism and bigotry. The field critically grapples with the various power structures and forms of oppression*

---

7 California Department of Education, "Ethnic Studies Model Curriculum," *https://www.cde.ca.gov/ci/cr/cf/esmc.asp.*
8 Ibid., "Introduction."
9 California Department of Education, "Ethnic Studies Model Curriculum," Chapter 4, pp. 14 and 236–237.

that continue to have social, emotional, cultural, economic, and political impacts.[10]

The word "intersectionality," in fact, appears regularly in the model coursework. Intersectionality is a critical technique for describing the overlapping layers of groups' victimhood. Under this concept, those who are not white can belong to more than one identity group (such as being Hispanic and transgender), and from those identifications, group members can claim to be oppressed in more than one way. You can multiply your level of victimization by being, say, a gay man from an ethnic minority—and multiply it even more if you are a gay woman from an ethnic minority. Any treatment that you find offensive because you are queer, you can add on top of that other offenses you find or perceive in the culture around you because you are an ethnic minority.

Kimberlé Crenshaw, law professor at Columbia Law School, and one of the original critical race theorists, developed intersectionality as a central component to critical race theory in the late 1980s. She says that "dominant conceptions of discrimination condition us to think about subordination as disadvantage occurring along a single categorical axis," that is, people regularly consider issues of bias according to one characteristic, such as race.[11] This is not enough, says Crenshaw. This form of analysis "erases" people. She says that minority individuals, black women especially, are "multiply-burdened," and "because the intersectional experience is greater than the sum of racism and sexism, any analysis

---

10 California Department of Education, "Ethnic Studies Model Curriculum," Introduction and Overview, p. 5.
11 Kimberlé Crenshaw, "Demarginalizing the Intersection of Race and Sex: A Black Feminist Critique of Antidiscrimination Doctrine, Feminist Theory and Antiracist Politics," *University of Chicago Legal Forum*, Issue 1 (1989), *https://chicagounbound. uchicago.edu/cgi/viewcontent.cgi?article=1052&context=uclf.*

that does not take intersectionality into account cannot suffi-ciently address the particular manner in which Black women are subordinated."

To critical race theorists, people's ethnic and gender iden-tities—not their actions, attitudes, or character—are essential because they determine how society keeps them down.

The survey of critical race theory (CRT) and education papers cited in Chapter 1 by María Ledesma and Dolores Calderón says that "CRT's commitment to intersectionality...also recognizes that oppression and racism are not unidirectional, but rather that oppression and racism can be experiences within and across divergent intersectional planes, such as classicism, sexism, ableism, and so on."[12] As applied to K–12 schools, they explain, ethnic studies courses have "provided CRT scholars with a robust foundation to draw upon the concept of intersectionality and flesh it out in their work."

Intersectionality is one of many critical concepts that state education officials included in California's ethnic stud-ies curriculum. In the final draft of the standards and model lesson plans, the coursework has "[centered] and [placed] high value on the pre-colonial, ancestral knowledge, nar-ratives, and communal experiences of Native People/s and people of color and groups that are typically marginalized in society."[13] Here, the priority is not only to discuss diver-sity and pluralism but to assume that some people are still "typically marginalized," regardless of whether someone with a certain skin color actually believes this to be true. The standards and lessons teach him that he is marginalized. The facts do not matter—racism is everywhere, whether you see it or not.

---

12   Ledesma and Calderón, "Critical Race Theory in Education."
13   Ibid.

Frantz Fanon's contributions to the critical worldview are included, as well. The coursework will "critique empire-building in history and its relationship to white supremacy"—not questioning whether the connection exists but assuming it is the case—along with "racism and other forms of power and oppression."[14]

Included in the list of recommended readings from California's ethnic studies curriculum is Howard Zinn's *A People's History of the United States*, a retelling of U.S. history that Fanon would appreciate. Zinn, a radical professor and activist, taught at Spelman College in Georgia and later at Boston University. He wrote *A People's History* in 1980, and the book was something of a cult classic for many years. Hollywood helped to renew interest in Zinn's work in the 1990s with the movie *Good Will Hunting*, released in 1997. In the film, Matt Damon's character, Will Hunting, tells the therapist played by Robin Williams: "If you want to read a real history book, read Howard Zinn's *A People's History of the United States*. That book will knock you on your ass."[15]

Indeed it will, but not for the reasons that Will Hunting would like. Readers get a sense of Zinn's perspective in *A People's History* from such claims as that the English arrival in North America, which any honest historian acknowledges involved bloodshed, disease, and hostile relationships between settlers and native tribes, was the result of "that special powerful drive born in civilizations based on private property."[16] According to Zinn, the settlers who established treaties with Native Americans, or who were seeking freedom for themselves from harsh European monarchs, have no redeeming qualities. Zinn also writes,

---

14   California Department of Education, "Ethnic Studies Curriculum," Chapter 3, p. 23.
15   Grabar, *Debunking Howard Zinn*, p. 10.
16   Zinn, *A People's History of the United States*.

My viewpoint, in telling the history of the United States, is...that we must not accept the memory of states as our own. Nations are not communities and never have been. The history of any country, presented as the history of a family, conceals fierce conflicts of interest (sometimes exploding, most often repressed) between conquerors and conquered, masters and slaves, capitalists and workers, dominators and dominated in race and sex.[17]

Such material can hardly be considered "ethnic studies for all students," as California officials described their ethnic studies course. In his afterword to the book added in 1999, Zinn says, "I wanted, in writing [*A People's History*], to awaken a greater consciousness of class conflict, racial injustice, sexual inequality, and national arrogance."[18]

One need not be politically conservative to find Zinn's work problematic. Writing for the American Federation of Teachers (AFT), the nation's second-largest teachers union, Sam Wineburg says that Zinn's book resembles the allegedly one-sided textbooks that educators intent on "decolonization" want removed. Wineburg says that "when *A People's History* draws on primary sources, these documents serve to prop up the main text, but never provide an alternative view or open up a new field of vision."[19]

He goes on: "Such a history atrophies our tolerance for complexity. It makes us allergic to exceptions to the rule. Worst of all, it depletes the moral courage we need to revise our beliefs in the face of new evidence."

Lessons that use Zinn's work do not teach students to consider that America's ideals of freedom and equality were the

---

17   Ibid.
18   Ibid.
19   Sam Wineburg, "Where Howard Zinn's *A People's History* Falls Short," *American Educator* (Winter 2012/2013), *https://www.aft.org/periodical/american-educator/winter-2012-2013/undue-certainty*.

profound climax of millennia of philosophies on the value of individuals and the possibility for human flourishing in a self-governed system. Zinn simply flips the hero-villain script of mid-twentieth-century cowboys-and-Indians TV shows and passes it off as history.

One more example from California's ethnic studies exemplifies the curriculum authors' efforts to ignore America's founding principles and focus on the guilt that should be bestowed on anyone who does not identify as "marginalized." In one of the model lesson plans, students are to read a section from *A People's History* and then from *A Patriot's History of the United States* by Larry Schweikart and Michael Allen, who have a decidedly different perspective on U.S. history than Zinn.[20] Those looking for an even-handed approach need go no further than the sample lesson's title, "This Is Indian Land: The Purpose, Politics, and Practice of Land Acknowledgement," to be disappointed.

Even before the readings, the lesson guide describes the purpose of the lesson as "recogniz[ing] that colonization is an ongoing process, and to inspire critically conscious action and reflection." Students are to "identify counter-hegemonic truth telling and reconciliation efforts." "Hegemony" is another concept that critical theorists developed. Critical thinker Antonio Gramsci, an Italian Communist Party leader during the early twentieth century, often referred to the dominant social and economic classes holding sway over ideas and institutions as "hegemonic." He described the hegemonic concept as "state-as-force."[21]

Students are to read an article from *Teen Vogue* and one from the Canadian Broadcasting Corporation about land belonging to aboriginal peoples. The latter article describes how students at a Toronto school are to participate in a schoolwide announce-

---

20 California Department of Education, "CDE-Recommended Edits: Sample Lessons and Topics," and Larry Schweikart and Michael Allen, *A Patriot's History of the United States: From Columbus's Great Discovery to the War on Terror* (New York: Sentinel, 2004).

21 David Forgacs, ed. *The Gramsci Reader* (New York: New York University Press, 2000), p. 195.

ment each morning that their school is built on land that was once inhabited by Native Americans.[22] The lesson plan then asks California students to create a "land acknowledgement statement and poster," admitting that they are guilty of maintaining the colonization of tribal lands.[23]

California's ethnic studies content is but one example of what is happening in states around the country. Public- and private-school educators in schools across the U.S. are adopting textbooks and lesson plans that teach children that they belong to tribes, and that America's laws and government are biased and will prevent students who are not white from succeeding—eclipsing any sense that students may have of the American dream.

The examples from classroom content in California also demonstrate that critical race theory is, in fact, taught in schools, despite claims to the contrary. AFT president Randi Weingarten made such a claim in July 2021, as mentioned in Chapter 1, and just weeks earlier, Representative Ilhan Omar (D-MN) said the same.[24] Journalists around the country have also said that critical race theory is not being taught in public schools.[25] These claims are impossible to defend when California's State Department of Education created a curriculum with an entire section on

---

22 Shannon Martin, "TDSB Schools Now Pay Daily Tribute to Indigenous Lands They're Built On," CBC, September 22, 2016, *https://www.cbc.ca/news/canada/toronto/tdsb-indigenous-land-1.3773050*.

23 California Department of Education, "CDE-Recommended Edits: Sample Lessons and Topics."

24 Caitlin McFall, "Ilhan Omar Denies Critical Race Theory Is Being Taught in Schools, Blames GOP for 'False Narratives,'" FoxNews.com, June 19, 2021, *https://www.foxnews.com/politics/ihan-omar-denies-critical-race-theory-is-being-taught-in-schools-blames-gop-for-false-narratives*.

25 John Battiston, "Ziegler Remains Firm LCPS Is 'Not Teaching Critical Race Theory,'" *Loudon Times-Mirror*, June 3, 2021, https://www.loudountimes.com/news/ziegler-remains-firm-lcps-is-not-teaching-critical-race-theory/article_146c1e8c-c3c9-11eb-9217-ebb5be4d3868.html, "Explained: The Truth about Critical Race Theory and How It Shows Up in Your Child's Classroom," *Education Post*, May 5, 2021, https://educationpost.org/explained-the-truth-about-critical-race-theory-and-how-it-shows-up-in-your-childs-classroom/, and Kiara Alfonseca, "Critical Race Theory in the Classroom: Understanding the Debate," ABC News, May 19, 2021, *https://abcnews.go.com/US/critical-race-theory-classroom-understanding-debate/story?id=77627465*.

intersectionality, one of critical race theory's central ideas. Or when officials from the Hayward Unified School District, a district located just south of Oakland on the east edge of the San Francisco Bay, release a memo to the school community saying that they have adopted California's ethnic studies curriculum and "will include critical race theory" in school instruction.[26]

But California is only the beginning.

NORTH CAROLINA:
"WHITENESS" IN EDUCATION SPACES AND IN SOCIAL STUDIES STANDARDS

Some North Carolina educators do not want parents to get in the way of critical instruction. In fall 2020, an independent journalist filed a public records request with Wake County Public Schools, the largest public school district in the state, to find out which materials the district's EdCamp Equity project was using to train teachers in critical ideas.[27] One handout available to participants at an EdCamp Equity "camp" held in February 2020 read, "You can't let parents deter you from the work...What do we do with parent push back?...Hard to let go of power/privilege...Loss of power." The handout then offers a brief explanation of critical race theory, saying that teachers must "analyz[e] every space with a critical lense [sic]." Critical race theory is described as a school of thought in which whiteness is the "dominant culture that permeates our country"— yet more evidence that critical race theory is being taught in schools. Professional development seminars are training teachers to include it in their classrooms.

26   Hayward Unified School District, "HUSD Board of Trustees Vote to Approve Ethnic Studies Policy," June 25, 2021, *https://www.husd.us/pf4/cms2/news_themed_display?id=1624611250631.*

27   A. P. Dillon, "Records Request Reveals 'Whiteness in Ed Spaces,' 'Affinity Groups' at WCPSS EdCamp Equity," LadyLiberty1885.com, September 5, 2020, *https://ladyliberty1885.com/2020/09/05/records-whiteness-in-ed-spaces-wcpss-edcamp-equity-2020/.*

District officials did not require teachers to attend the camp, but district teachers helped to organize the event and used school money to pay for the materials and speaker fees. Though Wake County officials denied that teachers were using critical race theory in "offerings within the district," according to reports, the EdCamp Equity slide presentation the journalist obtained began with a land acknowledgement picture, similar to the student assignment in California's ethnic studies described above.[28] Event organizers provided participants with a list of recommended readings that included writings by Howard Zinn, Learning for Justice materials, and #DisruptTexts.

Copies of the event notes also reveal that EdCamp Equity participants were to "dismantle" social studies in North Carolina—convenient timing for such a message, as state education officials began revising the state's social studies standards that year. Academic standards serve as guiding ideas for educators, and what happens inside the classroom once the teacher is charged with filling in the details on a lesson matters greatly. Yet academic standards reflect the subject matter that state departments of education officials and local school leaders decide are important. Standards and content are inseparable, then, and state officials' priorities are levied on local educators through academic standards.

As of July 2020, North Carolina's standards for high school American history included a section focusing on "how slavery, xenophobia, disenfranchisement, and intolerance have affected individual and group perspectives of themselves as Americans."[29] This rendering of the issue could be discussed

---

28 Dillon, "Wake County Schools' Administrator Denies Critical Race Theory District Offerings," *The North State Journal*, May 5, 2021, *https://nsjonline.com/article/2021/05/wake-county-schools-administrator-denies-critical-race-theory-district-offerings/*.

29 North Carolina Department of Public Instruction, "North Carolina Standards for American History," July 2020, *https://drive.google.com/file/d/1FqVEvoHLGNAZqRvHjGuQdjfiQbsNzcLz/view*.

from different viewpoints, but in a section on "turning points in American history in terms of perspective, causation, and change," there is a lesson plan that smacks of critical race theory's dogma surrounding the concept of white privilege. The lesson materials state that educators and students should "[d]istinguish the extent to which American foreign policy has advanced the interests of historically privileged groups over the interests of historically marginalized peoples."

Here, critical race theory's assumption that American interests *have* been discriminatory, not exploring *if* this is the case, is on display. The term "deconstruct" is used throughout the standards, pointing to the critical approach of focusing on the use of language and interpretations, not facts, to draw conclusions. For example, students are to "analyze the American economic system in terms of affluence, poverty, and mobility" by "deconstruct[ing] multiple perspectives of American capitalism in terms of affluence, poverty, and mobility."

These standards are rife with references to power and the use of government to "expand or restrict freedom and equality," and the theme of alleged discrimination that immigrants and "marginalized" groups face appears over and over.

The language used in these standards is from the fourth iteration of the material, which means that policymakers and reviewers had spent some time working through the ideas. In early 2021, local media reported that the standards had still caused "intense division" among members of the state board of education.[30] North Carolina's Lieutenant Governor Mark Robinson criticized the standards, especially the use of the term "systemic racism," which officials later removed.[31] Before drafters removed

---

30 Emily Walkenhorst, "How to Teach America's Negative History Prompts Debate on NC Board of Education," WRAL.com, January 27, 2021, *https://www.wral.com/how-to-teach-america-s-negative-history-prompts-debate-on-nc-board-of-education/19494741/*.

31 T. Keung Hui, "How Do You Teach America's 'Sins?' NC Board Still at Odds Over Social Studies Standards," *News & Observer*, February 3, 2021, *https://www.newsobserver.com/news/local/education/article248976850.html*.

the term, though, an editorial cartoon was published in local media that depicted an elephant (representing GOP officials such as Robinson who opposed the standards) in a KKK costume scratching out the state standards document with a pen. Offended by the crude and racialized caricature, Lieutenant Governor Robinson, who is black, and state board member Olivia Oxendine, of Native American descent, said the cartoon was "nothing short of bullying and should not be tolerated."[32]

In 2021, Robinson created a task force to investigate what his office called "indoctrination" across North Carolina schools.[33] The Fairness and Accountability in the Classroom for Teachers and Students (FACTS) task force released a report in August 2021 after reviewing five hundred allegations from parents and teachers of classroom instruction or activities that involved "fear of retaliation," "the sexualization of kids," "critical race theory," and "White Shaming," among other topics.[34] Teachers and parents sent FACTS hundreds of emails describing how their children were afraid to disagree with lessons on white privilege or presentations that criticized colorblind perspectives.

As the FACTS report and standards demonstrate, the culture war is raging in North Carolina schools. State board member Todd Chasteen was quoted by local media as saying, "We have to talk about the hard things, the failures, but we also have to build optimism and unity."[35] It is hard to be optimistic when your textbook says that your country systemically oppresses people.

Meanwhile, North Carolina Department of Education officials have posted a text on the agency's website that includes the asser-

32 Ibid.
33 David N. Bass, "Lt. Governor Announces Task Force on Bias, Indoctrination in Public Schools," *Carolina Journal*, March 16, 2021, *https://www.carolinajournal.com/news-article/lt-governor-announces-task-force-on-bias-indoctrination-in-public-schools/*.
34 The Office of Lt. Governor Mark Robinson, "Indoctrination in North Carolina Public Education," Fairness and Accountability in the Classroom for Teachers and Students Task Force, August 24, 2021, *https://drive.google.com/file/d/1NfHOpZGD4EeHcGD6y1AeVBuGUZkpNUia/view*.
35 Walkenhorst, "How to Teach America's Negative History Prompts Debate on NC Board of Education."

tion that "U.S cultural norms conflate race and class such that material wealth is associated with being White," which "fosters a sense of White racial entitlement and unearned privilege."[36] The outrageous and skewed text is included as part of the agency's "Equity" and "Social and Emotional Learning" (SEL) initiative. SEL is an instructional practice that has been increasingly common in schools around the U.S. for more than twenty years and is broadly described by advocates as a set of school services and activities that help students to develop "health identities."[37] SEL has been widely studied, and its effectiveness in school settings is beyond the scope of this book, but content such as this article on North Carolina's Department of Education website has made parents concerned that SEL has become a delivery mechanism for critical race theory's core ideas.[38]

One local reporter said that the debate over social studies among North Carolina education officials, parents, and policymakers was "a 'microcosm' of national political discourse surrounding race and

36   Robert J. Jagers, Deborah Rivas-Drake, and Brittney Williams, "Transformative Social and Emotional Learning (SEL): Toward SEL in Service of Educational Equity and Excellent," *Educational Psychologist* Vol. 54, No. 3 (2019), *https://www.tandfonline. com/doi/abs/10.1080/00461520.2019.1623032?journalCode=hedp20.*

37   Collaborative for Academic, Social, and Emotional Learning, "SEL Is...," *https:// casel.org/what-is-sel/,* and Stephanie Jones, et al., "Socio-Emotional Learning: What It Is, What It Isn't, and What We Know," *Education Next*, April 30, 2019, *https://www. educationnext.org/social-emotional-learning-isnt-know/.*

38   See, for example, Keely Quinlan, "Parents Bring Questions about Critical Race Theory, Social-Emotional Learning to School Board," *Clarksville Now*, August 24, 2021,   *https://clarksvillenow.com/local/parents-bring-questions-about-critical-race-theo- ry-social-emotional-learning-to-school-board/,* Reid Glenn, "Schools to Teach 'Social Emotional Learning,'" eMissourian.com, August 29, 2021, *https://www.emissou- rian.com/local_news/schools-to-teach-social-emotional-learning/article_72abddd6-0869- 11ec-8081-73f86585c380.html,* Grace Phillips, "Public Raises Concerns About CRT and SEL in Martinsville Schools," *Reporter-Times*, August 27, 2021, *https://www. reporter-times.com/story/news/local/2021/08/27/public-raises-concerns-crt-and-sel-mar- tinsville-schools/5614004001/,* and Dan Rosenfield, "No Opt-Out for Cedar Grove Social-Emotional Learning Curriculum," TapInto Verona/Cedar Grove, August 24, 2021, *https://www.tapinto.net/towns/verona-slash-cedar-grove/sections/education/articles/ no-opt-out-for-cedar-grove-social-emotional-learning-curriculum.*

the United States' racial history."[39] As we have seen in California, and will see again in other states, the reporter is correct.

OHIO STATE BOARD OF EDUCATION GETS COLD FEET

In 2020, the Ohio State Board of Education adopted a resolution stating that, "Equity is our [strategic] plan's greatest imperative" but the resolution goes on to say, "Whereas 'separate but equal' is no longer the law of the land...systemic inequity in education has relegated millions of children of color to under-resourced, struggling schools."[40]

Using the same language as diversity trainers and critical pedagogues, the resolution sounds like its authors have discovered the path to racial righteousness: "the starting point of our work in racial equity must be reflection and internal examination," straight from the playbook of critical race theorists. The board then commits to requiring diversity training programs for state education employees—the same diversity training programs that researchers have found ineffective at changing peoples' attitudes toward, and behavior regarding, racial bias, as is explained later in this chapter.[41] Then the board directed the state department of education to identify and share "curricular models and resources" that further this effort. The agency complied in the summer of 2020 by posting content espousing critical race theory's ideas on its website, with the agency's social studies email newsletter

39 Walkenhorst, "How to Teach America's Negative History Prompts Debate on NC Board of Education."

40 Ohio State Board of Education, "Resolution to Condemn Racism and to Advance Equity and Opportunity for Black Students, Indigenous Students and Students of Color," *July 14, 2020*, and Catherine Candisky, "Opponents Say State School Board's Anti-Racism Resolution Unjustified," *The Columbus Dispatch*, July 17, 2020, *https://www.dispatch.com/story/news/politics/2020/07/17/opponents-say-state-school-boardrsquos-anti-racism-resolution-unjustified/42088205/*.

41 See, for example, Frank Dobbin and Alexandra Kalev, "Why Doesn't Diversity Training Work?" *Anthropology Now*, Vol. 10, No. 2 (September 2018), *https://scholar.harvard.edu/files/dobbin/files/an2018.pdf*.

("Ohio Social Studies Signal") even including an announcement about the content in its July edition [42]

Board members were not unanimous in adopting the resolution, with one member calling the resolution's text "a slap in the face of those families and those individuals that go the extra mile to succeed," and another calling it "wrongheaded."[43] But the newsletter recommended Learning for Justice's[44] materials to prepare teachers to teach critical ideas.[45] The newsletter also promoted an article telling teachers to "[confront] their own biases" and argued that colorblindness "does not help" in "reducing racial prejudice or increasing racial understanding."[46] Following the adoption of the board's resolution, the state agency posted an "Anti-Racism Allyship Resource Starter Pack" with links to "anti-racist" articles.[47]

By November 2020, this starter pack had disappeared from the state department of education's website.[48]

The starter pack was filled with critical material. It started with "How White Women's Tears Threaten Black Existence," which argues that to "call the police on Black people, no matter the reasoning, is violent in and of itself simply because the act

---

42   Ohio Social Studies Signal, July 2020, *http://education.ohio.gov/getattachment/ Topics/Learning-in-Ohio/Social-Studies/Resources-for-Social-Studies/Ohio-Social-Studies- Signal-Newsletter/July-2020-1/Download-the-newsletter/SSSignalJuly2020Final.pdf.aspx- ?lang=en-US*, and Antiracist Allyship Starter Pack, "Resources & Tools Regarding Racism & Anti/Blackness [sic]," *https://docs.google.com/spreadsheets/d/e/2PACX-1vT- kmrhfhYUfCcTbp3NoDmxKZUAN7xMiVuhqIlNBizKz-Ih7yPPqTPFgYzmd5NgKtEdpVugB- 6GoZwPWR/pubhtml.*

43   Candisky, "Opponents Say State School Board's Anti-Racism Resolution Unjustified."

44   Under the group's former name, Teaching for Tolerance.

45   Ohio Department of Education, "Ohio Social Studies Signal," July 2020, *http:// education.ohio.gov/getattachment/Topics/Learning-in-Ohio/Social-Studies/Resources-for- Social-Studies/Ohio-Social-Studies-Signal-Newsletter/July-2020-1/Download-the-newsletter/ SSSignalJuly2020Final.pdf.aspx?lang=en-US.*

46   Candra Flanagan and Anna Hindley, "Let's Talk! Teaching Race in the Classroom," *Social Education*, Vol. 81, No. 1 (January/February 2017), pp. 62–66, *https://www. socialstudies.org/system/files/publications/articles/se_810117062.pdf.*

47   Antiracist Allyship Starter Pack, "Resources & Tools Regarding Racism & Anti/ Blackness [sic]."

48   Ohio Department of Education, "Ohio Social Studies Signal," November 2020, *http://education.ohio.gov/getattachment/86b6c417-1cf3-4496-ba06-7fbbabad0ad8/ SSSignalNov2020.pdf.aspx?lang=en-US.*

cannot be separated from historical context."[49] This may strike some black Americans as objectionable based on the results of a Gallup poll mentioned earlier that found that more than 80 percent of black Americans want police to spend the "same amount of time" or "more time" patrolling their local area.[50] Or "What Do We Do with White Folks?" which says that "even white money that is 'earned' is tainted by the labor and sacrifice of people of color—mostly Black and Native folks."[51] Other articles on the list include "In Defense of Looting" and "White People Have No Culture," where the (white) author claims: "White people do have culture. Our culture is that of colonization. Of genocide. Of taking. Of envy and fear."[52]

The starter pack also included the historically revisionist 1619 Project, work by "antiracist" activist professor Ibram X. Kendi, and of course, critical pedagogue Paulo Freire. For a board that resolved with such assurance that fixing systemic racism was its priority, its members suddenly lost the confidence to actually tell parents, taxpayers, and policymakers which ideas and materials they want educators to use to resolve the problem.

In November 2020, the Ohio State Board of Education included a statement in its social studies newsletter about the removal of the starter pack, saying that "the resource was removed from the webpage as it was determined to not meet the Department's standards for quality curricular resources."[53] Perhaps the state agency and its school board were not as confident in their prescription for achieving racial reconciliation as officials once thought.

---

49   Cameron Glover, "How White Women's Tears Threaten Black Existence," *Wear Your Voice*, May 15, 2018, *https://wearyourvoicemag.com/how-white-womens-tears-threaten-black-existence/*.

50   Saad, "Black Americans Want Police to Retain Local Presence."

51   Anthony James Williams, "What Do We Do with White Folks?" Medium, February 4, 2019, *https://medium.com/@anthoknees/what-do-we-do-with-white-folks-525a23dbead3*.

52   Lorena Wallace, "White People Have No Culture," Terra Incognita, February 28, 2018, *https://www.terraincognitamedia.com/features/white-people-have-no-culture2018*.

53   Ohio Department of Education, "Ohio Social Studies Signal," November 2020.

ILLINOIS' CULTURALLY RESPONSIVE TEACHING AND LEARNING STANDARDS

Illinois' policymakers have applied critical instruction to class-rooms through state-mandated teacher-certification requirements. In February 2021, lawmakers approved the Illinois State Board of Education's "Culturally Responsive Teaching and Learning Standards,"[54] developed by the Council of Chief State School Officers (a membership organization made up of the executives from state departments of education) and its Diverse and Learner-Ready Teachers task force.[55] The new standards for teacher-certifi-cation programs begin with the statement that "there is often not one 'correct' way of doing or understanding something, and that what is seen as 'correct' is most often based on our lived experi-ences," immediately calling to mind the Frankfurt School's rejec-tion of the possibility of authentic truth.[56] Teachers are to admit that they are biased, regardless of what they may think about them-selves; the standards say that teachers should assess "how their biases and perceptions affect their teaching practice and how they access tools to mitigate their own behavior (racism, sexism, homophobia, unearned privilege, Eurocentrism, etc.)."

Intersectionality is included ("Explore their [teachers'] own intersecting identities, how they were developed, and how they impact daily experiences of the world"), along with the "decolo-

---

54 Illinois State Board of Education, "Notice of Proposed Amendments: Title 23: Education and Cultural Resources, Subtitle A: Education, Chapter I: State Board of Education, Subchapter b: Personnel, Part 24: Culturally Responsive Teaching and Learning Standards for all Illinois Educators," *https://www.isbe.net/Documents/23-24RG-P.pdf*, and Amy Korte, "Illinois Lawmakers Approve Controversial 'Culturally Responsive' Teaching Rule," Illinois Policy Institute, February 23, 2021, *https://www.illi-noispolicy.org/illinois-lawmakers-approve-controversial-culturally-responsive-teaching-rule/*.

55 Illinois State Board of Education, "Diverse and Learner Ready Teachers," *https://www.isbe.net/dlrt*.

56 Illinois State Board of Education, "Notice of Proposed Amendments: Title 23: Education and Cultural Resources, Subtitle A: Education, Chapter I: State Board of Education, Subchapter b: Personnel, Part 24: Culturally Responsive Teaching and Learning Standards for all Illinois Educators."

nization" of books and course material ("Use a resource tool to assess the curriculum and assessments for biases").

What policymakers struck from the certification standards is as telling, in terms of the emphasis on critical race theory, as the new material. State officials struck the words "content knowledge" from the list of teacher priorities, along with the provision that teachers should understand the "major concepts, assumptions, debates, principles and theories that are central to the disciplines in which licensure is sought." Also removed was the instruction that teachers are to understand "the relationship of knowledge within the discipline to other content areas and to life and career applications" and that teachers should engage students in "generating and testing knowledge according to the process of inquiry and standards of evidence of the discipline."[57]

Now, instead of imparting knowledge and teaching facts, teachers are to recognize that "there are systems in our society, especially, but not limited to, our school system that create and reinforce inequities, thereby creating oppressive conditions," and teachers should research and offer "student advocacy content with real world implications."[58]

A survey of Illinoisans finds little support for these ideas. In a poll conducted by the American Council of Trustees and Alumni and an organization called eighteen92, 47 percent of respondents said that "schools should focus on teaching students about American founding principles and the documents that established the first free and democratic country in the world."[59] Half of respondents said, "Fighting racism means making sure that everyone regardless of race has the same opportunities and

---

57   Ibid.

58   Ibid.

59   American Council of Trustees and Alumni, "ACTA Survey: Illinois," March 11, 2021, *https://www.goacta.org/resource/new-acta-survey-finds-strong-opposition-to-politicizing-K–12-teaching-in-illinois/.*

equal protection under the law—but it's not the government's role to mandate equal outcomes for everyone."

Just 23 percent of those surveyed said that "teachers should embrace progressive viewpoints and perspectives when teaching U.S. history, to encourage students to advocate for social justice causes." Taking direct aim at the new teaching standards, 57 percent said, "Teacher preparation programs in Illinois should focus on making teachers better equipped to help students develop core skills and competencies, not on social justice or progressive politics." A whopping 84 percent said, "All people should be treated equally based on merit."[60]

ACTION CIVICS

Marx's tombstone, which is large enough to be a monument, reads: "The philosophers have only interpreted the world in various ways. The point however is to change it."[61] Through "action civics," educators and students exercise the Frankfurt School's ambitions in K–12 education. The concept drew widespread acclaim among progressive educators during President Barack Obama's administration in 2012, when the U.S. Department of Education released "Advancing Civic Learning and Engagement in Democracy: A Road Map and Call to Action." Given the title, it should come as no surprise that the report downplayed teaching facts, and advocated training students to become active— even activists—in politics.[62]

---

60 Ibid.
61 Elian Peltier, "With Cameras Monitoring His Grave, Karl Marx Still Can't Escape Surveillance," *The New York Times*, February 9, 2020, *https://www.nytimes.com/2020/02/09/world/europe/karl-marx-grave-london.html*.
62 U.S. Department of Education, "Advancing Civic Learning and Engagement in Democracy: A Road Map and Call to Action," January 2012, *https://www.ed.gov/sites/default/files/road-map-call-to-action.pdf*.

The 2012 report echoes many of the same themes cited by educators and parents about the need for more instruction in civics overall, making the initial claims of the report agreeable to many on either side of the political divide. The report's authors, led by then education secretary Arne Duncan, wrote that "unfortunately, civic learning and democratic engagement are add-ons rather than essential parts of the core academic mission in too many schools and on too many college campuses today."[63]

The Obama administration and critical theory-minded educators were keen on the "democratic engagement." Yet this engagement means something different from encouraging students to volunteer to pick up trash on the side of the road or register to vote when they are eighteen. The report's authors write: "The goals of traditional civic education, such as increasing civic knowledge, voter participation, or volunteerism, remain worth pursuing. However, the new generation of civic learning puts students at the center and includes both learning and practice—not just rote memorization of names, dates, and processes."[64]

Given the dismal performance of students on civics, history, and geography tests, along with the widespread lack of knowledge among everyday voters about government and current events, the Obama administration's de-emphasis of facts was puzzling. According to The Nation's Report Card, administered to a nationally representative sample of students in different subjects, including civics, average scores did not change at all between 2014 and 2018, and have only increased three points since 1998.[65] Among the nation's highest-achieving students, the share of children scoring at or above the "proficient" level, which is considered at or above a child's grade-level (eighth grade, in the case of the civics test), has

---

63 Ibid.
64 Ibid.
65 National Assessment of Educational Progress, "Civics 2018," *https://www.nationsreportcard.gov/highlights/civics/2018/*.

not changed since 1998. So K–12 schools are not adding students each year to the group that best understands general civic concepts.

The results on the Report Card's U.S. history test are not much better. Average scores on that test have not changed since 2006, with just a four-point increase since 1994. Here though, just 5 percent of black students and 7 percent of Hispanic students scored at the proficient level on the most recent test in 2018, compared with 21 percent of their white peers. The same gaps, then, in average scores between different ethnic groups are found in history as on the civics test. For a federal agency to simultaneously advocate that teachers train students to act on knowledge or information they do not fully understand is nothing short of education malpractice. But critical pedagogues are intent on action. An article in the *International Journal of Multicultural Education* captures the critical perspective, calling instruction that focuses on "respect for history and characteristics of people different from themselves" a "shallow 'heroes and holiday' approach."[66]

This intellectual position, however, helps to explain the adoption of aggressive student activism in schools around the country over the past decade. These school projects that engage students in activism are clearly partisan. In a 2018 report, Mikva Challenge, an action civics organization that operates in Southern California, Washington, DC, and Chicago, featured a student project that proposed gun control measures. Generation Citizen, also active in the action civics movement, created Vote16USA, an initiative to lower the voting age to sixteen.[67] In Wisconsin, the MacIver Institute, a government

---

66 Bree Picower, "Using Their Words: Six Elements of Social Justice Curriculum Design for the Elementary Classroom," *International Journal of Multicultural Education*, Vol. 14, No. 1, 2012, *https://ijme-journal.org/ijme/index.php/ijme/article/viewFile/484/677*.

67 Generation Citizen, "Democracy Doesn't Pause," 2020 Annual Report, *https://generationcitizen.org/wp-content/uploads/2020/12/GC_2020_Annulal_Report_FINAL_300dpi.pdf*.

watchdog, says that in the 2019–2020 school year, school districts across Wisconsin endorsed student marches during the school day for causes including climate change, gun control, and the Black Lives Matter movement.[68]

Given the shift away from teaching factual content in schools and the already low levels of student achievement in history and civics, young people would be even less prepared to evaluate the political and cultural issues before them in an election if the voting age were lowered.

PRIVATE SCHOOLS

In March 2021, former writer and editor at *The New York Times* and *The Wall Street Journal* Bari Weiss wrote a terrifying report of what private school parents are feeling as their tony independent schools adopt critical race theory training and curricula in their schools.[69] The parents she spoke with would only use pseudonyms for fear that they "could face profound repercussions if anyone knew they were talking." The parents said that their children are afraid to "speak up in class" and that the wave of "antiracist" materials "is making their kids fixate on race and attach importance to it in ways that strike them [the parents] as grotesque."

A review of some of the most expensive, competitive college preparatory schools in the country reveals what this fixation looks like. At Harvard-Westlake in Los Angeles, one of the schools Weiss discusses, the institution's "anti-racism" document begins reasonably enough: "Harvard-Westlake strives to be a diverse and inclusive community, united by the joyful pursuit of

---

68 MacIverNews, "Questionable Curriculum: Schools Walk Out on Education," MacIver Institute, July 2, 2020, *https://www.maciverinstitute. com/2020/07/questionable-curriculum-schools-walk-out-on-education/*.

69 Weiss, "The Miseducation of America's Elites," *City Journal*, March 9, 2021, *https:// www.city-journal.org/the-miseducation-of-americas-elites*.

educational excellence, living and learning with integrity, and purpose beyond ourselves."[70]

Hollywood stars Jake and Maggie Gyllenhaal, Tori Spelling of *Beverly Hills 90210* fame, and Jamie Lee Curtis are all alumni of Harvard-Westlake.[71] As of 2012, Denzel Washington and Steven Spielberg had sent their children there. Yet Weiss records a white mother's complaint: "They are making my son feel like a racist because of the pigmentation of his skin."[72]

And here's how: the school is redesigning its eighth-grade world history course

> *to center a non-European perspective on 19th and 20th century world history, focusing on political, social, and cultural history of Africa, Latin America, East Asia, South America, and the Muslim world. The course explores the impact of colonialism and imperialism on the non-European world and is **attentive to inequities of power, wealth, and privilege in every unit.**[73] (Emphasis added.)*

Sound familiar? These themes are identical to the ideas from Fanon, Herbert Marcuse, the Frankfurt School, Derrick Bell, bell hooks, and other critical theorists. Students are encouraged to "speak your truth," never mind *the* truth, and "keep an open mind," except when it comes to the ubiquity of racism and oppression everywhere, apparently. Seventh-graders will be taught about the "intersection of identity and racism within the criminal justice system," allowing intersectionality to make an appearance in middle school. School leaders are planning two

---

70 Harvard-Westlake, "Anti-Racism at Harvard-Westlake School," July 24, 2020, *https://www.hw.com/pdf/Anti-RacismatHarvard-Westlake.pdf.*

71 Christina Austin and Kirsten Acuna, "Check Out the Elite Schools Where Celebrities Send Their Kids," *Insider,* September 27, 2012, *https://www.businessinsider.com/where-celebrity-kids-go-to-school-2012-9.*

72 Weiss, "The Miseducation of America's Elites."

73 Harvard-Westlake, "Anti-Racism at Harvard-Westlake School."

new high school literature courses "centering on questions of racial inequalities," yet not in civics or history, but in literature. School officials are also changing the hard sciences. Revised course material will address "the effects of conscious and unconscious bias in science in 9th grade biology."

Harvard-Westlake is not unique in adopting these changes. Sidwell Friends in Washington, DC, where former presidents Bill Clinton and Barack Obama sent their daughters, adopted a statement that, again, sounds friendly at the start and takes a dark turn at the end: "Students and alumni called for justice, inviting the School to look inward, reflect on the student experience, and, amid political rancor, reckon with the nation's white-supremacist origins."[74]

It is worth pausing here to address this claim of white-supremacist origins specifically. As Sean Wilentz, Princeton scholar and author of *No Property in Man*, points out, "Organized anti-slavery politics originated in America."[75] The first abolitionist group in the world was the Pennsylvania Abolition Society, led by none other than Benjamin Franklin—and was formed originally in 1775, then rechartered in 1784. Vermont banned slavery in 1777. Rhode Island and Connecticut banned the importation of slaves in 1774,[76] and both states began what Wilentz calls "gradual emancipation laws" in 1784.[77] Lawmakers in Connecticut, New York, and New Jersey all made similar moves at this time. New Hampshire banned

---

74   Sidwell Friends, "Lead in the Light: Equity, Justice, and Community, Strategic Action Plan for Sidwell Friends School 2021–2023," *https://resources.finalsite.net/images/v1613661710/sidwell/wm37tyobjeujxdyfgc8o/2021EJCStrategicPlanBrochure0218.pdf.*
75   Sean Wilentz, *No Property in Man* (Cambridge, MA: Harvard University Press, 2018), (Kindle version, location 506).
76   Ibid., location 549.
77   Ibid., location 606.

slavery as part of its state constitution in 1783.[78] Slavery had been practiced for millennia throughout the world before it came to America, and Americans tried to abolish it early in the nation's young life. Did early Americans move fast enough against slavery? Obviously not, as the institution should never have been practiced in the first place. But is America based on white supremacy? Hardly.

Yet Sidwell Friends presses on. The school is also launching "student affinity groups," which segregate students by race for different activities. Public school officials in Chicago and New York City had been separating students and staff according to race for diversity training programs.[79] The U.S. Department of Education under then president Donald Trump began investigating an Illinois teacher's claims that she had been discriminated against through these segregated sessions discussing "White privilege," but the Biden administration cancelled the investigation just weeks after it began. The Southeastern Legal Foundation has since revived the lawsuit and as of this writing, the case is ongoing.[80]

---

78 Vermont State Archives & Records Administration, "Vermont Constitution–1777," *https://sos.vermont.gov/vsara/learn/constitution/1777-constitution/*, Alexandria Cannon, "Gradual Abolition Act of 1780," George Washington's Mount Vernon, *https://www.mountvernon.org/library/digitalhistory/digital-encyclopedia/article/gradual-abolition-act-of-1780/*, New York Historical Society, "When Did Slavery End in New York State?" *https://www.nyhistory.org/community/slavery-end-new-york-state*, State of New Hampshire, "State Constitution 1783," *https://www.nh.gov/glance/constitution.htm*, Peter P. Hinks, "Gradual Emancipation Reflected the Struggle of Some to Envision Black Freedom," Connecticut Historical Society, *https://connecticuthistory.org/gradual-emancipation-reflected-the-struggle-of-some-to-envision-black-freedom/*, and John Carter Brown Library, "Slavery and the Slave Trade in Rhode Island," *https://www.brown.edu/Facilities/John_Carter_Brown_Library/exhibitions/jcbexhibit/Pages/exhibSlavery.html*.

79 Houston Keene, "Biden Admin Suspends Probe into School Allegedly Segregating Students by Race; Rep. Owens Blasts Decision," FoxNews.com, March 11, 2021, *https://www.foxnews.com/politics/biden-admin-education-department-racial-segregation-burgess-owens*.

80 Sarah Parshall Perry, "Illinois School District Violates Civil Rights Law, Calls It 'Equity,'" The Daily Signal, August 4, 2021, *https://www.dailysignal.com/2021/08/04/illinois-school-district-violates-civil-rights-law-calls-it-equity/*, and Southeastern Legal Foundation, "Washington Examiner: Chicago-Area Lawsuit Blows Up Media Defenses of Critical Race Theory," *https://www.slfliberty.org/washington-examiner-chicago-area-lawsuit-blows-up-media-defenses-of-critical-race-theory/*.

According to the *New York Post*, a New York City public school principal was putting students and staff into affinity groups, too, even calling on parents to "'reflect' on their 'whiteness,'" and featuring a curriculum that lists eight "white identities."[81] These identities include "White Supremacist," "White Voyeurism," "White Confessional," and "White Critical," with the optimum identity being "White Abolitionist." Watchdogs have also found evidence of affinity groupings at schools in California and North Carolina.[82] In 2020 and 2021, the Wisconsin Institute for Law & Liberty warned the Madison Metropolitan School District twice about student affinity groups, calling the racial groupings "plainly unconstitutional."[83]

At Georgetown Day school, another college prep school in Washington, DC, where tuition is $45,060 for one high-school student, school leaders have announced that the school is requiring "annual anti-racism education for all faculty/staff."[84] Georgetown Day's program will align with the practices of the Alliance of White Anti-Racists Everywhere (AWARE), a group that says, "In order to challenge racism and dismantle white supremacy, white people need to unlearn racism and discover the ways we enact white privilege."[85] This sounds like something

81 Selim Algar and Kate Sheehy, "NYC School Asks Parents to 'Reflect' on Their 'Whiteness,'" *New York Post*, February 16, 2021, *https://nypost.com/2021/02/16/nyc-public-school-asks-parents-to-reflect-on-their-whiteness/*.

82 Parents Defending Education, "Piedmont Unified School District Separates Students by Race to Talk about Chauvin Trial; Uproar Ensues over Implication That White Students Need Support; Superintendent Promises to Be More Careful with Wording in the Future," *https://defendinged.org/incidents/piedmont-unified-school-district-separates-students-by-race-to-talk-about-chauvin-trial-uproar-ensues-over-implication-that-white-students-need-support-superintendent-promises-to-be-more-careful-wit/*, and Dillon, "Records Request Reveals 'Whiteness in Ed Spaces,' 'Affinity Groups' at WCPSS EdCamp Equity."

83 Wisconsin Institute for Law & Liberty, "Madison West High School, Again, Divides Virtual Family Conversations by Race," *https://will-law.org/will-urges-madison-superintendent-to-address-racially-segregated-school-discussions/*.

84 Georgetown Day, "Diversity, Equity, and Inclusion," *https://gds.myschoolapp.com/podium/push/default.aspx?s=416&i=425342&u=0*.

85 AWARE-LA, "What We Do," *https://www.awarela.org/what-we-do*.

that Bell or Crenshaw would have written. AWARE offers guidance on leading discussions, such as "Use facts sparingly, and ask first if they are open to hearing something you learned…" once again rejecting truth and facts in the name of critical theory.[86]

In Weiss's report, one of the parents she talked to was born under a communist regime and told Weiss, "I came to this country escaping the very same fear of retaliation that now my own child feels."[87]

ANTIBIAS TRAINING

School curricula are not the only resources that critical theorists have used to enmesh the critical worldview into the classroom. K–12 school officials are also hiring diversity trainers to "train" teachers and staff against bias. Although we should obviously reject and condemn bias and discrimination any place we find it, these training programs are assigned regardless of whether discriminatory incidents have occurred—exactly in line with the critical theme that racism and oppression are omnipresent.

Around the country, companies spend some $8 billion on diversity training every year, according to McKinsey & Company.[88] In recent years, "antiracist" Kendi has trained faculty in K–12 public school districts and on college campuses. In a presentation to the University of North Carolina School of Social Work, he cited intersectionality, among other concepts from critical race theory:

86   White People for 4 Black Lives, "How to Talk about Race During the Holiday Season," AWARE-LA, November 22, 2020, *https://www.awarela.org/news/2020/11/22/ how-to-talk-about-race-during-the-holiday-season.*

87   Weiss, "The Miseducation of America's Elites."

88   McKinsey & Company, "Focusing on What Works for Workplace Diversity," April 7, 2017, *https://www.mckinsey.com/featured-insights/gender-equality/focusing-on-what-works-for- workplace-diversity#.*

If we think of intersectionality in a very literal way...we can imagine a road, right outside our homes, as the road of racism. Down that road—half a block, a mile—it's going to intersect with another road, and that's the road of homophobia. And at that intersection is where, let's say, a Latinx queer person sits. So in other words, they're being affected by the cars on the racism road and they're also being affected by homophobia and the intersection. [89]

In 2020, Fairfax County Public Schools in Virginia paid Kendi some $20,000 to train school staff in his brand of "antiracism."[90] In 2020, the California Department of Education required all agency employees to undergo training to address "implicit bias and racism."[91] In Jacksonville, Florida, the Duval school district offered "unconscious bias" training for families.[92] In 2020, the Montgomery County School Board in Maryland spent nearly $500,000 on an "anti-racist audit" (local media pointed out that this expense was occurring at the same time as district officials prepared to cut $155 million from the school district budget).[93] Washington, DC, public schools have an equity strategy and programming team that has trained teachers, telling educators

89 University of North Carolina School of Social Work, "Highlights from Ibram X. Kendi's Presentation," November 6, 2020, *https://ssw.unc.edu/2020/11/highlights-from-ibram-x-kendis-presentation/*.

90 "Fairfax County Schools Defending $20K Presentation from Anti-Racism Scholar," Fox5 DC, September 25, 2020, *https://www.fox5dc.com/news/fairfax-county-schools-defending-20k-presentation-from-anti-racism-scholar*.

91 News release, "State Superintendent Tony Thurmond Announces Multi-Pronged Partnerships, Initiatives to Address Implicit Bias and Racism," California Department of Education, June 4, 2020, *https://www.cde.ca.gov/nr/ne/yr20/yr20rel41.asp*.

92 Joe McLean, "Duval County Public Schools to Offer Unconscious Bias Training for Families," News4Jax, June 22, 2020, *https://www.news4jax.com/news/local/2020/06/22/duval-county-public-schools-to-offer-unconscious-bias-training-for-families/*.

93 Montgomery County Public Schools, "Update on the Anti-Racism Systemwide Audit," *https://news.montgomeryschoolsmd.org/staff-bulletin/update-on-the-anti-racist-systemwide-audit/*, and Caitlynn Peetz, "MCPS Might Spend $450K on 'Anti-Racist System Audit,'" *Bethesda Magazine*, November 9, 2020, *https://bethesdamagazine.com/bethesda-beat/schools/mcps-might-spend-450k-on-anti-racist-system-audit/*.

that they "must acknowledge their own biases," regardless of what teachers think about themselves.[94]

According to Learning for Justice, "Every level of education has been affected by the presence of racial trauma."[95] Part of diversity training is to end "curriculum violence," which is defined as "classroom activities used to teach about difficult histories." This approach aligns with the decolonization movement and #DisruptTexts.

According to Harvard University researchers, these training programs are found around the country, at both the K–12 and postsecondary levels. Researchers Frank Dobbin and Alexandra Kalev surveyed 670 colleges in 2016 and found that two-thirds had diversity or bias training programs for faculty, 43 percent of which were mandatory.[96] Overall, Dobbin and Kalev estimate that 29 percent of all universities require faculty to participate in similar trainings.

There is a problem with such training, though, and the problem is not just that these trainers tell employees and educators to assume omnipresent discrimination, and to dismiss America's foundational promises: Research finds again and again that there is no evidence that antibias training has made any biased people less biased.

Dobbin and Kalev explain that educators and public officials have used diversity and antibias training for decades, and it "is likely the most expensive, and least effective diversity program around." They write that "two-thirds of human resources specialists report that diversity training does not

94 District of Columbia Public Schools, "Equity Strategy and Programming Team: Mindfulness as an Equity Practice" (under "Webinars and Pre-Recorded Content"), *https://dcps.dc.gov/equity.*

95 Stephanie P. Jones, "Ending Curriculum Violence," *Teaching Tolerance*, Issue 64 (Spring 2020), *https://www.learningforjustice.org/magazine/spring-2020/ending-curriculum-violence.*

96 Frank Dobbin and Alexandra Kalev, "Why Doesn't Diversity Training Work?" *Anthropology Now*, Vol. 10, No. 2 (September 2018), *https://scholar.harvard.edu/files/dobbin/files/an2018.pdf.*

have positive effects, and several field studies have found no effect of diversity training on women's or minorities' careers or on managerial diversity."

In one review of nearly one thousand studies on the effects of antiprejudice training, researchers at Harvard and Yale "conclude that the causal effects of many widespread prejudice-reduction interventions, such as workplace diversity training and media campaigns, remain unknown."[97] Another meta-analysis (a study combining the results of other studies in the same research area), looking at nearly five hundred papers reviewing different attempts to change implicit bias, found that measurements of changes to "implicit" bias "are possible," but "those changes do not necessarily translate into changes in explicit measures or behavior" and "effects are often relatively weak."[98] One review of the research in this area from 2017 finds that most of the changes in attitudes among participants did not last long after the training.[99]

A recurring theme is that even when changes in implicit bias are measured, they do not persist. A study of six thousand three hundred participants using nine different interventions for antibias training found that "none were effective after a delay of several hours to several days."[100]

Dobbin and Kalev explain that these training programs typically encourage people to "recognize and fight the stereo-

97 Elizabeth Levy Paluck and Donald P. Green, "Prejudice Reduction: What Works? A Review and Assessment of Research and Practice," *Annual Review of Psychology*, Vol. 60 (January 10, 2009), pp. 339–367, *https://www.annualreviews.org/doi/full/10.1146/annurev.psych.60.110707.163607*.

98 Patrick S. Forscher et al., "A Meta-Analysis of Procedures to Change Implicit Measures," PsyArXiv. August 9, 2019, *https://psyarxiv.com/dv8tu/*.

99 Carol T. Kulik and Loriann Roberson, "Common Goals and Golden Opportunities: Evaluations of Diversity Education in Academic and Organizational Settings," *Academy of Management Learning and Education*, Vol. 7 (2008).

100 C. K. Lai et al., "Reducing Implicit Racial Preferences: II. Intervention Effectiveness Across Time," *Journal of Experimental Psychology: General*, Vol. 145, No. 8 (2016), pp. 1001–1016, *https://doi.org/10.1037/xge0000179*.

types they hold, and this may simply be counterproductive."[101] A report in the *Journal of Applied Psychology* found that "individuals who received a high prevalence of stereotyping message expressed more stereotypes than those who received a low prevalence of stereotyping message."[102] Many white participants in such training feel "left out," according to the researchers.[103] Mandatory attendance is also not effective: "By mandating participation, employers send the message that employees need to change," again, irrespective of what the employees believe about themselves or their workplace.[104]

Remarkably, Dobbin and Kalev find that a message focused on colorblindness—a term explicitly rejected by critical race theorists—can be more effective. They write that the "message of multiculturalism, which is common in training, makes whites feel excluded and reduces their support for diversity, relative to the message of colorblindness, which is rare these days." Trainers, in fact, have reported animosity from participants after training sessions. The idea of "colorblindness" does not always appeal to black participants, but this resistance could be the result of critical race theorists' work to disparage the term.

Resistance to a colorblind perspective is certainly not found everywhere, nor is it necessarily representative, as demonstrated by the successful work of Robert Woodson, for example, including his 1776 Unites project.[105] This project consists mostly of black scholars who oppose the teachings of critical race theory

101 Dobbin and Kalev, "Why Doesn't Diversity Training Work?"
102 Michelle M. Duguid and Melissa C. Thomas-Hunt, "Condoning Stereotyping? How Awareness of Stereotyping Prevalence Impacts Expression of Stereotypes," *Journal of Applied Psychology*, Vol. 100, No. 2 (2015), pp. 343–359, *https://doi. org/10.1037/a0037908.*
103 Dobbin and Kalev, "Why Doesn't Diversity Training Work?"
104 Ibid.
105 See 1776 Unites, *https://1776unites.com, and Woodson Center, https://woodsoncenter.org/.*

and promote the ideas of individual responsibility and a shared appreciation of America's promise of freedom for everyone, regardless of background and ethnicity.

Dobbin and Kalev suggest that including this shared appreciation in training programs would be more effective in reducing bias than the multicultural, critical trend. "Perhaps the curriculum should emphasize multiculturalism but stress that the majority culture is an important part of multiculturalism," they write.[106]

○○○

Theologian and cultural commentator Reinhold Niebuhr, whose writings and teachings influenced Martin Luther King, Jr., aptly captured modern-day critical theorists and critical pedagogues when he described the communists of his day as "a fierce and unscrupulous Don Quixote on a fiery horse, determined to destroy every knight and lady of civilization; and confident that this slaughter will purge the world of evil."[107] The solution for America's schools and culture is to contribute to character formation and create a sense of a shared national history, not to create racial conflict in the classrooms or any values-related school activity. If students are not taught that racism in the twenty-first century is not the same as during the civil rights era or the nineteenth century, they are left with the false idea that the problems are identical today to the problems previous generations faced—and overcame.

Critical pedagogy's conscious replaying of oppression, as black author and documentary filmmaker Shelby Steele described in *The Content of Our Character*,[108] and calls for the admission of uncon-

---

106 Dobbin and Kalev, "Why Doesn't Diversity Training Work?"
107 Elisabeth Sifton, ed., *Reinhold Niebuhr: Major Works on Religion and Politics* (New York: Library of America, 2015), *https://a.co/335yCRa.*
108 Steele, *The Content of Our Character.*

scious bias, will not defeat evil. The critical worldview has created a sharp divide over what is taught, how instruction is delivered, and the kind of adults that critical theorists want students to become. Critical ideas are divisive and violate the values that Americans hold dear. Because critical theory condemns some of the most important ideas in American culture, it is a sign of the division in this country that two different White House administrations dedicated time and energy to opposite purposes on the subject between September 2020 (the creation of the 1776 Commission) and January 2021 (when the commission was rescinded).

At the center of this debate under two different administrations was the 1619 Project. President Trump mentioned the project by name in his September 2020 speech that created the 1776 Commission. Like *A People's History, The New York Times*'s 1619 Project is another attempt at revisionist history that leaves out important details, or simply gets the facts wrong. Entire books have been written to expose the project's factual errors.[109]

Northwestern University professor Leslie Harris, who was sympathetic to the project's aims and said it was "one of the most talked-about journalistic achievements," also "vigorously argued" against the project's claim that colonists fought the American Revolution to preserve slavery.[110] After Harris's essay describing how the *Times* ignored her objections was published in *Politico*, the *Times* adjusted the 1619 Project's text so that preserving slavery was named as *one* of the reasons why colonists rebelled against England, not the only reason.[111] The project's effort to

109 See, for example, Phil Magness, *The 1619 Project: A Critique* (Great Barrington, MA: American Institute for Economic Research, 2020), and Peter Wood, *1620: A Critical Response to the 1619 Project* (New York: Encounter Books, 2020).

110 Leslie M. Harris, "I Helped Fact-Check the 1619 Project. The Times Ignored Me," *Politico*, March 6, 2020, *https://www.politico.com/news/magazine/2020/03/06/1619-project-new-york-times-mistake-122248*.

111 Burke, Butcher, Gonzalez, and Kao, "The Culture of American K–12 Education: A National Survey of Parents and School Board Members."

reframe American history around slavery became a crusade that blinded the project's contributors to their own overstatements.

Historian Sean Wilentz also believed that the 1619 Project's purpose was an important one, but said that the essays contained factual inaccuracies and overstatements. Writing in *The Atlantic*, Wilentz said: "The opportunity seized by the 1619 Project is as urgent as it is enormous."[112] But just as with Harris's critique, Wilentz found that the *Times* used facts loosely (his article outlining his arguments was called "A Matter of Facts"). Wilentz notes the colonists' efforts to end the Atlantic slave trade near the end of the eighteenth century and that there "were no 'growing calls' in London to abolish the trade as early as 1776," as the project's lead essay argued.

Other than the small adjustment of the reference to the colonists' reasons for fighting the Revolutionary War, the *Times*'s editors refused to make corrections. Lead editor Jake Silverstein's response to historians' critiques is familiar, once readers review the critical emphasis on narrative over truth.

For example, scholars alerted the *Times* that Spanish explorers brought slaves to North America in the sixteenth century, well before England arrived with slaves in what would become Virginia in 1619.[113] Silverstein's answer on this point was fascinating. He did not deny that the *Times* may be wrong, but suggested the narrative matters more. "Though we stand by the logic of marking the beginning of American slavery with the year it was introduced in the English colonies, this feedback has helped us think about the importance of considering the prehistory of the period our project addresses," Silverstein writes.

---

112 Sean Wilentz, "A Matter of Facts," *The Atlantic*, January 22, 2020, *https://www.theatlantic.com/ideas/archive/2020/01/1619-project-new-york-times-wilentz/605152/*.

113 Jake Silverstein, "We Respond to the Historians Who Critiqued the 1619 Project," *The New York Times*, December 20, 2019 (updated January 19, 2021), *https://www.nytimes.com/2019/12/20/magazine/we-respond-to-the-historians-who-critiqued-the-1619-project.html*.

Helped them think about it? What does *The New York Times*'s consideration of this error do for the four thousand five hundred classrooms using the 1619 Project, including schools in Washington, DC, and Chicago, where approximately four of five black fourth-graders cannot read at grade level and are unlikely to find the correct material on their own?[114]

A nationally representative survey conducted less than one year after the 1619 Project's release finds little support for the project's main ideas, factual or not. Fifty percent of parents of school-aged children in the survey said they do not want schools "to use instructional material based on the idea that slavery is the 'center of our national narrative,'" compared with 42 percent in favor of such teaching.[115] Though parents were split on whether our "founding ideals of liberty and equality were false when they were written," 70 percent said that "slavery was a tragedy that harmed the nation, but our freedom and prosperity represent who we are as a nation, offering a beacon to those wanting to immigrate here."

CONCLUSION

This battle over what is taught in schools is not new. We cannot expect public schools to be free from political tension or debates over what is being taught. Horace Mann, considered the father of public schools in America, recognized this, writing that, "shall all teaching, relative to the nature of our government, be banished from our schools; and shall our children

---

114 The Nation's Report Card, "2019 Reading Trial Urban District Snapshot Report: District of Columbia (DCPS)," *https://nces.ed.gov/nationsreportcard/subject/publications/dst2019/pdf/2020016XW4.pdf*, and The Nation's Report Card, "2019 Reading Trial Urban District Snapshot Report: Chicago," *https://nces.ed.gov/nationsreportcard/subject/publications/dst2019/pdf/2020016XC4.pdf*.

115 Burke, Butcher, Gonzalez, and Kao, "The Culture of American K-12 Education: A National Survey of Parents and School Board Members."

be permitted to grow up in entire ignorance of the political history of their country?"[116]

Few groups are as partisan as teachers unions. When the New York City teachers union, the AFT, adopted the Black Lives Matter resolution, as described in Chapter 1, the local chapter was reflecting the position held by the central office. Both the AFT and the NEA, the nation's largest teachers union, supported the Black Lives Matter at School Week.[117] The NEA's list of materials includes a resource that says that disciplinary practices, such as suspension and expulsion, regardless of student behavior, results in the "spirit murder" of children.[118] A student could have threatened a teacher, fought with another student, or even physically harmed someone else, but the NEA's source, the Abolitionist Teaching Network (ATN) says that educators must "remove all punitive or disciplinary practices."

According to the ATN, all police should be banned from schools because they are part of an oppressive power structure. Schools should provide reparations to "children of color" who have faced discipline in schools for violent behavior. "Whiteness" is a form of oppression. White teachers should receive free anti-racist therapy. Standardized tests should be banned because personal merit cannot compete with privilege. The AFT resolved to compel union members to wear BLM T-shirts during the annual BLM Week of Action and "teach lessons about related topics," regardless of how union members feel about discrimination and

116 Horace Mann, "Report No. 12 of the Massachusetts School Board," 1848, *https://usa.usembassy.de/etexts/democrac/16.htm.*

117 American Federation of Teachers, "Black Lives Matter at School Week—Feb. 1–5, 2021," *https://www.aft.org/resolution/black-lives-matter-school-week-feb-1-5-2021,* and National Education Association, "Black Lives Matter at School," *https://neaedjustice.org/black-lives-matter-at-school/.*

118 Abolitionist Teaching Network, "Guide for Racial Justice & Abolitionist Social and Emotional Learning," August 2020, *https://img1.wsimg.com/blobby/go/8d4b8aa7-b12e-4df8-9836-081a29841523/downloads/ATN%20Guide%20to%20Racial%20and%20Restorative%20Justice%20in.pdf?ver=1621006231358.*

America's past.[119] Or how they feel about discussions of power and privilege today. And on and on.

Both unions also promoted the 1619 Project and continue to encourage educators to use the project in classrooms.[120] The NEA created a 1619 Project resource page that includes links to project lessons and Learning for Justice materials.[121] Philadelphia teachers union members advocated the use of materials that taught that men are "over-privileged" because of their gender.[122] In American culture, "white privilege…was similarly denied and protected." Educators should "give up the myth of meritocracy" and focus on "systems of dominance."

As the players struggle for possession of the K–12 stage, parents are right to ask whether their voices are being heard. Critical race theorists' penchant for hiding their activities conflicts directly with America's commitment to free speech and a free press, just as critical ideas conflict directly with liberty and equality. Increasingly, parents are speaking up.

In 2021, Parents Defending Education conducted a poll asking voters what they thought about critical race theory and the culture wars in schools today. Seventy percent of this nationally representative sample of Americans said that it is not important, or not at all important, for schools to teach students that

---

119 American Federation of Teachers, "Black Lives Matter at School Week—Feb. 1–5, 2021", Abolitionist Teaching Network, "Guide for Racial Justice & Abolitionist Social and Emotional Learning."

120 American Federation of Teachers, "Contributing Voices: Examining Essays from the 1619 Project with Nikole Hannah-Jones," *https://sharemylesson.com/teaching-resource/contributing-voices-examining-essays-1619-project-nikole-hannah-jones-329462.*

121 National Education Association, "The 1619 Project Resource Page," *https://neaedjustice.org/the-1619-project-resource-page/.*

122 Philadelphia Caucus of Working Educators, "Black Lives Matter in #PHLed," *https://docs.google.com/document/d/1UHtJqY8xdDOZM5QY39aRgQURRu-9jZhXQxUe_T2yYG0/edit*; Peggy McIntosh, "White Privilege: Unpacking the Invisible Knapsack," The National Seed Project, *https://nationalseedproject.org/Key-SEED-Texts/white-privilege-unpacking-the-invisible-knapsack*; Justice, "Resources for Educators," *https://www.dcareaeducators4socialjustice.org/black-lives-matter/resources#readings.*

"race is the most important thing about them."[123] Nearly three of four respondents said that "they opposed teaching students that white people are inherently privileged and black and other people of color are inherently oppressed." Sixty-nine percent of respondents opposed lessons that teach students that America is "structurally racist."

Parents wondering what critical ideas look like in practice need only consider what is taking place on college campuses around the U.S. The shout downs of speakers with unwoke opinions, the riots, and the cancel culture so prevalent on college grounds today are the incarnation of critical ideas.

How do we know? Just listen to what students are saying on campus.

---

123 Parents Defending Education, "Parents Defending Education National Poll: Americans Overwhelmingly Reject 'Woke' Race and Gender Policies in K-12 Education," May 10, 2021, *https://defendinged.org/commentaries/parents-defending-education-national-poll-americans-overwhelmingly-reject-woke-race-and-gender-policies-in-k-12-education/.*

CHAPTER 3

THE CRITICAL CAMPUS

What should parents and students expect from K–12 schools after critical race theory has taken root in classrooms?

Considering critical race theorists' aversion to facts, even in the hard sciences and math, critical ideas will not improve student achievement in foundational subjects like reading and mathematics. With research (and common sense) demonstrating that diversity training does not make people more tolerant or change their attitudes—perhaps even making them feel resentful about racial differences—diversity training does not equip teachers to teach children to be more empathetic. And, with the already low levels of knowledge about American civic responsibilities and history among students (and adults), we should not anticipate improved performance in these areas of study. Critical race theory reframes American history around identity groups and ethnicity, separating us into tribes, and rejects the principles of the civil rights movement.

To see what happens in an education environment that embraces critical ideas, we can look to postsecondary institutions, where these ideas have been commonplace for years.

We should not be surprised to find that students used words from the critical lexicon while they rioted inside the school library at Columbia University in 2018.[1] In April of that year, these students "marched into Butler Library calling to 'decolonize Columbia,' carrying signs and chanting slogans denouncing white supremacy."[2] True to critical form, students refused to stop shouting or leave even when law school dean Yadira Ramos-Herbert and campus security asked them to do so, saying that the rioters were "disrupting those trying to study."

According to reports, one student in the mob said, "You have acres of colonized land to study on…I hope you are being disturbed." The rioters held a banner that read "Decolonize Columbia University," conjuring the idea of intellectual and physical oppression at this $64,000-per-year institution that these rioting students *chose* to attend.[3]

Over the past decade, students, faculty, and rioters, including rioters from off campus, have participated in disruptive and sometimes violent activities at universities around the country. Because these incidents usually involve one group preventing another group from speaking or hosting a guest lecturer, some media and policymakers have recognized the wave of disruptive incidents as evidence of a free speech crisis on campuses[4]— while others have denied the reality before their eyes.[5]

---

1   Emma Buzbee, "Protestors Storm Butler Demanding 'Decolonization' of Curriculum, Campus Monuments," *Columbia Spectator*, April 25, 2018, *https://www.columbiaspectator.com/news/2018/04/25/protesters-storm-butler-demanding-decolonization-of-curriculum-campus-monuments/*.

2   Ibid.

3   Columbia University, "Student Financial Services: General Studies, 2020–2021," *https://www.sfs.columbia.edu/tuitions-fees-listing?trf_school=380&year-period=443*.

4   See, for example, Bradley Campbell, "The Free Speech Crisis on Campus Is Worse than People Think," *Quillette*, November 14, 2018, *https://quillette.com/2018/11/14/the-free-speech-crisis-on-campus-is-worse-than-people-think/*, and Jeremy Bauer-Wolf, "Free Speech Laws Mushroom in Wake of Campus Protests," *InsideHigherEd*, September 16, 2019, *https://www.insidehighered.com/news/2019/09/16/states-passing-laws-protect-college-students-free-speech*.

5   See, for example, Chris Ladd, "There Is No Free Speech Crisis on Campus," *Forbes*, September 13, 2017, *https://www.forbes.com/sites/chrisladd/2017/09/23/there-is-no-free-speech-crisis-on-campus/?sh=36a83ce928cb*.

Disruptions at universities over the past decade have infringed on individuals' First Amendment rights. But students' and professors' stated reasons for supporting these riots are as intellectually frightening as attempts to silence others are physically terrifying.

Consider: In 2017, Texas Southern University students shouted down Texas State Representative Briscoe Cain, calling him racist.[6] The lead rioter wore a Black Lives Matter T-shirt. Campus riots also took place that year at Middlebury College in Vermont, Evergreen State College in Washington State, and the University of California-Berkeley, to name just a few (more on these events below). In 2018, Duke University students demanded that the school president, Vincent Price, "get off the stage" during his speech to a group of alumni.[7] The students charged the stage "with signs and a megaphone," according to reports. In 2019, a University of North Carolina student repeatedly punched another student who had set up a display advocating for pro-life causes.[8]

There is no shortage of evidence that many, if not most, post-secondary institutions have a progressive bent both in school operations as well as instruction, the side of the ideological divide most receptive to Marxist influence. Conservatives have pointed to the ideological Left's increasing monopoly of ideas at universities for decades, touched off, perhaps, by William F. Buckley,

6   Stanley Kurtz, "Texas State Legislator Shouted Down at Texas Southern University," *National Review Online*, October 10, 2017, *https://www.nationalreview.com/corner/texas-legislator-shouted-down-tsu-briscoe-cain-campus-free-speech/*, and Texas Scorecard, "Protestors Storm Briscoe Cain Speech at TSU," YouTube.com, October 10, 2017, *https://www.youtube.com/watch?v=pWZSekfr24U.*

7   Adam Beyer and Sarah Kerman, "Group of Students Protests President Price's Alumni Address, Issues Demands," *The Chronicle*, April 14, 2018, *https://www.duke-chronicle.com/article/2018/04/041418-beyer-protest.*

8   Caleb Parke, "Liberal Student Arrested for Punching Pro-Lifer on UNC Campus, Triggered by Images of Aborted Children," FoxNews.com, May 9, 2019, *https://www.foxnews.com/us/liberal-student-arrested-punching-pro-lifer.*

Jr.'s *God and Man at Yale* in 1951. There, Buckley pointed to the erosion of capitalist tenets taught in economics departments.

Research finds that the share of professors on the left side of the partisan divide began increasing on campuses in the 1990s.[9] Former Hoover Institution fellow Samuel Abrams writes that Higher Education Research Institute surveys of professors from 1989 found that some 40 percent of respondents identified as liberal, and this figure jumped to 60 percent in 2014. During the same period, the share identifying as conservative halved from 20 percent to 10 percent.

Still, there are those who consider themselves to be on the ideological Left who have criticized critical race theory.[10] Comedian and long-time liberal critic of conservatives Bill Maher called critical race theory "hyperbole" and "insane" while lamenting that his condemnation of the theory aligned him with Fox News's Tucker Carlson on the issue.[11] Even writers at the World Socialist Web Site criticized *The New York Times*'s 1619 Project, so it is unfair to say that because more academics identify as politically liberal or progressive, they should automatically be considered Marxists or supporters of critical race theory.[12] But Marxist ideology and critical race theory have been spreading

---

9   Samuel J. Abrams, "There Are Conservative Professors. Just Not in These States," *The New York Times*, July 1, 2016, *https://www.nytimes.com/2016/07/03/opinion/sunday/there-are-conservative-professors-just-not-in-these-states.html.*

10   See, for example, the discussion of Bret Weinstein, the former Evergreen State College professor. Weinstein, for one, supported Senator Bernie Sanders and was an "outspoken supporter of the Occupy Wall Street movement." See Weiss, "When the Left Turns on Its Own," *The New York Times*, June 1, 2017, *https://www.nytimes.com/2017/06/01/opinion/when-the-left-turns-on-its-own.html.* Bari Weiss is also considered a liberal writer, and she is one of the founders of the Foundation Against Intolerance and Racism (FAIR). See Foundation Against Intolerance and Racism, "Board of Advisors," *https://www.fairforall.org/about/board-of-advisors/*, and Judith Miller, "The Illiberal Liberal Media," *City Journal*, July 14, 2020, *https://www.city-journal.org/bari-weiss-new-york-times.*

11   Jon Street, "WATCH: Leftist Bill Maher Rips into 'Insane' Critical Race Theory for 'Making People Crazy," *Campus Reform*, March 1, 2021, *https://www.campusreform.org/article?id=16931.*

12   World Socialist Web Site, "The New York Times' 1619 Project," *https://www.wsws.org/en/topics/event/1619.*

across college campuses for decades while the share of college professors identifying as ideologically liberal disproportionately outweighs those identifying as conservative—data points that we must acknowledge to accurately describe campuses today. If we can at least recognize the features of the higher education landscape, we can then better debate the ideas that are driving a wedge in our cultural institutions such as schools.

The current free speech crisis on campus is nothing less than a window into a culture where critical race theorists can freely apply their ideas. Many, if not most, college campuses today are populated with willing participants who consider ideologically different viewpoints as something to be stifled rather than debated. Policymakers, parents, and students must make the connection between the presence of critical race theory in classrooms and so-called diversity training and the recent wave of violence on campuses. Between 2015 and 2020, as disruptive events on campus made headlines, writers on both sides of the ideological divide were quick to notice the trend of shout downs and violence at universities. Greg Lukianoff and Jonathan Haidt's *The Coddling of the American Mind* and Heather Mac Donald's *The Diversity Delusion* are just a few of the titles in recent years that review the culture of campus unrest since 2010.

Some, like Mac Donald, and Haidt and Lukianoff, effectively connect today's racially charged social and political debates and campus shout downs. Critical race theorists, and critical theorists before them, have long argued that speech and violence are the same. We can use rioters' own words, along with their actions, to say unequivocally that the free speech crisis on campuses is inseparable from universities having adopted the ideology of critical race theory. Professors are not just teaching critical race theory as a historical artifact, but as a worldview that students should *apply to their lives,* turning theory into praxis, as the Frankfurt School intended.

After the list of campus shout downs and violence between students and off-campus rioters grew between 2015 and 2020, the progressive PEN America admitted in 2019 that the problems on campus could no longer be ignored. PEN says that free speech is "alive and well," but that there have been "recent incidents" that have "raised significant concerns about the heated climate for intellectual life on U.S. campuses and the implications for the rising generation of college-educated Americans," even if most of this activity had resulted in the silencing of conservative students and speakers.[13] *The Washington Post* and *The New York Times* published stories claiming that the free speech crisis was a myth. Yet, between 2015 and 2020, these same papers covered campus speech policies and shout downs at the University of California-Berkeley, Auburn University, Georgetown University, Evergreen State College, the University of Wisconsin, Texas A&M, and

---

13   Katherine Mangan, "If There Is a Free-Speech 'Crisis' on Campus, PEN America Says, Lawmakers Are Making It Worse," *Chronicle of Higher Education*, April 2, 2019, *https://www.chronicle.com/article/if-there-is-a-free-speech-crisis-on-campus-pen-america-says-lawmakers-are-making-it-worse/*, and PEN America, "And Campus for All: Diversity, Inclusion and Freedom of Speech at U.S. Universities," June 15, 2017, p. 8, *https://pen.org/wp-content/uploads/2017/06/PEN_campus_report_06.15.2017.pdf*.

Middlebury College, to name just a few, providing evidence that the free speech crisis on campus is no myth.[14]

Again, this growing list of incidents involving students disrupting campus activities or becoming violent is not just a signal that the First Amendment is threatened. In his 1995 lecture at the University of Illinois College of Law titled "Who's Afraid of Critical Race Theory?"—a lecture that helped to define critical race theory's main ideas—Derrick Bell said, "Most critical race theorists are committed to a program of scholarly resistance that they hope will lay the groundwork for wide-scale resistance."[15]

Forecasting that the application of critical race theory on campuses would create chaos, Heterodox Academy co-founder and author of *The Righteous Mind* Jonathan Haidt (coauthor with Lukianoff of *Coddling of the American Mind*) warned of the dangers inherent in the demands from student groups at some eighty universities in 2015, demands aligned with critical theory

---

14   Nick Miroff, "Protestors Shout Homeland Security Chief Off Georgetown University Stage," *The Washington Post*, October 7, 2019, *https://www.washingtonpost.com/immigration/protesters-shout-homeland-security-chief-off-georgetown-university-stage/2019/10/07/1f2892d2-e915-11e9-9c6d-436a0df4f31d_story.html*, Aaron Hanlon, "The New Threat to Free Speech Isn't Coming from the Left," *The Washington Post*, October 15, 2019, *https://www.washingtonpost.com/outlook/2019/10/15/real-threat-free-speech-campus-isnt-coming-left/*, Susan Svrluga, "UC-Berkeley Says 'Free Speech Week' Is Cancelled. Milo Yiannopoulos Is Coming Anyway," *The Washington Post*, September 23, 2017, *https://www.washingtonpost.com/news/grade-point/wp/2017/09/23/uc-berkeley-says-free-speech-week-is-canceled-milo-yiannopoulos-says-hes-still-coming-to-campus/*, and Thomas Fuller, "Berkeley Cancels Ann Coulter Speech over Safety Fears," *The New York Times*, April 19, 2017, *https://www.nytimes.com/2017/04/19/us/berkeley-ann-coulter-speech-canceled.html*, Katharine Q. Seelye, "Protestors Disrupt Speech by 'Bell Curve' Author at Vermont College," *The New York Times*, March 3, 2017, *https://www.nytimes.com/2017/03/03/us/middlebury-college-charles-murray-bell-curve-protest.html*, Jeremy W. Peters, "In the Name of Free Speech," *The New York Times*, June 14, 2018, *https://www.nytimes.com/2018/06/14/us/politics/campus-speech-protests.html*, and Christine Hauser, "Campuses Grapple with Balancing Free Speech and Security After Protests," *The New York Times*, March 29, 2017, *https://www.nytimes.com/2017/03/29/us/texas-aandm-speaking-policy-richard-spencer.html*.

15   Bell, "David C. Baum Memorial Lecture: Who's Afraid of Critical Race Theory?"

and critical race theory.[16] These demands included mandatory diversity training, that school officials admit "white privilege," that campus officials focus on "privilege, oppression, culture, society, and campus climate," and that campus leaders "decolonize" school curricula. As explained in Chapter 2, efforts at "decolonization" refer to removing classics of the Western canon from school curricula, including works whose very purpose is to oppose racism, such as *To Kill a Mockingbird.*

The groups making demands include student associations at Brown University, Clemson University, Dartmouth University, Harvard University, Portland State University, Sarah Lawrence College, the University of California-Berkeley, the University of Minnesota, the University of Virginia, and Yale University, to name just a few—many campuses that were also sites of shout downs or violent actions to block events or speakers in the past decade. Again, these incidents included forcible shout downs of college presidents.[17]

Demands for additional rights and emotional safety at some of the most expensive universities in the world have become absurd. At Sarah Lawrence College in Bronxville, New York (tui-

16   Jonathan Haidt, "Why Universities Must Choose One Telos: Truth or Social Justice," Heterodox: The Blog, October 21, 2016, *https://heterodoxacademy.org/blog/one-telos-truth-or-social-justice-2/*.

17   Jillian Lanney and Carolyn Cong, "Ray Kelly Lecture Cancelled Amidst Student, Community Protest," *The Brown Daily Herald,* October 30, 2013, *https://www.browndailyherald.com/2013/10/30/ray-kelly-lecture-canceled-amidst-student-community-protest/*, Julia Seymour, "Dartmouth's Free Speech Decline," RealClearEducation, November 6, 2020, *https://www.realcleareducation.com/articles/2020/11/06/dartmouths_free_speech_decline_110502:html,* College Fix Staff, "Protestors Disrupt David Horowitz Talk at Dartmouth," *The College Fix,* October 28, 2018, *https://www.thecollegefix.com/protesters-disrupt-david-horowitz-talk-at-dartmouth/*, Robby Soave, "Harvard President Lawrence Bacow to Activist Students Who Shut Down His Talk: 'The Heckler's Veto Has No Place' Here," *Reason,* April 12, 2019, *https://reason.com/2019/04/12/harvard-president-lawrence-bacow-disrupt/*, Butcher, "It's Not a College's Job to Protect Students from New Ideas," *Charleston Post and Courier,* September 14, 2020, *https://www.postandcourier.com/opinion/commentary/its-not-a-college-s-job-to-protect-students-from-new-ideas/article_53072cb4-2000-11e9-9e3f-b389ebac338e.html,* and Celine Ryan, "PSU Says Cowbell-Clad Protestor Who Shut Down Conservative Event Broke No Law. Experts Beg to Differ," Campus Reform, March 12, 2019, *https://www.campusreform.org/?ID=11970*.

tion: $69,000 per year, even without meals and student fees)[18], a student group calling itself the Diaspora Coalition took over a campus building for twenty-four hours and demanded, among other things, that administrators not punish students for occupying a school building, along with providing students free laundry detergent.[19] The group's letter with its demands opened in the style of the Frankfurt School's critical theorists, saying, "If healing is ever to take place, there must be action," connecting theory and praxis. Parents of these students should be shocked to learn that they are paying such large tuition bills each year for their children to attend a school where students claim there are "injustices imposed on people of color by this institution on a daily basis."

The letter says there are "racist white professors" at Sarah Lawrence, without naming any names. The letter demands that the college "offer classes that embody intersectionality, as defined by Kimberlé Williams Crenshaw, and address the racial diversity of the LGBTQ+ community instead of centering whiteness," which means that those of some ethnicities are deserving of more benefits on campus than others. And, of course, the letter included demands for mandatory diversity training.

Everyone should condemn hate, but the student group's demands do not describe an opposition to hatred so much as an alliance with progressive ideas, such as "land acknowledgement" and the creation of courses to study racial issues from critical race theorists' perspective. The group insists that the college "accept these demands [in the letter]" so that it can be "hailed as a progressive institution" and "embody its self-proclaimed progressive ideology and support all students against

---

18   Sarah Lawrence College, "Tuition & Costs: Academic Year 2021–2022," *https://www. sarahlawrence.edu/financial-aid/undergraduate/tuition.html.*

19   The Phoenix, "Demands: Westlands Sit-In 50 Years of Shame," March 11, 2019, *http://www. sarahlawrencephoenix.com/campus/2019/3/11/demands-westlands-sit-in-50-years-of-shame.*

an international rising tide of white supremacy and fascism." The letter equates the rejection of "hate" with the advancement of progressive ideology.

Student groups' letters are just the beginning. Students are also heeding Bell's call for "resistance" on campus.

Take Evergreen State College in Washington State. The "core themes" of this small liberal arts college (2,962 undergraduates in the 2020–2021 academic year) located five miles west of Olympia include "social justice" and "diversity and equity"—and in 2017, students took over campus and chased a professor into hiding because he publicly decried student separation by race.[20]

The events at Evergreen were more than a shout down, though it started with one. In previous years, black students at Evergreen would choose a day to not come to campus in a symbolic act protesting racism in America's past. But some student groups flipped the script in 2017 and told white people not to come to campus that day. As biology professor Bret Weinstein explained, in March 2017, he sent an email to faculty and staff objecting to the idea that some members of the campus community could force white members of campus to stay off campus for a day.[21] "I had challenged coercive segregation by race," Weinstein wrote in *The Wall Street Journal*. In his March email he wrote, "On a college campus, one's right to speak—or to be—must never be based on skin color." Weinstein, it should be noted, supported both Senator Bernie Sanders, the self-described democratic-socialist from Vermont, and the

---

20   U.S. Department of Education, "College Scorecard: The Evergreen State College," *https://collegescorecard.ed.gov/school/?235167-The-Evergreen-State-College,* Evergreen State College, "Evergreen's Mission," *https://www.evergreen.edu/about/evergreens-mission,* and Bret Weinstein, "The Campus Mob Came for Me—and You, Professor, Could Be Next," *The Wall Street Journal,* May 30, 2017, *https://www.wsj.com/articles/the-campus-mob-came-for-meand-you-professor-could-be-next-1496187482.*

21   Weinstein, "The Campus Mob Came for Me."

Occupy Wall Street movement.[22] He was no conservative wait-ing for an opportunity to provoke supporters of Evergreen's core themes, but a member of the campus community con-cerned that Evergreen had "slipped into madness."[23]

Weeks after Weinstein's message, students shouted Weinstein down during his own class and demanded that he resign. Then things got worse, and the need to protect free speech on campus became an afterthought.

In a film by Mike Nayna about the incident, which recounts Weinstein's experience, students are seen chanting at faculty, "Hey hey, ho ho, these racist teachers have got to go."[24] Such an accusation against professors, even at a school considered one of the most progressive in the country, was bound to happen.[25] Why? Professors had been teaching students to act this way. In Nayna's documentary, a professor at Evergreen is shown lecturing about how education is a "liberatory practice" and encouraging students to follow bell hooks's "engaged pedagogy," the critical activism described in Chapter 1.[26] The professor handed cards to students in her class with questions or statements written on them, then called on the students to read the cards aloud. The phrases and questions included "How do you know you are white?" and "Have you always been white?"

The documentary also features Robin DiAngelo's presenta-tions at Evergreen. DiAngelo, author of *White Fragility* and diver-

22 Weiss, "When the Left Turns on Its Own."

23 Weinstein, "The Campus Mob Came for Me."

24 Mike Nayna, "Part One: Bret Weinstein, Heather Heying & the Evergreen Equity Council," YouTube.com, January 17, 2019, *https://www.youtube.com/watch?v=FH2WeWgcSMh.*

25 Anemona Hartocollis, "A Campus Argument Goes Viral. Now the College Is Under Siege," *The New York Times*, June 16, 2017, *https://www.nytimes.com/2017/06/16/us/evergreen-state-protests.html,* and Weiss, "When the Left Turns on Its Own."

26 Mike Nayna, "Part Two: Teaching to Transgress," YouTube.com, March 6, 2019, *https://www.youtube.com/watch?v=A0W9QbkX8Cs&t=0s.*

sity trainer who charges between $50,000 and $75,000 for her training services, says, "I think racism depends on white people being really, really nice to everybody and just carrying on... And nothing will change or get interrupted and you will be supporting the default, and the default is the reproduction of whiteness and white supremacy."[27]

As the documentary unfolds, it becomes clear that the problem at Evergreen was not just the shout down of a professor, but a campus-wide mindset, a cult obsessed with racial identity, condemning anyone who questioned the idea that, as Weinstein said, people should be forced to apologize for not being a minority, and that all should be separated by skin color. As DiAngelo said in her training sessions at Evergreen, we are all fish, metaphorically, and "the water is whiteness. The water is white supremacy, that's the frame."[28] Eventually, students took over the main buildings on campus, some using baseball bats to randomly attack people who walked through parking lots at night, trapping the school president in his office and not letting him use the bathroom. Weinstein and his wife were eventually forced into hiding due to threats against their lives.[29]

This is the praxis, the application, of critical race theory on college campuses.

The Evergreen episode came during a year in which violence at universities was frequently in the news, especially involving lecturers being invited to campus only to be shouted down by disruptive students. Just months before the Evergreen incident, rioters at the University of California-

---

27   Key Speakers, "Robin DiAngelo: Fee Range," https://web.archive.org/web/202103 21060116/https://keyspeakers.com/bio.php?4602-robin-diangelo.

28   The Evergreen State College Productions, "Coming Together Speaker Series: Robin DiAngelo," March 9, 2016, *https://www.youtube.com/watch?v=wVddM1hzmvI.*

29   Hartocollis, "A Campus Argument Goes Viral. Now the College Is Under Siege."

Berkeley set fire to buildings and hurled explosive devices at students to prevent provocateur Milo Yiannopoulos, a flamboyant right-wing speaker, from speaking on campus in January 2017.[30] ABC News coverage of the event showed students holding a banner that read "This Means War." A young adult from the mob (it is not clear if the person was a student) was quoted by newscasters justifying this actual violence by characterizing speech as violence: "We will not tolerate racism or sexism or hate crimes and violence."[31] Meanwhile, other protestors held up a banner saying "Trump Must Go By Any Means Necessary," making one wonder about the group's commitment to nonviolence.

In my interview with Bradley Devlin, a University of California-Berkeley student involved with the school's College Republicans, the group that had invited Yiannopoulos to speak,[32] Devlin said, "I've never had a more helpless instance in my life. You pay an exorbitant security fee and [are] told that the people you've sold tickets to will be protected at this event."

"I had an M-80 firework thrown at me twice," Devlin said. "People tried to rush in and break the windows" in the building where Yiannopoulos was scheduled to speak.

Because Yiannopoulos is well known as an agitator, this incident might seem like a rare example, but similar incidents have occurred involving mild-mannered researchers and educators. Just two months after the Berkeley incident, Middlebury College students in Vermont shouted down American Enterprise Institute scholar Charles Murray, coauthor of *The Bell Curve*

30   Madison Park and Kyung Lah, "Berkeley Protests of Yiannopoulos Caused $100,000 in Damage," CNN.com, February 2, 2017, *https://www.cnn.com/2017/02/01/us/milo-yiannopoulos-berkeley*.

31   Good Morning America, "Milo Yiannopoulos Speech Protests Turns Violent at UC Berkeley," February 2, 2017, video, *https://www.youtube.com/watch?v=-PSYPrE5LrQ*.

32   Public Affairs, "Chancellor's Message on Campus Appearance of Milo Yiannopoulos," *Berkeley News*, January 26, 2017, *https://news.berkeley.edu/2017/01/26/chancellor-statement-on-yiannopoulos/*.

and author of *Coming Apart.*[33] Student shouting made it impossible to hear Murray's presentation and forced him to present his lecture in a secure room apart from the agitated crowd. The disruptive students prevented him from even beginning his presentation (the "uproar began," Murray says, "halfway through my first sentence"). Students held up signs reading "Resist Racism" and "Resist White Supremacy."[34] When Murray was leaving campus after his lecture in the secure room, rioters, including some in ski masks, physically assaulted him, as well as faculty member Allison Stanger. Rioters grabbed Stanger's hair and threw her to the ground, causing injury that would require medical treatment.[35]

Similar incidents would take place at William & Mary (involving the shout down of a representative of the American Civil Liberties Union); Clemson University; Georgetown University; the University of Pennsylvania, and many more.[36] In all of these incidents, disruptive students' objective was not just to be heard, but to make sure that others could *not* be heard. In some cases, they became violent in order to completely and utterly end any possibility of expression by those they tried to silence. According to critical race theory, the expression of ideas that challenge the theory's obsession with race is itself a harm.

---

33 Charles Murray, "Reflections on the Revolution in Middlebury," AEIdeas blog, March 5, 2017, *https://www.aei.org/society-and-culture/reflections-on-the-revolution-in-middlebury/.*

34 "Protestors Confront Scholar at Middlebury College," FoxNews, March 6, 2017, *https://www.youtube.com/watch?v=XJIxAS5Oy0c.*

35 Charles Murray, "Reflections on the Revolution in Middlebury," AEIdeas blog, March 5, 2017, *https://www.aei.org/society-and-culture/reflections-on-the-revolution-in-middlebury/.*

36 Jeremy Bauer-Wolf, "Free Speech Advocate Silenced," *Inside Higher Ed,* October 6, 2017, *https://www.insidehighered.com/news/2017/10/06/william-mary-students-who-shut-down-aclu-event-broke-conduct-code,* Butcher, "It's Not a College's Job to Protect Students from New Ideas," and "There's Little Sympathy for Campus Mobs," In Defense of Liberty, October 26, 2019, *https://www.indefenseofliberty.blog/2019/10/26/campus-mobs-pyrrhic-victories-audience-members-disgusted-by-recent-shout-downs/,* and "Student Protestors Disrupt University of Oregon President's University Speech," *The Oregonian,* October 6, 2017, *https://www.youtube.com/watch?v=A5NlKpjS1Sk.*

At Rutgers, students interrupted a university board of trustees meeting, pushing past security, singing "Solidarity forever, for the union makes us strong" while demanding a fifteen-dollar-per-hour minimum wage for student workers.[37] A video shows campus officials standing by helplessly as students occupy the room where the board meeting was about to begin. "If we don't get it, shut it down!" the rioters chanted. Observers will notice this chant regularly across campus shout downs. Harvard students shouted the same slogan at school president Lawrence Bacow in 2019, for example.[38] Again, the students' goal was not to have their ideas heard, but to make sure that *other people* could not express themselves. Setting aside the evidence that minimum-wage mandates hurt the least-skilled and lowest-paid workers the most, the students' methods are clearly in line with critical theorists' calls to engage in resistance, even practice violence and take away others' expressive rights to accomplish their goals.

These incidents and others should be condemned as violations of individuals' free speech rights. When we listen to the language that students and rioters use in committing the disruptions, we find ourselves having the language of the Frankfurt School, Freire, Frantz Fanon, and other critical theorists shouted back at us. At the University of Oregon, a student with a megaphone who helped to shout down the school president said that professors were "teaching them to deprioritize everything that we care about"; later, in an interview with local media, another student said, "expect resistance to anyone who opposes us."[39] Of note: this university maintains a multicultural center run by stu-

---

37 Daniel J. Munoz, "Rutgers Student Activists Disrupt Board of Trustees, Call for Minimum Wage Increase," *Tap Into New Brunswick*, December 13, 2017, *https://www.tapinto.net/towns/new-brunswick/articles/rutgers-student-activists-disrupt-board-of-truste*.

38 Soave, "Harvard President Lawrence Bacow to Activist Students Who Shut Down His Talk: 'The Heckler's Veto Has No Place' Here."

39 "Student Protestors Disrupt University of Oregon President's University Speech," *The Oregonian*.

dent groups that have hosted the likes of revisionist historian Howard Zinn and radical activist Angela Davis.[40]

Davis is a former student of critical theorist Herbert Marcuse,[41] and is a legend in the underground community. Her involvement with a group that took over the Marin County Courthouse in California and killed a Superior Court judge in 1970 cemented her place in radical chic lore.[42] University of California-Los Angeles (UCLA) officials dismissed her from her faculty position that year because of her "inflammatory language" (though in 2014, UCLA made Davis a Regents' lecturer, and she taught a graduate seminar).[43] She twice ran for vice president on the Communist Party USA's ticket.[44] She is currently a distinguished professor emerita for the University of California-Santa Cruz's Feminist Studies Department.[45] One can hardly believe that students are opposed to violence when they endorse the ideas of figureheads of violent movements who never renounced their past.

$$\text{O O O}$$

In March 2019, three University of Arizona students—later known as the Arizona Three—interrupted a presentation by U.S. Customs and Border Protection (CBP) agents in a university building, making it impossible for students to hear the agents speak. One of the three students, Denisse Moreno Melchor, had noticed the agents addressing the university's Criminal Justice

---

40 University of Oregon, "Events Calendar: Multicultural Center," *https://calendar.uoregon.edu/group/multicultural_center*.

41 Explorations in Black Leadership, "Brandeis University: Herbert Marcuse," University of Virginia Arts & Sciences, *https://blackleadership.virginia.edu/videos/davis-angela/ad08*.

42 Bryan Burrough, *Days of Rage* (New York: Penguin Books, 2015).

43 UCLA, "Angela Davis," *https://optimism.ucla.edu/stories/angela-davis/*.

44 James Brooke, "Other Women Seeking No. 2 Spot Speak Out," *The New York Times*, July 29, 1984, *https://archive.nytimes.com/www.nytimes.com/books/98/03/08/home/davis-vp.html*.

45 UC Santa Cruz, "Angela Y Davis," Humanities, *https://humanities.ucsc.edu/academics/faculty/index.php?uid=aydavis*.

Association (CJA). The CJA is a student group that had invited the CBP agents to talk about careers in law enforcement.[46] According to university police, the three agitated students ultimately forced the agents to leave and interfered with "the peaceful conduct of an educational institution."[47] At least one of the students was caught on video cursing at the agents as they walked to the parking lot, calling them "murder patrol" and "KKK."[48]

When members of the CJA called campus security, hoping to put an end to the disruption so that the event could continue, another of the Arizona Three shouted, "White man and white woman calling the police!" when members of the student group called campus security so that the event could continue. Melchor later told the student newspaper that she started "chanting, disrupting that space until they [the officers] left. Literally walked them all the way to their cars until they left."

The Arizona Three filmed the disruption, threatening to stay and scream at the agents and call them murderers if the officers continued to speak to the group of students.[49] Eventually CJA members gave up, and members of the Arizona Three can be seen following the officers to the parking lot.

The event convinced university leaders to hold a "campus conversation" that April, where students, faculty and staff could

46   Eddie Celaya, "The Saga of the 'Arizona 3': The Story So Far," *The Daily Wildcat*, April 15, 2018, *https://www.wildcat.arizona.edu/article/2019/04/n-arizona-3-roundup*.

47   Rachel Leingang, "University of Arizona Charges 3rd Student in Border Patrol Protest," *The Arizona Republic*, April 5, 2019, *https://www.azcentral.com/story/news/local/arizona-education/2019/04/05/university-arizona-protest-border-patrol-3rd-student-charged/3379687002/*.

48   Butcher, "Arizona Case Shows the Difference Between Campus Free Speech and Harassment," The Daily Signal, April 23, 2019, *https://www.dailysignal.com/2019/04/23/arizona-case-shows-the-difference-between-campus-free-speech-and-harassment/*, and Curt Prendergast, "Criminal Charges Dismissed Against 3 UA Students After Confrontation with Border Patrol," Tucson.com, April 23, 2019, *https://tucson.com/news/local/criminal-charges-dismissed-against-3-ua-students-after-confrontation-with-border-patrol/article_e325ecd4-e58c-548f-b27d-1c9c0dc492ba.html*.

49   Professor Walker, "University of Arizona Students Harass Border Patrol Recruiters," April 2, 2019, video, *https://www.youtube.com/watch?v=4OmFtYMvrG0*.

discuss the incident.[50] Comments at this event were reveal-ing. One student said that school officials needed "to take into account the…disproportional harms and oppression that people of color face at the university," then in Marcusian fashion added,

> *we need to reject this idea that…free speech means the same thing for everybody. I think it means a very different thing for a young white man to demand free speech on a campus versus people who for generations have been oppressed and who on a daily basis face microaggressions.*[51]

Marcuse, the original member of the Frankfurt School whom historian Stuart Jeffries described as most open to "polit-ical militancy,"[52] explained the critical concept of unequal rights in 1965. Marcuse wrote: "It should be evident by now that the exercise of civil rights by those who don't have them presupposes the withdrawal of civil rights from those who pre-vent their exercise, and that liberation of the Damned of the Earth presupposes suppression not only of their old but also of their new masters."[53]

Radical professor Ibram X. Kendi echoes this in his work when he says the answer to discrimination is more discrimina-tion.[54] In the upside-down worlds of critical theory and critical race theory, in which speech is a kind of violence, freedom is also a type of oppression. To be free requires government to restrict the liberty of others who differ from us, just as to be antiracist is to favor racial discrimination.

---

50   University of Arizona, "Campus Conversation," April 23, 2019, *https://www.youtube.com/watch?v=74eBgKzr3WY*.
51   Ibid.
52   Stuart Jefferies, *Grand Hotel Abyss* (London: Verso, 2016), p. 4.
53   Herbert Marcuse, "Repressive Tolerance," in Robert Paul Wolff, Barrington Moore, Jr., and Herbert Marcuse, *A Critique of Pure Tolerance* (Boston: Beacon Press, 1965).
54   Kendi, *How to Be an Antiracist*, pp. 18–19.

A University of Arizona student at the campus conversation said in his remarks, "It's very easy to say we need to be civil, but, again, you don't understand because of your white male privilege what these people experience on a daily basis." The two-hour event was frequently interrupted by rioters who interfered with faculty speaking on the panel, as well as interrupting the college president, shouting statements like, "this is the time where we speak up or we shut [others] up. There is nothing else for us."[55]

At the University of Oklahoma, officials were quite direct in saying that student speech should be censored in class if it does not align with critical race theory's dogma. In an April 2021 antiracist workshop, a woman identified as a university faculty member said that professors can limit what students say in class. According to the recording, the professor said, "One of the fears is that we're going to get in trouble for this, right? Like we can't tell students that they can't say something in class. But we can! And let me tell you how...The law is on the side of educators. In the classroom, free speech does not apply."[56]

Teachers may, of course, limit speech in the classroom in order to prevent disruptions and ensure that the class follows the lesson plan. That is not what this professor was talking about. On the contrary, given critical theory's principle that speech is a form of violence and power, this professor was arguing that free discussion should be curtailed so that educators can force students to believe or profess a specific philosophical or moral position. In 2020, school officials announced that all faculty, students, and staff would be required to participate in

---

55 University of Arizona, "Campus Conversation."
56 Carly Mayberry, "University of Oklahoma's Anti-Racist Workshop Training Violates Free Speech, Nonprofit Says," *Newsweek*, June 23, 2021, *https://www.newsweek.com/university-oklahomas-anti-racist-workshop-training-violates-free-speech-nonprofit-says-1603580*, and news release, "OU Launches Mandatory Diversity Training for all Students, Faculty, and Staff," University of Oklahoma, August 27, 2020, *https://www.ou.edu/web/news_events/articles/news_2020/ou-launches-mandatory-diversity-training-for-all-students-faculty-and-staff.*

so-called diversity training as part of a plan to make the school a place of "belonging and emotional growth."[57] But if faculty who are leading diversity training programs are censoring students who do not affirm the critical race theory agenda, some people will inevitably not belong. They will be forced either to silence their true beliefs or to leave.

In November 2019, State University of New York-Binghamton (SUNY-Binghamton) students also made no pretense of a willingness to allow a planned event to proceed. They attacked a set of display tables set up by the Young America's Foundation (YAF) and SUNY-Binghamton's College Republicans. After shouting at members of YAF and the College Republicans, rioting students flipped the tables over and destroyed the flyers and signs.[58] John Restuccia, then president of the College Republicans, said that he has more than one hour's worth of footage documenting the destruction of his group's materials. He told me in an interview, "Eventually, we were surrounded by two hundred people. We had to be escorted out of the area by campus police."[59]

Just days later, the YAF and Restuccia's group hosted a lecture featuring economist Arthur Laffer. As soon as Laffer, former advisor to both Democratic Governor of California Jerry Brown and Republican President Ronald Reagan, took the lectern to speak, students began shouting.[60] Loud chants and applause followed, making it impossible to hear Laffer's comments. One student near the front of the auditorium was heard saying, "We are tired of being murdered by this adminis-

---

57   News release, "OU Launches Mandatory Diversity Training for all Students, Faculty, and Staff."

58   Young America's Foundation, "Crazed Leftists Mob Conservative Students at Binghamton University," YouTube, November 15, 2019, *https://www.youtube.com/watch?v=_X2-96 gt9MI&t=242s*.

59   Phone interview with John Restuccia, November 21, 2019.

60   "Protestors Shout Down Arthur Laffer Event at Binghamton University," *Binghamton Review*, November 19, 2019, video, *https://www.youtube.com/watch?v=eTqlmDar_hg*.

tration," though it is unclear to which administration (university leadership or the White House) he was referring. Another student brought him a megaphone, and the first student referenced "America's legacy of slavery and racial oppression." The disruptive students then began chanting "Free speech! Free speech!"—without any sense of irony—as they silenced the person who was invited to speak at this event. Eventually, police cancelled the event, pulling rioters down from the desks on which they were standing.

Restuccia and local media would later report that the university offered students who disagreed with Laffer and YAF's positions a different room in which to hold their event, but, clearly, the rioting students' objectives did not include the coexistence of competing opinions on campus.

No students were sanctioned for their behavior at the event, despite the destruction of property prior to Laffer's planned speech. But as evidence of further confusion created by the strains of critical theory's ideas of oppression and intolerance on campus, SUNY-Binghamton officials announced the formation of a committee to review police activities— and not because of the Laffer incident. Rather, after George Floyd's tragic death in May 2020, when a Minneapolis police officer kneeled on Floyd's neck for a prolonged time, SUNY-Binghamton administrators announced the creation of a Campus Citizen Review Board, cochaired by the campus's vice president of diversity, equity and inclusion, to review campus security officers' actions and job performance.[61] The university's press release about this board made no mention of the violence at the Laffer event.

---

61 State University of New York-Binghamton, "Office of the President: University Statements, Campus Citizen Review Board to Review University Police Department's Policies, Practices, Procedures, Actions and Resources," August 26, 2020, *https:// www.binghamton.edu/president/statements.html.*

SUNY-Binghamton's administration is not the only one to embody the critical perspective on campus life. In a letter to Princeton's president signed by hundreds of faculty members, Princeton professors claimed that the university was infected with systemic racism, and borrowed language straight from the Frankfurt School, Freire, and other critical theorists.[62] "Anti-Blackness is foundational to America," the letter begins, an idea echoed by the "diversity" statements from tony K–12 college prep schools, such as Sidwell Friends, that say that the "origins" of America are based on white supremacy, as explained in Chapter 2.[63] The Princeton faculty says that antiblackness "plays a powerful role at institutions like Princeton, despite declared values of diversity and inclusion." The signatories also allege that administrators have been negligent about racial issues: "Indifference to the effects of racism on this campus has allowed legitimate demands for institutional support and redress in the face of micro-aggression and outright racist incidents to go long unmet."

The letter ended with demands that school officials hire "exponentially" more faculty of color (without mentioning anything about the qualifications of the individuals that school leaders will hire—their race is apparently sufficient). The university community is to be educated "about the legacy of slavery and white supremacy" and "Princeton's ties to and culpability in slavery and white supremacy." The letter calls for diversity training for everyone on campus, of course.

The idea that racism is rampant on the campus of Princeton University is absurd. Rather than stand up for the university's

---

62   Brett Tomlinson, "Faculty Members Propose an Anti-Racism Agenda," *Princeton Weekly*, July 13, 2020, *https://paw.princeton.edu/article/faculty-members-propose-anti-racism-agenda*.

63   Sidwell Friends, "Lead in the Light: Equity, Justice, and Community, Strategic Action Plan for Sidwell Friends School 2021–2023," *https://resources.finalsite.net/images/v1613661710/sidwell/wm37tyobjeujxdyfgc8o/2021EJCStrategicPlanBrochure0218.pdf*.

reputation, university president Christopher Eisgruber said that he had already "charged my Cabinet in June [2020] to develop plans to combat systemic racism at Princeton and beyond."[64] Eisgruber says that racism "persist[s]" at the prestigious university and wants to make the school "fully inclusive."

There is just one problem with Eisgruber's response to the letter from faculty: if Princeton must "address [systemic racism] within our own community," that means that the school has racial discrimination that has gone unaddressed—or at least unallayed—by school officials. This means that individuals who are part of the campus community are violating federal law.

The U.S. Department of Education was prepared to take Eisgruber at his word that the university had perpetuated systemic racism. Federal officials sent him a letter in fall 2020 explaining that Washington has a responsibility to investigate such accusations and to punish them, in part by withholding federal funds.[65] U.S. Department of Education officials noted that Princeton had received some $75 million in federal spending under the federal Higher Education Act alone, spending that requires university officials to abide by the Civil Rights Act of 1964. The agency's letter cited Eisgruber's own words, which claimed that racism is "embedded in structures of the University itself."

The U.S. Department of Education wrote, "Based on its [Princeton's] admitted racism, the U.S. Department of Education ("Department") is concerned Princeton's nondiscrimination and equal opportunity assurances in its Program

---

64 Princeton Office of Communications, "Letter from President Eisgruber on the University's Efforts to Combat Systemic Racism," September 2, 2020, *https://www.princeton.edu/news/2020/09/02/letter-president-eisgruber-universitys-efforts-combat-systemic-racism.*
65 Robert King, Assistant Secretary, Office of Postsecondary Education, U.S. Department of Education, "Letter to Princeton University President Christopher Eisgruber," September 16, 2020, *https://www.princeton.edu/sites/default/files/documents/2020/09/Princeton-Letter-9-16-20-Signed.pdf.*

Participation Agreements from at least 2013 to the present may have been false."

Translation: Princeton promised that it was following federal civil rights laws so that it could receive federal spending, but now the school president himself claimed that school policies are systemically racist. (After the incident at SUNY-Binghamton in November 2019, the Education Department also sent school officials a letter with concerns about how administrators handled the incident.)

University officials found themselves in a catch-22. If the school agreed with the federal letter, it might have to repay millions in federal spending and face a federal investigation. If the school denied systemic racism on campus, school officials would lose the favor they were trying to curry with social justice warriors, who want all who are not "oppressed" to admit that they are oppressors.

This is critical race theory's ultimate paradox: if you admit you are racist, you are; if you deny you are racist, that also means you are racist.

Faced with an impossible situation just weeks away from a U.S. presidential election, Princeton officials appeared to simply wait and reframe the issue. "The University will respond to the Department of Education's letter in due course," read a Princeton press release, adding, "It is unfortunate that the Department appears to believe that grappling honestly with the nation's history and the current effects of systemic racism runs afoul of existing law."[66] The delay tactic worked. Once Joe Biden

---

66   Princeton University, "University Statement on U.S. Department of Education Letter Regarding Nondiscrimination Practices," September 17, 2020, *https://www.princeton. edu/news/2020/09/17/university-statement-us-department-education-letter-regarding-nondiscrimination.*

was sworn in as president in January 2021, his administration dropped the investigation the next month.[67]

OOO

Obviously, no one in a campus community should accept racist behavior. Critical race theory, however, states that racist acts are everywhere, happening all the time—and that they are sustained by university policies. Yet colleges have done more in the name of diversity over the past thirty years than perhaps any sector of American society. Research conducted by my Heritage Foundation colleague Jay Greene, and James Paul, a distinguished doctoral fellow at the University of Arkansas, finds that universities are awash in staff working on "diversity, equity, and inclusion" (DEI).[68] They find that among sixty-five universities in the "Power 5" athletic conferences (the Atlantic Coast Conference, the Big 10, the Big 12, the PAC 12, and the Southeastern Conference), the schools had, on average, 4.2 times the number of staff working on DEI initiatives as those working with students with special needs. The schools employed 1.4 times more DEI staff than history professors, and 3.4 DEI staff members for every one hundred tenured or tenure-track faculty members.

Another review conducted by researchers at the American Enterprise Institute (AEI) and the Heritage Foundation of the top twenty colleges of education according to *U.S. News & World Report* rankings, found that "attention to [equity, race,

---

67   Anika Agarwal, "Department of Education Drops Investigation into Princeton," *The Daily Princetonian*, February 10, 2021, *https://www.dailyprincetonian.com/article/2021/02/department-of-education-princeton-discrimination-investigation-systemic-racism*.

68   Jay P. Greene and James D. Paul, "Diversity University: DEI Bloat in the Academy," Heritage Foundation *Backgrounder* No. 3641, July 27, 2021, *https://www.heritage.org/sites/default/files/2021-07/BG3641_0.pdf*.

and diversity] is ubiquitous."[69] "Among the top-ranked colleges of education," researchers wrote, "48 percent of the faculty had a research interest or area of study that included one of the diversity keywords [such as discrimination, inclusion, human rights, or race]."[70] Twenty-four percent of the professors' biographies and areas of research reviewed had "race, diversity, or equity as their *primary* area of study" (emphasis in the original). It should shock no one that the AEI and Heritage Foundation researchers estimate that "at least between one-third and one-quarter of scholars who focus on race and diversity do so as critical theorists."[71]

Progressives who dismiss the free speech crisis should consider the larger question of critical race theory's influence on college communities. And because critical ideas are at odds with Americans' sense of national identity and the formation of individual character, they should consider how critical race theory makes it nearly impossible for faculty, students, and staff to communicate with each other.

Critical ideas create this chasm between educators and students, students and students, and college officials and policymakers. Just as racist and communist institutions, such as slavery and the USSR, were not be defeated without strong, sustained belief that freedom is worth fighting for, so, too, critical race theory's neoracist and neo-Marxist applications can only be stopped by the same. Furthermore, Americans must answer the critical worldview with something else. Before

---

69   Frederick M. Hess and Lindsey M. Burke, "Does Race Get Short Shrift in Education Research and Teacher Training?" Heritage Foundation *Issue Brief* No. 6073, April 5, 2021, *https://www.heritage.org/education/report/does-race-get-short-shrift-education-research-and-teacher-training*.
70   Ibid.
71   Ibid.

turning to this response, though, we will look more closely at how some faculty and students describe life on campus today.

OOO

K–12 is not the only level of education in which there was once a belief in teaching a shared set of facts, ideas, and values to prepare young people for civic life. Anthony Kronman, Yale law professor and former dean of Yale Law School, observes in *Education's End: Why Our Colleges and Universities Have Given Up on the Meaning of Life,* that his institution's curricular focus a century ago on a fixed set of classic Western philosophers and writers was widely shared by other institutions. At that time, colleges and universities were places where students were taught a shared cultural canon, the principles of a common humanist philosophy—which prioritized universal scientific principles and a philosophy of shared human values and human rights—and where they could also learn character values. Critical theory and pedagogy are designed to address these subjects in a very specific way—by opposing the values of the Enlightenment, including not only individual dignity and civil behavior, ideas on which civil society rests, but even the idea of objective reality.[72]

Higher education institutions have turned their attention from teaching character and civic virtues, and focused either on the "hard" sciences, or on "soft" social science research. Over the past 150 years, college educators have refocused their schools' mission from training for life to training for the workforce. We can describe the recent trend in K–12 schools in much the same way. Since 2001, public school officials have

---

72   Anthony T. Kronman, *Education's End: Why Our Colleges and Universities Have Given Up on the Meaning of Life* (New Haven: Yale University Press, 2007), Kindle edition, location 396.

faced increasing pressure to improve student skills in reading and math, unquestionably necessary given the dismal test scores, but this pressure has resulted in other subjects, such as history and civics, receiving less time in the classroom. With the indelible components of character formation being part of civics instruction, in particular, critical race theorists have taken advantage of the vacuum created by the elimination of character-oriented teaching.

College professors used to value tradition, with a "more stable and holistic view of knowledge, one that stressed the continuity of human knowledge from each generation to the next and the capacity of a well-educated mind to grasp it as a whole," Kronman says. "It underscored the role that teachers play as keepers of tradition," he writes.[73] As students enter college, then, they lack the tools to recognize the dangers of the critical worldview, or to recognize what civic—and civil—behavior should look like. K–12 students' poor performance on measures of civic and history knowledge does not help, either. (More on this in Chapter 4.) College educators' departure from this perspective has made it easier for some students to accept the critical dogma without hesitation because they have so little knowledge of history and civics.

Writing in the early 1990s, around the same time that Arthur Schlesinger was warning of the growing threat from critical ideas in the form of "multiculturalism," the brilliant economist Thomas Sowell recognized the same problems. In *Inside American Education*, he wrote, "The ideological component of multiculturalism can be summarized as a cultural relativism which finds the predominance of Western civilization in the world or in the schools intolerable. Behind this attitude is often a seething hos-

---

73   Ibid., location 640–641.

tility to the West…"[74] Yet many students, and even professors, at postsecondary institutions do not recognize the disruption to civil society in America that "multiculturalism" and critical theory cause. For others, of course, this disruption is the point.

Critical theory has spoiled the pursuit of truth, the "art of living," in the academy, Kronman says. Sowell agrees:

> *What is also salient are the multiculturalists' educational methods, geared toward leading students to a set of pre-selected beliefs, rather than toward developing their own ability to analyze for themselves, or to provide them with adequate factual knowledge to make their own independent assessments.*[75]

As explained in Chapter 1, critical race theorists have abandoned any sense of truth as well as its importance. Once we understand the critical view of "narrative" as being more important than facts, questions about life and its meaning become vulnerable to the intellectual occupation of critical race theory's radical, sometimes violent, and always destructive dogma.

STUDENTS DESCRIBE THE CAMPUS CLIMATE

Recent surveys have allowed students to describe what it feels like to live in an environment dominated by the intolerance of critical race theory. The Knight Foundation surveyed college students in 2020 and found that only 68 percent think that free speech rights are "extremely important" to democracy.[76] Eighty-one percent of respondents "widely support a campus environ-

---

74   Thomas Sowell, *Inside American Education: The Decline, the Deception, the Dogmas* (New York: The Free Press, 1993), p. 71.

75   Sowell, *Inside American Education*, p. 71.

76   Knight Foundation, "The First Amendment on Campus 2020 Report: College Students' Views of Free Expression," 2020, *https://knightfoundation.org/wp-content/uploads/2020/05/First-Amendment-on-Campus-2020.pdf.*

ment where students are exposed to all types of speech, even if they may find it offensive," but in a sign of students holding two incompatible ideas at once, 78 percent of students also approved of "safe spaces," where students would be "free from threatening actions, ideas or conversations."

So-called safe spaces are often part of discriminatory policies, making the spaces part of the fold of critical race theory's applications. These are physical spaces that university officials reserve for students from certain ethnic backgrounds or who claim to be or feel oppressed.[77] Schools should certainly offer students the chance to meet with mental health professionals, but far too often, "safe spaces" are rooms with bean bags, puppies, crayons, and Play-Doh. Students congregate in these spaces and are "infantilized," as one author described the activities, and students ignore their responsibility to respond to the changes in the world around them (some schools offered students safe spaces after Donald Trump won the 2016 presidential election, for example).[78]

Student fears about intolerant critical dogmas come to the fore in questions about schools' intellectual and social climate. The Knight Foundation survey found that 76 percent of respondents believe that programs that college officials describe as attempts to enhance "diversity" actually "come into conflict with free speech rights." Sixty-three percent said that "the climate on their campus deters students from expressing themselves openly, up from 54 percent in 2016." Although 90 percent or more of respondents said that female, politically liberal male, Hispanic, black, LGBT and white students can

---

77   Michael S. Roth, "Don't Dismiss Safe Spaces," *The New York Times*, August 29, 2019, *https://www.nytimes.com/2019/08/29/opinion/safe-spaces-campus.html*.

78   Kim Kozlowski, "Students Seek Safe Spaces, Dialogue After Election," *The Detroit News*, November 21, 2016, *https://www.detroitnews.com/story/news/education/2016/11/21/students-seek-safe-spaces-dialogue-election/94175310/*.

"freely express their views," just 73 percent said the same of conservative students.

Even some college *presidents* feel it is appropriate to shout down speakers on campus (the "heckler's veto"). In an American Council on Education survey from 2018, 15 percent of the college presidents surveyed said that it was sometimes acceptable to shout down speakers or to try to "prevent [speakers] from talking," with the implication that physical force could be used to do so.[79] In another inconsistent twist, 100 percent of presidents said it was never appropriate to use violence to stop a speech—but why would anyone be sure that, if an enraged mob shouts so loud and so long that a speech has to be cancelled, this group will not resort to violence? The behavior of officials at Evergreen State College and Princeton, who conceded to the demands of student mobs and activist faculty rather than defend the principle of free speech can hardly give other professors or lecturers confidence that the school administration will support their rights to listen and be heard.

In another Knight Foundation survey, this one from 2019, 58 percent of college students said that it is "sometimes" or "always" acceptable to deny the news media access to a college campus to report on campus protests.[80] Although 60 percent of respondents said that "these days too many people are easily offended over the language that others use," 17 percent of respondents— nearly one in five—said that it is "always" or "sometimes" acceptable to use violence to "stop a speech protest or rally." Fifty-one

---

79 Lorelle L. Espinosa, Jennifer R. Crandall, and Philip Wilkinson, "Free Speech and Campus Inclusion: A Survey of College Presidents," American Council on Higher Education, April 9, 2018, *https://www.higheredtoday.org/2018/04/09/free-speech-campus-inclusion-survey-college-presidents/*.

80 Knight Foundation, "Free Expression on College Campuses," College Pulse, May 2019, *https://kf-site-production.s3.amazonaws.com/media_elements/files/000/000/351/original/Knight-CP-Report-FINAL.pdf*.

percent said that is it "always" or "sometimes" acceptable to shout down speakers or to prevent them from talking.

A survey conducted in 2020 at the University of North Carolina (UNC) offers similar, discouraging findings. More than a quarter of students said they would "endorse blocking or interrupting events featuring speakers with whom they disagree." Though students said that political issues did not "come up" regularly in class and "generally" perceived their professors as open-minded, many students were concerned that if they "express their sincere political views openly, instructors and/or peers will think less of them, or do something to embarrass them."[81] Seventeen percent of conservative students reported keeping "an opinion related to class to themselves" more than ten times, compared with 4 percent of students identifying as moderate and 1.5 percent of students identifying as liberal. Curiously, among those who reported self-censoring less often (between six and ten times), 13 percent of conservatives kept their opinions to themselves that many times, while no liberal students reported doing so (5 percent of moderates reported self-censoring between six and ten times).

Nearly 12 percent of respondents in the UNC survey—more than one in ten—were conservative students who were "extremely" concerned that other students would "file a complaint" against them if they gave their own opinion in a class on a political topic. Less than 1 percent of both liberal and moderate students were extremely concerned.

In fact, in 2017, the Foundation for Individual Rights in Education found 231 colleges and universities that were operating "bias response teams," which allow individuals to report on something another student said or did, anonymously on

---

81   Jennifer Larson, Mark McNeilly, and Timothy J. Ryan, "Free Expression and Constructive Dialogue at the University of North Carolina at Chapel Hill," March 2, 2020, p. 1, *https://fecdsurveyreport.web.unc.edu/wp-content/uploads/sites/22160/2020/02/ UNC-Free-Expression-Report.pdf.*

some campuses.[82] These reports could trigger action by university staff. At the University of Michigan, the bias response team fielded reports with the instruction that "the most important indication of bias is your own feelings," not the facts surrounding an incident.[83]

A group called Speech First sued the University of Michigan in a case titled *Speech First v. Schlissel et al.*, a case that drew interest from the U.S. Department of Justice. The Justice Department described the university's "Statement of Student Rights and Responsibilities" prohibiting "harassment," "bullying," and "bias" as unconstitutional "because it offers no clear, objective definition of the violations."[84] The Justice Department also said that "the University's Bias Response Policy chills protected speech through its Bias Response team."

The school eventually settled and agreed to disband its bias response team.[85] The university also agreed to revise its definitions for the terms "harassment" and "bullying" in university handbooks.[86]

The University of Michigan case is but one example that lends credibility to student complaints that they fear to speak their minds on campus because of what others might do to them. Free speech advocates have filed similar suits at

82   Foundation for Individual Rights in Education, "Bias Response Team Report 2017," *https://www.thefire.org/research/publications/bias-response-team-report-2017/report-on-bias-reporting-systems-2017/*.

83   News release, "Speech First Files Federal Lawsuit Challenging University of Michigan Speech Code and Bias Response Team," Speech First, May 8, 2018, *https://speechfirst.org/litigation/speech-first-files-federal-lawsuit-challenging-university-of-michigan-speech-code-and-bias-response-team/*.

84   News release, "Justice Department Files Statement of Interest in Michigan Free Speech Case," U.S. Department of Justice, June 11, 2018, *https://www.justice.gov/opa/pr/justice-department-files-statement-interest-michigan-free-speech-case*.

85   William A. Jacobson, "Appeals Court Reinstates Lawsuit Challenging U. Michigan 'Bias Response Team,'" Legal Insurrection, September 24, 2019, *https://legalinsurrection.com/2019/09/appeals-court-reinstates-lawsuit-challenging-u-michigan-bias-response-team/*.

86   Speech First, "Speech First v. U. of M; Settlement Agreement," October 28, 2019, *https://speechfirst.org/court-battles/speech-first-v-u-of-m-settlement-agreement/*.

the University of Central Florida, Iowa State University, the University of Texas, and the University of Illinois.[87] These bias response teams, along with the violent disruptions of campus events, are all part of the environment that those exercising critical race theory's worldview have created on university campuses. Students who fear disagreeing openly with the majority mindset are not paranoid. They are right to be afraid.

OOO

Despite the free speech crisis on campuses today, despite the riots and embarrassing headlines about college no longer being a place where students can have open discussions, and despite the racial discrimination that is inseparable from critical race theory, many university officials remain committed to expanding the use of the theory on their campuses.

At Arizona State University (ASU), the nation's seventh-largest university by enrollment, school officials announced the hiring of a professor who teaches music according to critical race theory.[88] In "Speak No Evil: Talking Race as an African American in Music Education," professor Joyce McCall wrote that "colonization, institutionalized Whiteness, and managing pluralistic platforms" are "specific structures that...legitimize an oppressive social order" in music.[89]

---

87 Speech First, "Court Battles: Protect Free Speech," *https://speechfirst.org/court-battles/*.

88 Josh Moody, "10 Colleges with the Most Undergraduate Students," *U.S. News & World Report*, September 29, 2020, *https://www.usnews.com/education/best-colleges/the-short-list-college/articles/colleges-with-the-most-undergraduates*, Ben Zeisloft, "ASU Welcomes New Prof Who Focuses on Applying 'Critical Race Theory' to Music," *Campus Reform*, July 27, 2021, *https://campusreform.org/article?id=17889*, and news release, "Critical Race Theory Scholar Joins ASU School of Music, Dance and Theater," Arizona State University, July 21, 2021, *https://news.asu.edu/20210721-critical-race-theory-scholar-joins-asu-school-music-dance-and-theatre*.

89 Joyce M. McCall, "Speak No Evil: Talking Race as an African American in Music Education," in Brent C. Talbot, ed., *Marginalized Voices in Music Education* (New York: Routledge, 2018).

At Princeton, school officials hired a "sociocultural and medical anthropologist" who is committed to critical race theory.[90] This professor will be teaching a course on the Black Lives Matter movement and require students to read a book by Angela Davis, the UC-Santa Cruz professor described earlier, who was once on the FBI's most-wanted list.[91] In February 2021, ASU's student government and the Black African Coalition (BAC) cohosted a virtual event featuring Davis and paid her $15,000 for the speech.[92]

OOO

Critical race theory brings with it a drastic jargon—which is little surprise, since it is overwhelmingly focused on the use and restriction of language. Along with bizarre new definitions for words like "racist" and "violence," practitioners of this ideology have also embraced the term "microaggression" to refer, as Richard Delgado and Jean Stefancic explain in *Critical Race Theory*, to

> *one of those many sudden, stunning, or dispiriting transactions that mar the days of women and folks of color. Like water dripping on sandstone, they can be thought of as small acts of racism, consciously or unconsciously perpetrated, well-*

90 Christian Lubke, "Princeton Offers '#BlackLivesMatter' Course with Readings by an Avowed Marxist," The College Fix, August 6, 2021, *https://www.thecollegefix.com/princeton-offers-blacklivesmatter-course-with-readings-by-an-avowed-marxist/.*

91 Princeton University, Office of the Registrar, "Course Details: #BlackLivesMatter," *https://registrar.princeton.edu/course-offerings/course-details?term=1222&courseid=016062,* and Federal Bureau of Investigation, "Most Wanted History Pictures: 309. Angela Davis," *https://www.fbi.gov/wanted/topten/topten-history/hires_images/FBI-309-AngelaYvonne Davis.jpg/view.*

92 Mike LaChance, "Communist Angela Davis Paid $15,000 for a Virtual Speech at Arizona State U.," Legal Insurrection, August 11, 2021, *https://legalinsurrection. com/2021/08/communist-angela-davis-paid-15000-for-a-virtual-speech-at-arizona-state-u/,* and Ben Zeisloft, "EXCLUSIVE: ASU Student Government Paid Communist $15,000 for Virtual Speech," *Campus Reform,* August 10, 2021, *https://campusreform.org/article?id=17960.*

ing up from the assumptions about racial matters most of us absorb from the cultural heritage in which we come of age in the United States.[93]

Where most people might detect (non-race-related) rudeness or nothing at all, "antiracist" activists see racism, pure and simple. Yet alleged microaggressions are so micro that they often cannot be detected at all. As early as the 1970s, academic journals published articles arguing that ethnic minorities must "be *taught* to recognize these micro-aggressions" (emphasis added), making clear that the very acts are matters of interpretation.[94]

For example, in September 2017, Lipscomb University president Randy Lowry issued a public apology after he and his wife hosted a dinner for black students and used centerpieces for the tables that contained stalks of barley, wheat, and sunflowers, along with stalks of cotton.[95] The menu for the night included macaroni and cheese, greens, and corn bread, and Lowry's critics said he had failed at "cultural inclusivity." Lowry said, "I'm very sorry if anyone was offended by that, but there was absolutely no intention to set up a menu that would in any way make a statement. It was just one of the options for a good dinner."[96]

In the past decade, researchers and commentators have often credited Derald Wing Sue, a professor of psychology and education at Columbia University, with reigniting the notion

---

93   Delgado and Stefancic, *Critical Race Theory: An Introduction*, p. 2.

94   Chester M. Pierce, "Psychiatric Problems of the Black Minority," *American Handbook of Psychiatry* (New York: Basic Books, 1974), p. 28, *https://www.freepsychotherapybooks.org/ebook/psychiatric-problems-of-the-black-minority/*.

95   Rick Seltzer, "More than Cotton," *Inside HigherEd*, September 19, 2017, *https://www.insidehighered.com/news/2017/09/19/lipscomb-president-apologizes-again-after-menu-choices-dinners-african-american-and*.

96   Ibid.

of microaggressions for this generation.[97] Microaggressions are slippery, though, even in Wing Sue's description, because they have "invisibility to the perpetrator." Anyone who does not have microaggressions directed at him is guilty of causing harm, because "all citizens are exposed to a social conditioning process that imbues them with prejudices…that lie outside their level of awareness." So, unless someone is committing a microaggression against us personally, we cannot recognize it and, due to social conditioning, we probably don't recognize the microaggressions that we ourselves commit. When someone claims that an action is a microaggression, the accused may not have any way of knowing what he has supposedly done wrong.

Microaggressions present a paradox similar to critical race theory's picture of racism: if you admit to committing a microaggression, you have done so; if you are accused of committing a microaggression and deny it, this means you have committed a microaggression.

That makes having a conversation about preventing or dealing with microaggressions impossible. Everyone is required, as a function of this principle, to live either in a constant state of anxiety that someone, somewhere is being offended by something we may have done or failed to do—or to live in a state of tense readiness to pounce on a perceived slight, no matter how "invisible to the perpetrator." The very idea that black people— or anyone with an ethnic minority background in the U.S.—are so delicate that they may suffer traumatic psychological harm from the existence of a table centerpiece made of cotton—is itself denigrating to black people.

---

97 Derald Wing Sue, *Microaggressions in Everyday Life: Race, Gender, and Sexual Orientation* (Weinheim, Germany: Wiley, 2010), e-book, and Hahna Yoon, "How to Respond to Microaggressions," *The New York Times*, March 3, 2020, *https://www.nytimes.com/2020/03/03/smarter-living/how-to-respond-to-microaggressions.html.*

Musa Al-Gharbi, who holds a fellowship in Columbia University's Sociology Department, writes that there simply is not enough evidence about the actual harm from microaggressions to warrant governmental, academic or even social responses. He writes that

> *it seems highly plausible that poorly conceived or implemented policies intended to address microaggressions could either endanger the free exchange of ideas, lead to unjustly severe consequences for minor (even unintentional) infractions, heighten animus between minority and majority groups, or even exacerbate the harm caused by microaggressions.*[98]

Al-Gharbi explains that researchers studying microaggressions emphasize "an *absence of evidence* regarding the prevalence of harm of microaggressions," though this does not necessarily mean that there is also *"evidence of absence."* "It is in *everyone's* interest to address the profound conceptual and evidentiary shortcomings of the MRP [microaggression research program] literature to date," Al-Gharbi says. (Emphasis in original.)

Although many conservative and progressive individuals may disagree over the existence of "microaggressions," even some progressives have spoken out against the general atmosphere of cowardice that the prevailing attitudes about psychological safety on campus have created. Greg Lukianoff and Jonathan Haidt explain this issue of perceived safety in *Coddling of the American Mind.*[99] They and others have pointed to self-described progressive activist and CNN contributor Van Jones's lecture at the University of Chicago in 2017 where he said, "I'm against bigots and against bullies," but, "I don't

---

98   Musa Al-Gharbi, "Microaggressions: Strong Claims, Inadequate Evidence," Heterodox: The Blog, January 30, 2017, *https://heterodoxacademy.org/blog/microaggressions-macro-debate/*.

99   Greg Lukianoff and Haidt, *The Coddling of the American Mind* (New York: Penguin Press, 2018), p. 89.

want you to be safe ideologically. I don't want you to be safe emotionally. I want you to be strong. That's different. I'm not going to pave the jungle for you. Put on some boots and learn how to deal with adversity."[100]

Fortunately, despite the long list of universities whose school officials want their school to be considered "woke," there are some schools whose leaders have recommitted their institutions to free speech and common sense. University of Chicago leadership has released statements saying the same. In 2016, the dean of students wrote a message to incoming freshmen that stated, "We do not support so-called 'trigger warnings,' we do not cancel invited speakers because their topics might prove controversial, and we do not condone the creation of intellectual 'safe spaces' where individuals can retreat from ideas and perspectives at odds with their own."[101]

Even some progressives, such as those at PEN America, see the value in protecting free speech and this freedom's unique place in American history. Student and faculty who "justify censorship" actually "risk giving free speech a bad name." PEN researchers write:

> *If a new generation comes to see it as an ossified, irrelevant, even inimical concept, core freedoms that have been vigilantly guarded throughout American history could be in peril. Free speech advocates face an urgent task of articulating how to reconcile unfettered expression with acute demands for great equality and inclusion and, indeed, how both goals are mutually complementary and reinforcing.*[102]

---

100 University of Chicago Institute of Politics, "Van Jones on Safe Spaces on College Campuses," February 24, 2017, *https://www.youtube.com/watch?v=Zms3EqGbFOk.*

101 Scott Jaschik, "U Chicago to Freshmen: Don't Expect Safe Spaces," *InsideHigherEd,* August 25, 2016, *https://www.insidehighered.com/news/2016/08/25/u-chicago-warns-incoming-students-not-expect-safe-spaces-or-trigger-warnings.*

102 PEN America, "And Campus for All," p. 6.

Protecting free speech is just part of the necessary work to preserve freedom and equality of opportunity in America, however. Critical race theory's goals do not prepare students for life after college, nor do they prepare them to recognize America's unique contributions of ordered liberty. Critical race theory also does not accept the declaration that all men and women are created equal. Allan Bloom recognized this in the Black Power movement that arose alongside, and persisted after, the civil rights movement in the 1960s and 1970s. Critical race theorists most certainly adopted the guiding principles of the Black Power movement—these academic and social movements are nearly indistinguishable. Bloom writes,

> *The Black Power movement that supplanted the older civil rights movement—leaving aside both its excesses and its very understandable emphasis on self-respect and refusal to beg for acceptance—had at its core the view that the Constitutional tradition was always corrupt and was constructed as a defense of slavery. Its demand was for black identity, not universal rights. Not rights but power counted.*[103]

This is the intellectual centerpiece of any critical theory: everything in life can be reduced to competition for power.

Today, with the "woke" crowd's definition of "equality and inclusion" borrowing exclusively from the critical canon's twisted ideology of tolerance for some, and condemnation according to ethnicity, social justice activists will find that cherished rights, such as free speech, do not fit into the critical worldview. Universities must choose truth and build on

---

103 Allan Bloom, *The Closing of the American Mind: How Higher Education Has Failed Democracy and Impoverished the Souls of Today's Students* (New York: Simon & Schuster, 1987), p. 33.

the lessons from great thinkers and leaders of the past. As Kronman explains:

> We acknowledge their authority not because they are Western. That has nothing to do with it. We acknowledge their authority because they express the universal moral and political aspirations of all humankind, and though the West has done some terrible things in the name of these aspirations, and has selfishly exploited their appeal, that is no reason to impeach their authority, which rests on transcendent foundations.[104]

CONCLUSION

K–12 and postsecondary instructors cannot avoid the responsibility they bear as educators to help students to separate right from wrong, understanding which character traits sustain people's lives, thereby keeping the community in which they live a healthy one.

The challenge for all of us today is to see the pernicious influence of critical race theory in K–12 education, on college campuses, and in the general culture. Yale's Kronman says the diversity craze on campuses, with its training sessions and courses focused on racial tribes "are merely expressions of power" that are "corrosive of the attempt to explore the question of life's purpose and meaning."[105]

As individuals and communities, we must recognize the overlap between education content and character formation as a crucial factor that defines the culture in which we live. In doing so, we can develop a different theory—a "civil" theory that defines the way we celebrate America's identity as a land of possibilities

---

104 Kronman, *Education's End*, Kindle, locations 1807 and 1809.
105 Ibid., location 100.

for everyone, no matter our skin color. We can acknowledge the failures of past Americans to live up to our creed without resolving that we are a nation beyond redemption that must be disrupted, as critical race theorists threaten to do.

CHAPTER 4

SOLUTIONS

Neither students nor adults have a working understanding of American history or civics. K–12 educators devote noticeably little attention to civics, in particular, while revisionist historians, who want American history to be presented as a failure, have captured media headlines and, increasingly, textbooks. According to *Education Week*, fourteen states have no civics or government course requirements at all.[1] Just nineteen states require students to take a civics exam to graduate. In most of the states that do require students to take a civics test before graduating, lawmakers adopted the requirements in the past decade, which means the requirements are relatively new.[2]

Although no single test can demonstrate that a student or adult has a complete grasp of civics, the questions on the U.S. Citizenship and Immigration Services' civics test can reasonably be considered the bare minimum we should expect students (and new citizens to know). Questions (and answers) include:

---

1   "Data: Most States Require History, But Not Civics," *Education Week*, October 24, 2018, *https://www.edweek.org/teaching-learning/data-most-states-require-history-but-not-civics*.

2   Brenda Iasevoli, "Another State to Require Testing in Civics," *Education Week*, June 8, 2018, *https://blogs.edweek.org/edweek/curriculum/2018/06/another_state_to_require_testing.html*.

What is the supreme law of the land? (U.S. Constitution)

Name <u>one thing</u> the U.S. Constitution does. (Forms the government; defines powers of government; defines the parts of government; protects the rights of the people)

What does the Bill of Rights protect? ([The basic] rights of Americans; [the basic] rights of people living in the United States)

What founding document said the American colonies were free from Britain? (Declaration of Independence)[3]

Prospective citizens must only score sixty out of one hundred in order to pass, and as of June 2021, 91 percent of applicants for citizenship passed the test.[4] According to a survey from 2018 that asked current citizens questions from this test, however, just 36 percent of Americans could earn a passing score.[5]

As stated earlier, critical race theorists have stepped into this vacuum created by a lack of civic and cultural understanding. Critical race theory has long festered in universities and become standard in teachers colleges, especially. College professors are no longer concentrating on helping young adults to answer questions about life's purpose and what this means for America's shared national identity, discussions that would help the next generation of employees, parents, and leaders understand the problems with "wokeness." As students apply critical race theory to their lives on campus, some of the most prestigious American universities have recently been the sites

---

3   Most questions are multiple choice. U.S. Citizenship and Immigration Services, "128 Civics Questions and Answers (2020 Version)," *https://www.uscis.gov/sites/default/files/document/crc/M_1778.pdf.*

4   U.S. Citizenship and Immigration Services, "Applicant Performance on the 2008 Version of the Naturalization Test," *https://www.uscis.gov/citizenship/learn-about-citizenship/the-naturalization-interview-and-test/applicant-performance-on-the-naturalization-test.*

5   News release, "National Survey Finds Just 1 in 3 Americans Would Pass Citizenship Test," Woodrow Wilson National Fellowship Foundation, October 3, 2018, *https://woodrow.org/news/national-survey-finds-just-1-in-3-americans-would-pass-citizenship-test/.*

of violent riots where students recite words and phrases from the critical lexicon. Meanwhile, diversity trainers and educators in K–12 schools, as well as those on university campuses, are proselytizing a worldview rooted in Marxism that teaches students to search out ever more ways to feel victimized.

Under critical race theory, America is not ours to share, but ours to destroy. Critical race theorists claim that oppression, not liberty, is the defining feature of this nation. Radical professor Ibram X. Kendi says that the critical worldview—what he calls "antiracist" (yet is based on answering discrimination with more discrimination)—"can become real if we focus on power instead of people."[6]

As Americans, we must respond to this unholy crusade. Parents, policymakers, and educators, especially, should make themselves a part of the solution because so much of our "habitus" comes from the people who make up our families, communities, and schools.[7]

As explained in the introduction, habitus is the idea that members of a culture communicate most effectively when they have a set of shared assumptions about right and wrong. We do not have to agree on everything, but neighbors are far more likely to live side by side hospitably if one neighbor is not burning crosses in the yard next door, for example. Aristotle, Thomas Aquinas, and other thinkers from antiquity discussed the idea of habitus in their writings, but twentieth-century scholars attribute the development of the concept over the past fifty years to the French social scientist Pierre Bourdieu.[8] Bourdieu studied

---

6   Kendi, *How to Be an Antiracist*, p. 11.

7   Hunter, *The Death of Character: Moral Education in an Age Without Good or Evil.* See also Pierre Bourdieu, *Outline of a Theory of Practice*, trans. by Richard Nice (Cambridge, MA: Cambridge University Press, 1977), p. 78.

8   Thomas Medvetz and Jeffrey J. Sallaz, "Introduction: Pierre Bourdieu, a Twentieth-Century Life," *The Oxford Handbook of Pierre Bourdieu*, April 2018, *https://www.oxfordhandbooks.com/view/10.1093/oxfordhb/9780199357192.001.0001/oxford-hb-9780199357192-e-1*, and Cary J. Nederman, "Nature, Ethics, and the Doctrine of 'Habitus': Aristotelian Moral Psychology in the Twelfth Century," *Traditio*, Vol. 45 (1989–1990), pp. 87–110, *https://www.jstor.org/stable/27831241?seq=1*.

sociology, anthropology, and philosophy, and his description of habitus is one that aptly describes what anthropologist Laura Bohannan was struggling with in her conversation with the Tiv, also described in the introduction.

Bourdieu says that "habitus" refers to "dispositions," or "distinctions between what is good and what is bad, between what is right and what is wrong, between what is distinguished and what is vulgar."[9] When a group of people, a culture, shares assumptions about these choices, these assumptions help to define what the members of that culture understand as appropriate ways to respond to different questions.

University of Virginia (UVA) professor James Davison Hunter, who is also executive director of the Institute for Advanced Studies in Culture at UVA, explains it this way:

> *Habitus refers to the taken-for-granted assumptions that prevail in a particular society or civilization that make our experience of the world seem commonsensical. At the most basic level of experience, habitus operates as a system of dispositions, tendencies, and inclinations that organizes our actions and defines our way of being. Socialized as children into this habitus, we live with an intuitive feeling about the nature of the world around us. Culture, in this way, becomes so deeply embedded into our subjective consciousness that the ways of the world seem "natural" to us.[10]*

Critical race theory teaches an entirely different habitus than America's constitutional republic, a nation based on the idea that all men are created equal and should be treated equally

---

9 Pierre Bourdieu, "Physical Space, Social Space and Habitus," University of Oslo, Vilhelm Aubert Memorial Lecture, May 15, 1995, *https://archives.library.illinois.edu/erec/University%20Archives/2401001/Production_website/pages/StewardingExcellence/Physical%20Space,%20Social%20Space%20and%20Habitus.pdf.*

10 Hunter, *The Death of Character*, p. 291.

under the law. Again, in contrast to America's creed, critical race theory "questions the very foundations of the liberal order, including equality theory, legal reasoning, Enlightenment rationalism, and neutral principles of constitutional law." Critical race theorists say that the notions of equality and liberty in the Declaration of Independence come from a "voice that does not speak for everyone, but for a political faction trying to constitute itself as a unit of many disparate voices."[11]

These claims reject America's founding ideas and the notion of a shared national identity. Certainly, policymakers and citizens should hold U.S. law (and lawmakers) accountable for ensuring that our laws do not perpetuate racism or allow discriminatory treatment. In 1995, U.S. Supreme Court Justice Clarence Thomas captured this essential mission for American law when he wrote, "Government sponsored racial discrimination based on benign prejudice is just as noxious as discrimination inspired by malicious prejudice."[12]

Notably, *White Fragility* author Robin DiAngelo also cites Bourdieu's discussion of habitus.[13] DiAngelo, remember, is the diversity trainer whose lectures at Evergreen State College represented the racial discord that critical race theory creates and preceded the campus meltdown described in Chapter 3. DiAngelo argues that white people resist the "antiracist" movement because it is an "interruption to the racially familiar."[14] As critical race theorist Derrick Bell said, racism is permanent,[15] so DiAngelo argues that when white people are informed of this,

11   Delgado and Stefancic, *Critical Race Theory: An Introduction*, p. 3, and
      Angela Harris, "Race and Essentialism in Feminist Legal Theory,"
      Stanford Law Review, Vol. 42, No. 3 (February 1990), pp. 581–616.
12   *Adarand Constructors v. Pena* (93-1841), 515 U.S. 200 (1995).
13   Robin DiAngelo, *White Fragility: Why It's So Hard for White People to Talk About Racism*
      (Boston, MA: Beacon Press, 2018), location 1843, (Kindle edition).
14   Ibid.
15   Bell, *Faces at the Bottom of the Well: The Permanence of Racism*.

their habitus is disrupted, causing them to be defensive, which DiAngelo calls "fragility."

This cynical perspective both embraces critical race theory's divisive principles and rejects a belief about America's creed that dates at least as far back as Benjamin Franklin and the first abolitionists: racism is incompatible with America's founding ideals. It is our ideals that largely form our habitus. When we reject critical race theory in all its racial prejudice, we are rejecting a theory that runs directly counter to the ideas of freedom and equality under the law on which the founding fathers based this nation.

OOO

Critical theory, especially critical race theory and critical pedagogy, have found their way into our schools, churches, workplaces, and elsewhere in the form of curricula and "diversity" training seeking to disrupt, not improve, American culture. The critical threats are cultural issues, not just legal questions about following the Civil Rights Act. As theologian and ethicist Reinhold Niebuhr wrote, "Man's capacity for justice makes democracy possible; but man's inclination to injustice makes democracy necessary."[16] The "capacity for justice" is a cultural subject that is reflected in the government of that culture—especially in representative government. Schools occupy a crucial place in policy and society and must be part of the discussion about what critical ideas are doing to our communities.

A *Newsweek* commentator sympathetic to critical ideas explains the debate this way: "It's about who gets to define what it means

---

16   Reinhold Niebuhr, *Reinhold Niebuhr: Major Works on Religion and Politics* (New York: Library of America, 2015) p. 483.

to be American, who gets to define how U.S. institutions work."[17] Terrifyingly, he is absolutely correct.

Hunter says that a basic inability to agree on values and issues of character formation as a culture affects cultural institutions (such as schools) and those in those institutions (such as teachers, students, and families). Hunter writes about the different components of social and public life affected by a people's habitus:

The confusion over these rather basic issues [of values and character] spills out into public controversies over gender, sexuality, the family; over the nature of art, faith, and life itself; over the meaning of justice, public welfare, tolerance, and liberty; over the purpose of schools, philanthropy, technology and markets...[18]

Schools are at the forefront of cultural changes because everyone has some relationship to a school, having either attended one, sent his children to one, or paid taxes to fund a public school (or paid tuition to send his child to a private school or pay for homeschooling services), or all of these. We depend on schools as part of our social fabric. University of Virginia professor emeritus and Core Knowledge Foundation founder E.D. Hirsch writes, "Our early thinkers about education thought...the school would be the institution that would transform future citizens into loyal Americans. It would teach common knowledge, virtues, ideals, language and commitments."[19] Schools help to form this nation's habitus and are institutions that represent our culture. This is

---

17 Marcus Johnson, "The Republican Push to Ban Critical Race Theory Reveals an Ugly Truth," *Newsweek*, May 5, 2021, *https://www.newsweek.com/republican-push-ban-critical-race-theory-reveals-ugly-truth-opinion-1588684.*

18 Hunter, *The Death of Character*, p. 292.

19 E. D. Hirsch, *The Making of Americans: Democracy and Our Schools* (New Haven: Yale University Press, 2009), p. 4.

an objective observation, something that is true whether we agree with what educators are teaching or not. And this is why it matters that parents and policymakers and taxpayers pay attention to what is happening in schools, and engage with teachers, in order to preserve schools as places where students can pursue truth.

But with the critical content that teachers and administrators are teaching now, the transformation of American students will hardly result in what the founders intended. The chaos on college campuses is but one example. The riots in cities across the country in 2020, and the 1776 Commission/1619 Project debates, are yet more evidence of how our social fabric, of which schools are an important part, is splitting—splintering, no less—when we do not share basic ideas about our national character and founding ideals. Conservatives, too, should recognize that the storming of the U.S. Capitol on January 6, 2021, is also evidence of a splintering culture.

We do not have to take sides in explaining these events to recognize that neither critical theory nor critical race theory holds an answer. In fact, critical theory's Marxist ideas of dividing the world between oppressors and the oppressed, the intolerance of competing worldviews, and loosely issued calls for "resistance" are disrupting what we once knew as foundational ideas such as justice, equality, and self-reliance.

These are the character traits that the 1776 Commission's report called distinctly American, saying that Americans

> *have shared a history of common struggle and achievement, from carving communities out of a vast, untamed wilderness, to winning independence and forming a new government, through wars, industrialization, waves of immigration, technological progress, and political change....*

Americans yearn for timeless stories and noble heroes that inspire
them to be good, brave, diligent, daring, generous, honest, and
compassionate.[20]

But the report's leftist critics called it "racist" and a "great lie" despite the report's acknowledgement of Americans' failures to live up to this country's creed, including through the institution of slavery.[21] Among the critics was Kimberlé Crenshaw, the architect of intersectionality, and Kendi. By calling attention to America's creed and rejecting the critical race theorists' adherence to "systemic racism," the 1776 Commission ran afoul of the critical intolerance that is now widespread in K–12 curricula and in the ivory tower. Writing of his generation, some sixty years ago, Niebuhr knew that Marxist ideas are an assault on time-tested virtues: "The notion of a society which achieves social harmony by prudence and a nice balance of competitive interests, is challenged by communism with the strategy of raising 'class antagonisms' to a final climax of civil war."[22]

Let us make sure that it does not come to that again.

One of critical theory's many glaring shortcomings is the lack of specifics for creating the equality or social reforms that its proponents claim to seek. Stuart Jeffries, cited in Chapter 2, whose *Grand Hotel Abyss* traces the origins of the Frankfurt School, says that critical theory's "self-imposed task was to negate the truth of the existing order rather than producing

---

20   1776 Commission Report, *https://f.hubspotusercontent10.net/hubfs/397762/The%20 President's%20Advisory%201776%20Commission%20-%20Final%20Report.pdf.*

21   Maegan Vazquez, "Trump Administration Issues Racist School Curriculum Report on MLK Day," CNN, January 18, 2021, *https://www.cnn.com/2021/01/18/politics/1776-commission-report-donald-trump/index.html,* and Derrick Clifton, "How the Trump Administration's '1776 Report' Warps the History of Racism and Slavery," NBC, January 20, 2021, *https://www.nbcnews.com/news/nbcblk/how-trump-administration-s-1776-report-warps-history-racism-slavery-n1254926.*

22   Niebuhr, *Reinhold Niebuhr: Major Works on Religion and Politics,* p. 644.

blueprints for a better one."[23] High-profile critical race theorists today embrace the same approach—that of describing the problem (whether real or alleged) while offering few solutions—a criticism that comes even from Left-of-center publications. In a 2019 *New Yorker* article profiling arguably the two most visible and talked-about contemporary critical race theorists, Ibram Kendi and Robin DiAngelo, author Kelefa Sanneh says: "It may take many years to determine whether a policy produces or sustains racial inequity."[24] Kendi, for one, appears to be in no hurry. Sanneh describes a policy in New York that prohibits employers from asking job applicants about their criminal history or credit scores. "These measures are designed in part to help African American applicants, who may be more likely to have a criminal record, or to have poor credit," Sanneh explains.

The outcomes have not been measurably better for minority workers. Sanneh points out that "some studies suggest that such prohibitions make black men, in general, less likely to be hired," then asks whether Kendi would consider those who support such policies to be racist. "In Kendi's framework," Sanneh says, "the only possible answer is: wait and see."

Sanneh then says of Kendi's bestselling *How to Be an Antiracist*, "He offers a provocative new way to think about race in America, but little practical advice." Sanneh is also not convinced of DiAngelo's methods, whose focus is on diversity training—the effectiveness of which has been challenged by hundreds of studies. Sanneh says, "It's not clear what the effect of these seminars is," and while trainers attempt to change peoples' "implicit bias," Sanneh echoes the research cited earlier

---

23 Stuart Jeffries, *Grand Hotel Abyss: The Lives of the Frankfurt School* (New York: Verso, 2016), p. 323.

24 Kelefa Sanneh, "The Fight to Define Racism," *The New Yorker*, August 12, 2019, *https://www.newyorker.com/magazine/2019/08/19/the-fight-to-redefine-racism/amp.*

in these pages that "there is scant evidence that implicit bias reliably affects behavior"—making the effects of diversity training inconclusive or ineffective at best, and fostering hostility in participants at worst.

○○○

We—families, taxpayers, policymakers—need solutions to pressing cultural questions about power and discrimination. We can start in our schools by asking educators and students to consider not just a list of pertinent facts, but by considering *why* knowledge is important.

More than a decade ago, Hirsch, wrote, "The reason that our eighteenth-century founders and their nineteenth-century successors believed schools were crucial to the American future was not only that the schools would make students technically competent."[25] He said that reformers "argue that these technical problems can be solved," but that the initial purpose of American schooling was to "assimilate not just the many immigrants then pouring into the nation but also native-born Americans who came from different regions and social strata into the common American idea."

Our founding fathers believed that schools were important institutions because they could impart a similar canon of knowledge to all children. Hirsch and other education historians point to Benjamin Rush, writer, educator, and signer of the Declaration of Independence, and his listing of different subjects that he thought schools should teach every child. These subjects include languages, eloquence, history and chronology, commerce, chemistry, and "practical legislation," as he explained in his 1786 essay "Thoughts upon the Mode of Education Proper

---

25   Hirsch, *The Making of Americans.*

in a Republic."[26] Hirsch echoes Rush and says that the founders expected schools to "teach common knowledge, virtues, ideals, language, and commitments."[27]

Postsecondary educators in the nineteenth century had similar goals. In *Education's End*, Yale University's Anthony Kronman writes that, historically, many leading postsecondary institutions, such as Yale, used the same classic works to teach the time-honored ideas of virtue and civility. Kronman explains that although the courses "varied in certain details," instructors' objectives were to impart knowledge to students and to help students have some understanding of the same knowledge so that the common understanding would foster communication within our culture.[28]

For Rush and the Founders, citizens' knowledge and character were important for supporting liberty and America's democratic institutions. They emphasized the value of knowledge and virtues as these ideas connected to religious faith, though the civic purpose of this habitus was the preservation of civil society: "The only foundation of a useful education in a republic is to be laid in religion. Without this, there can be no virtue, and without virtue there can be no liberty, and liberty is the object and life of all republican governments."[29] Even for those skeptical of religion, then, the founders emphasized the importance of knowledge for the purpose of understanding character not just for salvation, but to sustain democracy and liberty. "Only a virtuous people are capable of freedom," Benjamin Franklin said.[30]

---

26 Benjamin Rush, "Thoughts upon the Mode of Education Proper in a Republic," 1786, ExplorePAhistory.com, *https://explorepahistory.com/odocument.php?docId=1-4-218*.
27 Hirsch, *The Making of Americans.* "Commitments," here, refer to civic participation at its most basic level, from voting to volunteering.
28 Kronman, *Education's End*, location 577.
29 Rush, "Thoughts upon the Mode of Education Proper in a Republic."
30 National Center for Constitutional Studies, "Only a Virtuous People Are Capable of Freedom," *https://nccs.net/blogs/articles/only-a-virtuous-people-are-capable-of-freedom.*

The purpose in this brief review of the history of public schools' content is not to argue in favor of standardized education, nor for the presence of public schools at the expense of any other form of education. Hirsch, for one, advocates national standards, but the Common Core standards movement that swept through K–12 schools over the past decade has not corresponded with improved student achievement.[31] K–12 education is a state and local concern, which means that education initiatives led by Washington can only be implemented through coercion. President Barack Obama's administration, for one, lured states to adopt national standards with additional federal money.[32] Former Brookings Institution senior fellow Tom Loveless says, "Despite the [common standards'] intuitive appeal, standards-based reform does not work very well in reality. One key reason is that coordinating key aspects of education at the top of the system hamstrings discretion at the bottom."[33]

We do not have to either support or oppose national standards in order to reject critical race theory's discriminatory applications, though. Hirsch explains that what he calls the New Left uses "power" and "equality" as its chief terms.[34] He writes, "There are many things to criticize about the New Left—its lack of practicality, for example, and its elitist jargon-ridden discourse. Especially suspect intellectually and ethically is the substitution of group identity for individual identity."[35] On this point, Hirsch doesn't mince words. In 2009, a full ten years before the 1619 Project and other examples of critical race theory made head-

31 Mary Clare Amselem, et al., "Rightsizing Fed Ed," Cato Institute *Policy Analysis* No. 891, May 4, 2020, *https://www.cato.org/sites/cato.org/files/2020-04/PA_891_DOI.pdf.*
32 Secretary Arne Duncan's Remarks at the 2009 Governors Education Symposium, "States Will Lead the Way Toward Reform," U.S. Department of Education Archived Information, June 14, 2009, *https://www2.ed.gov/news/speeches/2009/06/06142009.html.*
33 Tom Loveless, "Why Common Core Failed," Brookings Institution, March 18, 2021, *https://www.brookings.edu/blog/brown-center-chalkboard/2021/03/18/why-common-core-failed/.*
34 Hirsch, *The Making of Americans*, p. 61.
35 Ibid., p. 63.

lines, Hirsch wrote that "identity politics has emphasized membership in subgroups over participation in the larger national community and has viewed traditional goals like assimilation and Americanization with suspicion."[36] Hirsch says that "the curricular views of the New Left have done little to promote the general welfare, raise the *economic* status of blacks and Hispanics, or provide the basis for effective job retraining in the information economy." (Emphasis in original).[37]

Parents and policymakers can oppose common national standards and still agree with those who advocate these standards that educators should share a commitment to the pursuit of truth and a belief that facts matter. The knowledge of facts preserves character and virtues, which themselves matter for maintaining a culture based on liberty and in which people have the freedom to pursue their potential. Writing for the British Jubilee Centre for Character and Virtues, Stephen Earl and James Arthur said that "virtues and character are critical to individual excellence, contribute to societal flourishing, can be exercised in all human contexts, and, more importantly, are educable."[38] The teaching of facts about when and why individuals made important choices that had societal impacts, and were based on an individual understanding of virtue, lies at the intellectual intersection where knowledge and morals meet—the intellectual building blocks of a culture.

We should frame education around the values and character traits that have stood the test of time, and on which communities have relied for generations in pursuit of a more just, more equal, society. America has the legal framework to sustain equal pro-

---

36 Ibid., p. 65.
37 Ibid., p. 63.
38 Stephen Earl and James Arthur, "Character and Academic Attainment: Does Character Education Matter?" The Jubilee Centre for Character and Virtues, University of Birmingham, *https://www.jubileecentre.ac.uk/userfiles/jubileecentre/pdf/insight-series/Insight_Briefing_Paper_JA_SE.pdf.*

tection under the law, and whether critical theorists admit it or not, Americans also have a shared history in which our founders began to create a nation based on liberty and democracy despite the obvious failure of previous generations to live out the meaning of America's creed.

Our responsibility as citizens is to fulfill this promise to ourselves and to future generations. Instead of a new list of content for educators to teach, policymakers, community leaders, educators, and families should frame instruction around beliefs and character traits that Americans need to understand so they can live in and contribute to a civil society.

Critical race theorists are doing the opposite: instead of teaching math, "Equitable Math" proponents advocate resistance to capitalism; to teach about other cultures, California's ethnic studies curriculum instructs students to be resentful and seek out evidence of victimization using "decolonization" and "intersectionality." Such divisive and antiknowledge ideology is present in K–12 and postsecondary curricula around the country.

Parents and educators should share with students the knowledge and ideas that help them to understand the American dream—the dream that Swedish economist and sociologist Gunnar Myrdal described in *An American Dilemma,* his groundbreaking review of race in American society from 1938 to 1940, as "being able to grow to the fullest development as man and woman, unhampered by the barriers which had slowly been erected by older civilizations, unrepressed by social orders which had developed for the benefit of classes rather than for the simple human being of any and every class."[39]

---

39 Gunnar Myrdal, *An American Dilemma,* p. 5. It was at the invitation of the Carnegie Corporation that Myrdal explored the social and economic problems of black *Americans.*

For educators and students to reach this goal, parents and other adults who are influential in a child's life should focus discussions of America's past, the national ethos, and race relations around three main ideas:

First, Americans failed to live up to their country's national creed in the past. This fact is not a shortcoming of the national creed, but the inability of prior generations to fulfill it. The commitment to life, liberty, and the pursuit of happiness and of human equality under God and the law—beliefs central to America's creed—are the ideas that can overcome the divisive and anti-human ideas of critical theory and provide a sense of national identity we can all celebrate.

Second, black Americans' success in building a culture and participating in the economy even under the worst of conditions has been extraordinary. We—all of us—should celebrate these accomplishments and teach the attitudes and behaviors that made these successes possible. These achievements are part of America's shared experience. This recognition in no way minimizes the vicious discrimination that black Americans once faced. Instead, it elevates black success as an example of *human* success.

Third, our society will be defined by our cultural disposition on how we treat those with whom we disagree. One of the most time-tested beliefs, which has survived for centuries, is that we should love our enemies. This is one of the foundational values of the Christian worldview on which the founders based our constitutional republic, and one of the most important principles of the civil rights movement. Critical race theory is rooted in conflict and a perpetual search for enemies, oppressors, and victims. No nation can long survive when adults teach these ideas to the next generation.

We can use these three ideas to build a different theory, a theory that counters critical race theory's racial bias. Call this a "civil theory."

RACE AND AMERICA'S PAST

Racial discord was and is a challenge in American culture. Critical race theorists are not wrong to draw attention to actual racial problems, but their obsession with viewing everything in society through the lens of race is the wrong response to healing America's racial divides. The bigger problem is that critical race theory is reviving racial divisions and stoking racial resentment that this country, as a whole, fought so admirably to overcome. Critical race theory is turning the past into the present and future.

This is the first shared idea for educators and students: as part of our history, America failed to live up to its promise of equality for all. America is the only nation, though, where the founding citizens established a creed that allowed future generations to develop laws and a habitus that could not be maintained unless the laws and cultural assumptions condemned discrimination and racism. These subjects of racism, and America's creed of life, liberty, and the pursuit of happiness for all, are, at the most basic level of understanding, moral and cultural issues.

Perhaps no one covered this expansive topic or established the connection between race and morality as well as Myrdal in his two-volume *American Dilemma*. Historian Arthur Schlesinger called *American Dilemma* "the first full-dress, comprehensive study of black-white relations" and a "powerful work," and considered it required reading for anyone trying to understand

America's national character.[40] Myrdal devotes much of his fifteen hundred pages to pointing out the inconsistencies that existed in the 1940s between white Americans' actions and existing law, along with data demonstrating the impact of discrimination on Americans who are black.

As Kendi points out, *American Dilemma* "has been called the 'bible' of the civil-rights movement."[41] Kendi, however, focuses on passages that encourage black assimilation into mainstream American culture, which Kendi rejects outright, and claims—falsely—that Myrdal says that American culture is only white culture.[42] For example, Kendi quotes Myrdal saying that "American Negro culture is…a distorted development, or a pathological condition of the general American culture," but Kendi leaves out that Myrdal goes on to explain that any harmful behaviors by black Americans are the results of despicable white racism against them.[43] Myrdal says that high crime rates and family instability, for example, "are mainly forms of social pathology which, for the most part, are created by the caste pressures."[44]

Given the importance of Myrdal's contribution to the topic of race in America, his writings deserve a closer look. Myrdal begins *American Dilemma* with a broad concept that connects all of his evidence to a much larger issue: "the problem of Good and Evil in the world."[45] Myrdal writes, "At bottom our problem is the moral dilemma of the American—the conflict between his moral valuations on various levels of consciousness and generality."[46]

---

40 Arthur M. Schlesinger, *The Disuniting of America: Reflections on a Multicultural Society*, revised and enlarged edition (New York: W. W. Norton & Company, 1998), p. 178.
41 Kendi, *How to Be an Antiracist*, p. 83.
42 Ibid., pp. 33, 83, and 84.
43 Myrdal, *An American Dilemma*, p. 612, and Kendi, p. 83.
44 Myrdal, *An American Dilemma*, p. 614.
45 Ibid., p. 79.
46 Ibid., location 1562.

The issue of race is "primarily a moral issue... It is a moral issue that this problem presents itself in the daily life of ordinary people; it is as a moral issue that they [ordinary people] brood over it in their thoughtful moments."[47]

When people of certain ethnic backgrounds treat those of a different skin color as less valuable, or, as critical race theorists do today, as guilty by association because of their (white) race, this creates a moral dilemma and has implications for all of society. Such a culture cannot establish civil interactions where all people have the same opportunities to achieve their human potential. Myrdal writes, "The unity of a culture consists in the fact that all valuations are mutually shared in some degree...This cultural unity is the indispensable basis for discussion between persons and groups. It is the floor upon which the democratic process goes on."[48]

But Myrdal found that Americans in the 1940s and before had not lived up to their own national creed, which is the "ideological foundation of national morale."[49] Thus we—all Americans—were not keeping a shared national identity. "Americans of all national origins, classes, regions, creeds, and colors, have something in common: a social ethos, a political creed. It is difficult to avoid the judgment that this 'American Creed' is the cement in the structure of this great and disparate nation," Myrdal writes.[50]

The failure to live up to our national ethos and ideals, though, was a problem of behaviors and actions based on people's moral understanding, not a problem with the creed itself. Even with Myrdal's conclusion that Americans had not lived up to their creed, he still believed that this creed created a way for

---

47   Ibid., location 1631.
48   Ibid., locations 1590 and 1598.
49   Ibid., p. 5.
50   Ibid., p. 3.

individuals to transform society and government to fulfill the creed's promises: "But in taking the broad historical view, the American Creed has triumphed. It has given the main direction to change in this country."[51] Because the American creed "represents the national conscience," the "average American" cannot help but recognize a "palpable conflict between the status actually awarded [black Americans] and those ideals."[52]

Calvin Coolidge once remarked on the significance of the Declaration of Independence as not just the proclamation of a new nation, but as a transcendent statement on the value of every person: "There is something beyond the establishment of a new nation, great as that event would be, in the Declaration of Independence which has ever since caused it to be regarded as one of the great charters that not only was to liberate America but was everywhere to ennoble humanity."[53]

This analysis of the American ethos is the opposite of critical race theorists' dogma. Critical race theorists assume the worst about America and Americans, even when they are at their best: Derrick Bell, for instance, argued that those white Americans who purged American law of discriminatory provisions, or who celebrated decisions, such as *Brown v. Board of Education*, were not fulfilling our national creed, but sustaining their own "sense of racial superiority" and "[sacrificing] the rights of blacks."[54] All the "commitments" for equality "came about when those making them saw that they, those they represented, or the country could derive benefits that were at least as

---

51   Ibid., p. 7.
52   Ibid., p. 23.
53   Calvin Coolidge, "The Inspiration of the Declaration of Independence," speech delivered on July 5, 1926, Calvin Coolidge Presidential Foundation, *https://www. coolidgefoundation.org/resources/inspiration-of-the-declaration-of-independence/*.
54   Bell, "White Superiority in America," in Delgado and Stefancic, eds., *The Derrick Bell Reader.*

important as those blacks would receive."[55] Bell called his belief "Interest convergence."[56] Critical race theorist Richard Delgado summarizes Bell's position:

American civil rights law is not aimed at improving conditions for blacks, except on the rare occasions when doing so coincides with whites' self-interest. Instead, our system of civil rights statutes and case law serves a homeostatic function, assuring that society has exactly the right amount of racism.[57]

Such cynicism, like DiAngelo's "white fragility," insults the sacrifices of soldiers, lawmakers, and activists—both white and black—who fought and struggled to fulfill America's promise.

More than a century before *American Dilemma*, Thomas Jefferson wrote, "Nothing is more certainly written in the book of fate than these people [black Americans] are to be free."[58] Jefferson himself failed to live up to this belief, but Myrdal argues that America's ethos simply could not uphold discrimination in law or custom. Americans had to see racism's "very inconsistency with the American creed."[59] Myrdal stresses that Americans had to turn to their shared sense of identity that is based on equality under the law, along with life, liberty, and the pursuit of happiness. American culture, any sense of community, would not last otherwise.

Writing some twenty years before the 1964 Civil Rights Act was passed, Myrdal said, "Great changes are working underneath the visible surface, and a dynamic situation full of pos-

---

55   Bell, "The Role of Fortuity in Racial Policy-Making," in Delgado and Stefancic, eds., *The Derrick Bell Reader*, p. 41.
56   See Bell, "*Brown v. Board of Education* and the Interest-Convergence Dilemma," in Delgado and Stefancic, eds., *The Derrick Bell Reader*, p. 33.
57   Delgado, "Derrick Bell and the Ideology of Racial Reform: Will We Ever Be Saved?" *Yale Law Journal*, Vol. 97, No. 5 (April 1988), *https://www.jstor.org/stable/796520*.
58   Myrdal, *An American Dilemma*, p. 85.
59   Ibid., p. 75.

sibilities is maturing."[60] He wrote prophetically at the time that "at least the legal foundations for Negro disenfranchisement is [sic] gradually withering away," which he said "is the main explanation for the calm before the storm."[61] And, of course, the civil rights movement would follow shortly after *American Dilemma*'s release.

This history and legacy of moral relevance was and is necessary for a proper civic education, Myrdal said. Given the "calm before the storm" during Myrdal's time, and the racial storm in which we find ourselves today, as Myrdal warned, "The more urgent it is also to speed up the civic education of these masses who are bound to have votes in the future."[62] Here again, questions of civic responsibility, character, policy, morals, and culture are inseparable from education. Over and over again, we find ourselves arriving at the recognition that character matters in education because character matters for culture—and education matters because it is such a vital part of our culture.

In his 1990 book *The Content of Our Character*, Shelby Steele says that although "[b]lacks still suffer from racism," the lives of black Americans "are more integrated than they have ever been before. Race does not determine our fates as powerfully as it once did, which means it is not the vital personal concern it once was. Before the sixties, race set the boundaries of black life."[63] Antiblack racism still exists, but it is no longer a defining feature of American life.

Brown University professor Glenn Loury puts it this way: "The 'America ain't all it's cracked-up to be' posture that one hears so much of these days is, in my view, a sophomoric indul-

---

60   Ibid., p. 513.
61   Ibid., p. 514.
62   Ibid., p. 519.
63   Steele, *The Content of Our Character*.

gence for blacks at this late date. In fact, our birthright citizenship in what is arguably history's greatest republic is an inheritance of immense value."[64]

THE LEGACY OF BLACK RESILIENCE

The second shared idea on which we should base educational content and cultural discussion, including civics and social studies in K–12 schools, is that all Americans should want the extraordinary legacy of black Americans' perseverance against all odds to represent the strength and grace of American character.

University of Texas professor John Sibley Butler's *Entrepreneurship and Self-Help Among Black Americans* is a meticulous record of how the resilience and fortitude of African Americans before, during, and after slavery and the Jim Crow era are remarkable achievements. Butler explains that for centuries, minority ethnic groups around the world used economic advancement and entrepreneurship to make a place for themselves in societies when they could not do so through government or other cultural vehicles.

Butler explains, "In other words, when this Afro-American experience is compared to those of other groups which have experienced hostility throughout history, it is revealed as a case consistent with the special types of adjustments to society that other groups have had to make."[65] Butler cites the experience of Japanese Americans before, during, and after World War II as just one example, and says that the "road toward eco-

---

64 Glenn Loury, "Whose Fourth of July? Blacks and the 'American Project,'" 1776 Unites, February 9, 2021, *https://1776unites.com/essays/whose-fourth-of-july-blacks-and-the-american-project/*.

65 John Sibley Butler, *Entrepreneurship and Self-Help Among Black Americans: A Reconsideration of Race and Economics*, revised edition (Albany: SUNY Press, 2005) (Kindle edition, locations 4844–4845).

nomic stability and general peace of mind for the Japanese was paved with systemic discrimination and constant struggle."[66] This does not trivialize the black experience under slavery and Jim Crow, but rather emphasizes that black Americans as well as Japanese Americans took advantage of the indiscriminate, colorblind features of capitalism, which allowed them to be financially successful in American society even when facing systemic discrimination and exclusion.

Specifically, Butler says "there is an emphasis on entrepreneurship which develops as a result of discrimination, oppression, and racism."[67] He says, "The literature on Afro-American entrepreneurship, both slave and free, is systematic testimony to the spirit of enterprise even under troublesome conditions."[68] Without question, black Americans "are woven historically into the economic fabric of America."[69]

Researchers including Butler and others whom he cites provide a wealth of data demonstrating the success of black businessmen and women. In 1838, for example, a pamphlet published in Philadelphia found 656 black people working in fifty-seven different jobs, including blacksmiths, carpenters, and tailors.[70] A black sail maker who was living in Philadelphia during this period had forty employees—including black and white individuals. Records from 1839 show that nearly five hundred, or one-third, of Americans who were black and had been slaves in Ohio had earned enough money to purchase their freedom.[71]

---

66   Ibid., locations 241–242.
67   Ibid., locations 639–640.
68   Ibid., location 830.
69   Ibid., locations 683–684.
70   Ibid., location 706.
71   Ibid., location 825.

In 1847, the value of the real estate holdings of black Americans in Philadelphia was worth $400,000, the equivalent of more than $13 million today, and by 1856, black Americans held property that was worth double this amount, according to Abram Harris in *The Negro as Capitalist*.[72] In New York, the property held by black Americans doubled in value between 1833 and 1853, when the worth was estimated at $1 million (the equivalent of approximately $27 million to $32 million today). Nearly four thousand black Americans even owned slaves in 1830—a fact merely reminding us of what should be obvious, namely that people of any color can be bad, or good, or a mix of both.[73] Also in the 1840s, a group of free black Americans in New Orleans speculated on cotton futures prices, and the wealthiest of this group had a personal fortune worth some $13 million in today's dollars at his death in the 1890s.[74]

Butler says that free black Americans also "dominated the restaurant business before the Civil War."[75] Between 1860 and 1900, black Americans were responsible for some of the most significant inventions, including the process of "preparing coconut for domestic use," the locomotive smoke stack, lawn sprinklers, the railway signal, the ironing board, and a variation on the printing press.[76] By 1910, black Americans were "just as likely as white Americans to be employers, and almost as likely as whites to be self-employed."[77] What a truly awesome

---

72   Abram L. Harris, *The Negro as Capitalist: A Study of Banking and Business Among American Negroes* (New York: Haskell House Publishers, 1936), p. 6. My calculations using data from Federal Reserve Bank of Minneapolis, "Consumer Price Index, 1800-," *https://www.minneapolisfed.org/about-us/monetary-policy/inflation-calculator/consumer-price-index-1800-.*

73   Ibid., p. 4.

74   Butler, *Entrepreneurship and Self-Help Among Black Americans*, location 756, and African American Registry, "Thomy Lafon," *https://aaregistry.org/story/thomy-lafon-used-his-wealth-to-help-the-needy/.* See also Abram L. Harris, *The Negro as Capitalist*, p. 22.

75   Butler, *Entrepreneurship and Self-Help Among Black Americans*, location 770.

76   Ibid., locations 866–928.

77   Ibid., locations 662–663.

achievement, given the daily hurdles and roadblocks that black Americans faced.

Compare this to critical race theorists' belief in "Marx's dazzling analysis of capitalism and his conviction that the laws of historical materialism would bring on the revolution of the proletariat as inevitably as the sun rises," and Paulo Freire's critical idea that "the oppressed, as objects, as 'things,' have no purpose except those their oppressors prescribe for them."[78] Or, consider the Smithsonian Institution's National Museum of African American History and Culture's infographic described in Chapter 1, in which the museum derisively called such behaviors as being polite and the idea that "hard work is the key to success" evidence of "whiteness."

Butler rejects such ideas outright. "There is nothing permanent, as can be seen in the presentation of data in this work, about underclass status."[79] Furthermore, those who are oppressed or disadvantaged should not reflexively turn to disruption, resistance, or violence; Butler says that "after the people develop a sense of self-help, values pertaining to education, family, and self-motivation follow almost automatically."[80]

With this reference to "self-help," Butler adds yet another dimension to the significance of black Americans' successes under racist conditions. He explains that because legal and cultural conditions resulted in black Americans striving for success with little or no help from public institutions or government, black Americans developed a tradition of self-help and self-reliance that Americans, regardless of their skin color, can and should pass from one generation to the next.

---

78   Angela Harris, "Compassion and Critique," *Columbia Journal of Race and Law*, Vol. 1, No. 3 (2021), pp. 326–352, *http://blogs.law.columbia.edu/abolition1313/files/2020/08/Angela-Harris-Compassion-and-Critique-1.pdf*, and Paulo Freire, *Pedagogy of the Oppressed* (New York: Continuum, 2005), p. 60.

79   Butler, *Entrepreneurship and Self-Help Among Black Americans*, location 5030.

80   Ibid., locations 4992–4993.

One example of such self-help is that black Americans used church gatherings not just for worship but also to discuss their challenges and suffering in society and business. Church communities would respond by issuing loans to those in need, which created a banking system for communities that were blocked from banking elsewhere.[81] These communities also created the first insurance companies for black Americans, as white insurers would not issue policies to them.[82]

The African Methodist Episcopal (AME) Church system was also central in creating the first universities for black students, "owned and operated by Afro-Americans."[83] AME Church members gave millions of dollars to found these institutions beginning around the middle of the nineteenth century, and by 1907, AME churches supported twenty-two colleges for black students.[84] These schools, along with private K–12 schools for black children supported by churches around the same time, were "educational efforts [that] served as one of the backbones for the development of Afro-American business."[85] Butler says, "Because of economic stability, parents of self-help groups are more able to launch their children into professional occupations within the larger economic sector because of the importance that the group places on education."[86]

This tradition of self-help and individual agency is still celebrated by some today, including former civil rights activists such as Steele. "The elimination of discrimination will always be largely a collective endeavor, while racial development will

81   Ibid., location 1353.
82   Ibid., location 1529.
83   Ibid., location 1373.
84   Ibid.
85   Ibid., location 1526.
86   Ibid., location 95.

always be the *effect* that results from individuals within the race bettering their own lives," Steele says.[87] (Emphasis in original.) "The former requires group solidarity, collective action, and a positive group identity," says Steele, "while the latter demands individual initiative, challenging personal aspirations, focused hard work, and a strong individual identity.[88]

Butler concludes that, "Despite the barriers thrown up by white America, [black Americans] produced the great men and women who made their marks in history."[89] Americans who were black worked toward self-actualization, to fulfill their own personal ambitions. They were entrepreneurs despite racist treatment and discriminatory policies. They emphasized family and community and religious activities. They saw education as the ladder to success and created opportunities when there were none. Who would not want to embrace this as part of a shared national identity?

LOVE YOUR ENEMIES

A *New York Times* bestselling devotional book caused quite a stir when readers found a prayer authored by a Mercer University professor of theology who wrote, "Dear God, please help me to hate white people."[90] The professor, who teaches courses in "pastoral care and counseling," said that she wants God to help her "at least want to hate them. At least, I want to stop caring about them, individually and collectively. I want to stop caring about

---

87   Steele, *The Content of Our Character*, p. 158.
88   Ibid., p. 158.
89   Butler, *Entrepreneurship and Self-Help Among Black Americans*, locations 4900–4901.
90   Nicole Fallert, "'Help Me to Hate White People': Entry in Bestselling Prayer Book Stokes Controversy," *Newsweek*, April 8, 2021, *https://www.newsweek.com/help-me-hate-white-people-entry-bestselling-prayer-book-stokes-controversy-1582043*, *and* Chanequa Walker-Barnes, "Prayer of a Weary Black Woman," in Sarah Bessey, ed., *A Rhythm of Prayer* (New York: Convergent, 2021), p. 69.

their misguided, racist souls, to stop believing that they can be better, that they can stop being racist."[91]

This prayer is just one step beyond Derrick Bell's claim that any efforts to improve the quality of life for black Americans are really attempts by white Americans to maintain power—in line with bell hooks's observation in *Teaching to Transgress* that "we are living in a culture of domination."[92] Or with Angela Harris's view that: "Challenging power relations, as critical theorists love to do, means provoking anger, disquiet, anxiety, and even fear in those with a settled understanding of who they are and where they belong."[93]

Such ideas will not allow people to communicate or co-exist, let alone build a community and sustain a culture. These ideas are a far cry from the deeply insightful voices of the civil rights movement. Contemporary critical race theorists, such as Kendi, reject the leaders of this era, saying that he does not need "another shaming lesson about how [Martin Luther King, Jr.] died for me."[94]

Most Americans know of Martin Luther King, Jr.'s call to judge one another by the content of our character, not the color of our skin. But since Kendi and other critical minds consider colorblindness to be "a mask to hide racism," we can consider another of King's lessons—one that originated well before the civil rights movement.[95] King wrote an entire series of sermons on the idea of loving one's enemies. He said, "Returning hate for hate multiplies hate, adding deeper darkness to a night already devoid of stars."[96] King stated:

---

91   Ibid.
92   bell hooks, *Teaching to Transgress* (New York: Routledge, 1994), p. 27.
93   Angela Harris, "Compassion and Critique," p. 328.
94   Kendi, *How to Be an Antiracist*, p. 99.
95   Ibid., p. 9.
96   Martin Luther King, Jr., *A Gift of Love: Sermons from* A Strength to Love *and Other Preachings* (Boston: Beacon Press, 1981), p. 49.

Upheaval after upheaval has reminded us that modern man is traveling along a road called hate, in a journey that will bring us to destruction and damnation. Far from being the pious injunction of a Utopian dreamer, the command to love one's enemy is an absolute necessity for our survival. Love even for enemies is the key to the solution of the problems of our world.[97]

Sensing the continued fragmenting of American society in this generation, author and former president of the American Enterprise Institute Arthur Brooks wrote a book titled *Love Your Enemies* in 2019. He explains that "love" in this sense and the way in which King discusses love in this context are not romantic notions, obviously, or even just emotions. Brooks explains his point by quoting Saint Thomas Aquinas, the thirteenth-century Roman Catholic theologian, who said "To love is to will the good of the other."[98]

This call to will the good of someone else is not far from Myrdal's description of America's racial conflicts as moral issues, or even words attributed to Abraham Lincoln that ask "do we not destroy our enemies when we make them our friends?" Brooks argues that we should focus our policy or cultural positions "on the moral values we share—compassion and fairness—rather than those held by only part of the population."[99] This was Myrdal's approach in arguing that all Americans, no matter their color or country of origin or any other immutable characteristic, help to create their national identity. We are sharing this nation together. Kendi, by focusing on the desire for equal *outcomes* for everyone, and by advo-

---

97   Ibid., p. 45.
98   Arthur C. Brooks, *Love Your Enemies: How Decent People Can Save America from the Culture of Contempt* (New York: Broadside Books, 2019), (Kindle edition, location 21).
99   Ibid., location 1455.

cating discrimination if necessary to achieve this end, promotes an approach that has an inherently limited reach.

We need not retreat from the pursuit of truth, or from the knowledge that America's culture of ordered freedom and representative government are profound, for us to also love our enemies. We can share moral values and still not agree on every policy enacted to answer the problems of war, or a pandemic, or a financial recession. But we *can* pursue policy ideas out of a desire for the best uses of the resources we have—not for the sake of victory over our ideological opponents.

If Americans are not ready to consider loving their enemies, there are smaller steps they can take to finding common ground. E. B. White, who wrote the children's classic *Charlotte's We*b, was also an essayist who wrote regularly for *The New Yorker* and *Harper's* magazine on government and culture. In 1946, while considering the newly formed United Nations, White pointed out that America is home to people from many different ethnic backgrounds ("think of the impurity of its bloodlines and of how no American ever won a prize in a dog show"). "Peace is to be had," White says, "when people's antagonisms and antipathies are subject to the discipline of law and the decency of government."[100]

"Do not try to save the world by loving thy neighbor; it will only make him nervous. Save the world by respecting thy neighbor's rights under law and insisting that he respect yours (under the same law)," White says.[101] Here again, we need not retreat from standing firm in our beliefs. Indeed, we should hold fast to them, because our beliefs are our basis for building families and communities and, ultimately, a nation.

---

100 E. B. White, *On Democracy* (New York: Harper, 2019), p. 67.
101 Ibid., p. 67.

Americans must at least be willing to respect each other's rights, and they must teach their children to do so. The University of Virginia's Hunter writes that, "We Americans see all around us the fragmentation of our public life, our increasing inability to speak to each other through a common moral vocabulary, the emptying loss of an unum holding together a complex plurality of people and cultures."[102]

King saw the same in 1963: "Have we not come to such an impasse in the modern world that we must love our enemies— or else? The chain reaction of evil—hate begetting hate, wars producing more wars—must be broken, or we shall be plunged into the dark abyss of annihilation."[103]

Taken together—(1) acknowledging the meaning of our founding documents, as well as past failures to live up to them, (2) recognizing the success of black Americans under the most difficult of circumstances as a credit to those individuals, and as part of America's identity that we should all celebrate, and (3) loving our enemies (or at least aspiring to do so)—these three concepts form the basis for a response to critical race theory, matching one theory with another. These three ideas are "civil" at their very core, humbly acknowledging America's imperfections, while honoring the unique features of our constitutional republic. Most important perhaps, a civil theory gives us something to unite around and aspire to—not something that divides, disrupts, and, in the end, destroys everything it touches.

---

102 Hunter, *The Death of Character*, p. 21.
103 King, *A Gift of Love*, p. 49.

POLICY SOLUTIONS

In 2021, the mainstream media filled the headlines with stories about how lawmakers were "banning" critical race theory.[104] The implication was that anyone who opposed critical race theory's racially discriminatory ideas was out of touch with the mainstream or otherwise holding on to prejudice from America's past. There was, in fact, resistance to critical race theory in the form of state and federal legislation. State lawmakers in more than half of all U.S. states introduced proposals to reject the use of critical race theory's racial bias in schools. The proposals varied according to the needs that state lawmakers identified, but the proposals had notable similarities that did more to *reject* critical race theory's racial prejudice than *ban* its discussion in schools. In fact, some proposals explicitly said that although educators and students cannot *apply* critical race theory in the form of mandatory affinity groupings, homework assignments according to skin color, or classroom assignments that ask students to affirm that individuals can be guilty of racism based on their skin color, the provisions did not prevent the discussion of racial, or otherwise controversial, issues in the classroom.

In Texas, for example, officials proposed new education standards for social studies instruction that included the teaching of the U.S. Constitution and the Declaration of Independence, along with material from the Lincoln-Douglas

---

104 Jack Dutton, "Critical Race Theory Is Banned in These States," *Newsweek,* June 11, 2021, *https://www.newsweek.com/critical-race-theory-banned-these-states-1599712,* Lauren Camera, "Bills Banning Critical Race Theory Advance in States Despite Its Absence in Many Classrooms," *U.S. News & World Report,* June 23, 2021, *https://www.usnews.com/news/education-news/articles/2021-06-23/bills-banning-critical-race-theory-advance-in-states-despite-its-absence-in-many-classrooms,* and Evan Gerstmann, "Should the States Ban Critical Race Theory in Schools?" *Forbes,* July 6, 2021, *https://www.forbes.com/sites/evangerstmann/2021/07/06/should-the-states-ban-critical-theory-in-schools/?sh=385d0a2111a0.*

debates and Alexis de Tocqueville's *Democracy in America*.[105] The proposed standards also prohibit a state agency or school administrator from compelling a teacher to discuss public policy issues of the day.

Some of the provisions of these state proposals may improperly limit the discussion of ideas in the classroom. In Texas's proposal, again, one provision says that no educator may "make part of a course" any ideas that are part of critical race theory. These ideas include the belief that individuals could be "inherently" oppressive due to their skin color, and that "an individual should be discriminated against or receive adverse treatment solely or partly because of his or her race or sex."[106] These concepts are unarguably part of critical race theory's core principles and have no place in a K–12 classroom or anywhere else. However, a teacher could consider "making a topic part of a course" to mean simply including the idea in a class discussion. And, students should learn that critical race theory is steeped in prejudice, so officials should be careful to remove any ambiguity about whether teachers and students may discuss critical race theory in the classroom—all the better to discover the depths of its depravity.

Lawmakers must prevent the *application* of critical race theory through affinity groupings and the discriminatory behaviors described in these pages. Texas lawmakers debated this section ("make part of a course") of their proposal and others, eventually continuing the discussion in at least two special legislative sessions after the regular session ended.[107]

Also problematic are provisions that ban specific content, such as the 1619 Project. As described in Chapter 2, this *New*

---

105 Texas Legislature, 87th Regular Session, H.B. 3979, *https://capitol.texas.gov/tlodocs/87R/billtext/pdf/HB03979I.pdf*.

106 Ibid.

107 As this book went to press, lawmakers were still debating this proposal.

York Times Magazine feature contains factually inaccurate references and misleading historical analyses. Yet attempts by some lawmakers to ban even the presence of the 1619 Project in classrooms embraces the same elements of the cancel culture that are part of critical race theory.[108] Teachers have a responsibility to teach students how to investigate and interpret materials such as the 1619 Project. Furthermore, there are few actions that make a book or article more appealing than declaring the piece to be contraband, which means that banning certain material may have an effect that is the reverse from what lawmakers intended. Yes, some teachers may want to teach the 1619 Project as truth, but parents have the responsibility to be aware of what their children are learning. When they object, parents should talk to their child's teacher and principal and go to the school board with their concerns, ultimately being prepared to choose a new school if education officials refuse to listen. (Of course, far too many parents still do not have the option of sending their children to a different school.)

We cannot be logically consistent, or effective, if we advocate the banning of certain materials from classrooms while believing that the pursuit of truth should be part of a school's mission, if not one of its central features. Few explained this responsibility as clearly and succinctly as the University of Chicago's statement on free expression from 2015. This statement, adopted by nearly one hundred colleges and universities, says that it is "not the proper role of a University to

---

108 South Carolina General Assembly, 124th Session 2021–2022, H. 4343, *https://www. scstatehouse.gov/sess124_2021-2022/bills/4343.htm*, and Michigan Legislature, 2021 Session, Senate Bill 460, *http://www.legislature.mi.gov/(S(qnfzqiklrxie5y32rf4el5mh))/ mileg.aspx?page=GetObject&objectname=2021-SB-0460.*

attempt to shield individuals from ideas and opinions they find unwelcome, disagreeable, or even deeply offensive."[109]

K–12 schools are different from postsecondary institutions—students are younger, for one. And the court cases involving First Amendment freedoms in K–12 schools also differ from the opinions on free speech on college campuses (public school officials may limit the expressive rights of public-school teachers in the course of their duties[110]). Still, for educational institutions at all levels to prepare students for adulthood by equipping them to determine truth from falsehood is a sound goal. To distinguish between what is true and what is not, teachers will have to discuss materials that must be refuted.

State officials do not have to ban materials or ideas from the classroom to prevent the application of critical race theory's racial prejudice, and preventing prejudice should be a prime objective. Lawmakers do not even have to use the words "critical race theory" to prohibit the use of this worldview in school operations. First, proposals that try to preempt or respond to critical race theory's application can say specifically that nothing in a proposal prevents teachers or students from discussing controversial ideas.[111]

Second, lawmakers should focus their proposals on preventing any public official from compelling a teacher or student to affirm or believe any idea, especially ideas that would violate the race-related provisions of the Civil Rights Act of 1964. Title VI of this act states: "No person in the United States shall, on the ground of race, color, or national origin,

---

109 University of Chicago, "Report on the Committee of Free Expression," *https://provost.uchicago.edu/sites/default/files/documents/reports/FOECommitteeReport.pdf*, and FIRE, "Chicago Statement: University and Faculty Body Support," June 15, 2021, *https://www.thefire.org/chicago-statement-university-and-faculty-body-support/*.

110 *Garcetti v. Ceballos*, 547 U.S. 410 (2006).

111 The Heritage Foundation, "Protecting K-12 Students from Discrimination," June 18, 2021, *https://www.heritage.org/article/protecting-k-12-students-discrimination*.

be excluded from participation in, be denied the benefits of, or be subjected to, discrimination under any program or activity receiving Federal financial assistance."[112]

Since the primary way of *applying* critical race theory in schools clearly violates Title VI, state lawmakers must reinforce the idea that teachers and school officials may not practice the theory in schools. Lawmakers in Idaho included a prohibition on "compelled speech" in their proposal, and members of Congress used similar language in a proposal introduced for Washington, DC, public schools (a school district under federal jurisdiction).[113] Usually, federal activity in K–12 schools should be viewed with suspicion or outright opposition (see the discussion of Common Core earlier in this chapter). But this federal proposal for the nation's capital appropriately applies only to a district under federal supervision and, appropriately and urgently, rejects critical race theory's racial bias.

Lawmakers must design these proposals carefully because court judges will be the ones who decide critical race theory's fate in schools. Parents and teachers have already filed lawsuits against the application of critical race theory in the classroom, including a suit a teacher filed in Illinois saying that a school near Evanston used mandatory affinity groupings for teachers and students for different school activities.[114] The U.S. Department of Education began an investigation into these claims in late 2020, but after the 2020 election, the

---

112 42 U.S. Code § 2000d(b).

113 Sixty-sixth Legislature of the State of Idaho, First Regular Session, 2021, House Bill No. 377, *https://legislature.idaho.gov/wp-content/uploads/sessioninfo/2021/legislation/H0377. pdf*, and 117th Congress, 2021-2022, H.R. 3937, *https://www.congress.gov/member/glenn-grothman/G000576?q={%22search%22:[%22grothman%22]}&s=2&r=1&page Sort=dateOfIntroduction%3Adesc.*

114 Southeastern Legal Foundation, "*Deemar v. Evanston/Skokie School District 65*," *https:// www.slfliberty.org/case/deemar-v-evanston-skokie-school-district-65/.*

new administration dropped the case.[115] In Nevada, a mother filed a lawsuit against a public charter school that her son said required him to affirm privilege based on his skin color.[116]

At the same time, the nation's largest teachers union has committed its members to applying critical race theory. The NEA voted at its annual meeting in 2021 to "share and publicize" information on critical race theory and "educate" its members on the ideology.[117] With lawmakers introducing provisions that reject the theory, parents and teachers filing lawsuits against the theory's applications, and political interest groups, such as unions, supporting use of the theory, court cases are inevitable. Lawmakers should consider proposals that prevent teachers and students from being forced to believe or profess critical race theory, and should base proposals on the Civil Rights Act, which already outlaws the theory's racist applications.

CONCLUSION

As reflections of our culture, K–12 schools cannot avoid cultural battles. As Schlesinger recognized, "The schools and colleges of the republic train the citizens of the future. Our public schools in particular have been the great instrument of assimilation and the great means of forming an American identity."[118] We do not have to agree in full with Schlesinger's assessment of public schools (families, houses of worship, and private organi-

---

115 Carl Campanile, "US Dept. of Education Curbs Decision on Race-Based 'Affinity Groups,'" *New York Post*, March 7, 2021, *https://nypost.com/2021/03/07/education-dept-curbs-decision-on-race-based-affinity-groups/*.

116 Joshua Dunn, "Critical Race Theory Collides with the Law," *Education Next*, May 19, 2021, *https://www.educationnext.org/critical-race-theory-collides-with-law/*.

117 National Education Association, "New Business Item 39: Adopted as Modified," July 2021. This item is no longer available on the internet, but screenshots are available here, for example: *https://twitter.com/realchrisrufo/status/1411473898491678720?lang=en*.

118 Schlesinger, *The Disuniting of America*.

zations play vital roles, too) to consider that he is not alone in holding these expectations. Public schools play an important role in reflecting and transmitting shared ideas.

In a RAND study cited in Chapter 1, in which social studies teachers were the least confident in the importance of facts in K–12 instruction, not all the findings are so discouraging. Most educators even cited specific behaviors that should be part of our habitus. In fact, 76 percent of the teachers said that it is "absolutely essential" to teach students "to have good work habits such as being timely, persistent, and hardworking."[119] These are the very same ideas that critical race theorists decry as "white values" and evidence of systemic racism. Again, as also described in Chapter 1, the National Museum of African American History and Culture listed "hard work" and the nuclear family as "Aspects & Assumptions of Whiteness & White Culture in the United States" on its website before this material, like the Ohio Department of Education material described in Chapter 2, was removed after public outcry.[120]

Debates over character formation and our sense of national identity overlap with conversations about the purpose of schools, student achievement, and cultural reflections of ourselves in our schools. Observers were concerned with these issues two hundred years ago, thirty years ago, twenty years ago, and still are today. Schlesinger writes, "The debate about the curriculum is a debate about what it means to be an American." Schlesinger says that "in no arena is the rejection of an overriding national identity more crucial that in our system of education."[121]

---

119 Laura S. Hamilton, Julia H. Kaufman, and Lynn Hu, "Truth Decay: Social Studies Teachers' Perspectives on Key Civic Outcomes in 2010 and 2019," RAND, 2020, *https://www.rand.org/pubs/research_reports/RRA112-4.html.*

120 Rod Dreher, "Smithsonian's Anti-White Propaganda," *The American Conservative,* July 15, 2020, *https://www.theamericanconservative.com/dreher/smithsonian-whiteness-anti-white-propaganda/.*

121 Schlesinger, *The Disuniting of America,* p. 21.

The concerns are also personal—issues of character—as well as communal. As Schlesinger recognizes: "What students are taught in schools affects the way they will thereafter see and treat other Americans."[122]

Schlesinger's "what it means to be an American" is a notion that involves teaching facts to children, but also concerns character formation. On the topic of school mission statements and the renaming of schools especially, what may appear to be a straightforward policy responsibility for education officials is indelibly linked to civic concepts. In these policy choices, decision-makers are reflecting the character traits they want to prioritize.

We must take seriously the threats we find to a shared sense of national character. Creating (and rescinding) the 1776 Commission, renaming schools, and being concerned when school curricula emphasize (or not) one person over another are all ideas that matter, and not just for policy reasons. These issues and others in and outside K–12 schools are important because at the very center of the discussion is the representation, communication, and teaching of the virtues and character that generations of Americans have honored and remembered. Today, more and more Americans are learning to dishonor and forget.

Hunter, whose definitions of culture and habitus were introduced at the beginning of this chapter, explains that schools and the imparting of values to children reflect the desires of society at large. "One need not listen very long to realize that children have become a code for speaking about our own desires, commitments, and ideals, and the world we wish to create," Hunter says.[123]

---

122 Ibid., p. 22.
123 Hunter, *The Death of Character.*

If schools are abandoning character formation, abandoning America's traditions of individual liberty and responsibility as the basis for civil society, they are betraying the trust that citizens impart to educators to perpetuate our way of life. Future generations must have the opportunity to build a life for themselves and their families, protecting the possibility—not the guaranteed outcome—of the American dream.

In *The Closing of the American Mind*, Allan Bloom asked, "But when there are no shared goals or vision of the public good, is the social contract any longer possible?" The critical worldview that is implanted in our K–12 schools and universities, directing instruction and school cultures, is intentionally tearing apart our social fabric. The beginnings of a civil theory presented here respond to critical race theory, reviving beliefs that Americans once held as incontrovertible. This civil theory is meant to give us something on which we can rebuild a habitus—and pass on to the next generation.

CHAPTER 5

CONCLUSION

Scarlett Johnson describes her Wisconsin town in the Mequon-Thiensville school district as "quiet, friendly, nice." But in a story that will sound familiar to parents around the country, over the past year, she began noticing not-so friendly and nice material that some of her children, high school students, were working on via Zoom during the 2020 school closures due to the COVID-19 pandemic. As she said in an interview, "Everything is being viewed through the lens of race." [1] There is division among the parents in her community on this issue now—"so divisive and so unnecessary," Scarlett says.

Much of the material was "focused on making kids social justice warriors." Scarlett explains that she does not want to ignore difficult discussions about race and discrimination: "I just wanted them to have a liberal education, truly in the sense of the word," she said. Yet, educators from her children's school district have been taken in by "equity" training programs where presenters pushed the "oppression" narrative, complete with recommendations that educators rely on staples from the critical race theory canon, such as *Pedagogy of the Oppressed* and *White Fragility*.[2]

---

1   Author interview with Scarlett Johnson, May 14, 2021.
2   Material provided by Scarlett Johnson.

Scarlett says that Mequon-Thiensville officials adopted many of the same critical race theory-themed goals of the Elmbrook School District, a district twenty miles away. There, "equity" training presentations informed teachers that "oppression, marginalization are historical, structural, cultural, and systemic..."[3] Although one presentation says that there should be "high quality teaching and learning for all learners," the presenters completely absolved students of any responsibility for their future. "The system is responsible for prevention of student failure," the presentation said. Instruction should be based on "identity relevant teaching," the presenters said, and quoted from critical pedagogue bell hooks.

The message is clear: students are no longer responsible for outcomes in their lives, and teachers should adjust instruction according to a student's classification in some sort of tribe. Consistent with critical theory's rejection of authentic truth, a principle that critical race theorists adopted, the presentation says: "Educators should teach based on who the student is, vs [sic] to a preconceived normative." That is, there is no truth that applies to everyone. There are different truths for different students.

A "norm" or "normative" idea is similar to the concept of habitus described in Chapter 4. People from all different ethnic and religious backgrounds and belief systems inhabit America's pluralistic society, so some communities may regard one norm as important while others value different norms. America's "melting pot" or "salad bowl" or any other metaphor means that our national creed can allow different cultures to exist simultaneously because Americans can exercise their

---

3   Elise M. Frattura and Colleen A. Capper, "Integrated Comprehensive Systems for Equity," presentation to the Mequon-Thiensville and Elmbrook school districts, provided by Scarlett Johnson.

freedoms to speak and act and worship as long as they do not interfere with others' rights to do the same. The legal bound aries around these freedoms have expanded and contracted under different presidential administrations, but America's unique gift to world history is its successful—imperfect, but successful—experiment in ordered liberty. Critical race the- ory's norms, though, like those of critical theory before it, are not attempting to create a shared set of assumptions that are bound by the rule of law. If everyone has a right answer based on his or her experience—a "diverse normative"—there are no shared assumptions on which communities can base responses to external forces, such as a pandemic, war, or eco- nomic collapse, all of which the U.S. has experienced or been a part of in the past decade alone.

The Mequon-Thiensville and Elmwood "equity" presenta- tions are consistent with the new teacher-certification standards in Illinois, which were described in Chapter 2, and state that "there is often not one 'correct' way of doing or understanding something, and that what is seen as 'correct' is most often based on our lived experiences."[4] Ibram Kendi's ideas of measuring intelligence "by how knowledgeable individuals are about their own environments" naturally follow.[5]

Diversity trainers in Mequon-Thiensville and Elmwood told educators that schools have a "culture of marginaliza- tion" based on immutable characteristics, along with religion. The presentation finished by recommending works by Robin

---

4   Illinois State Board of Education, "Notice of Proposed Amendments: Title 23: Education and Cultural Resources, Subtitle A: Education, Chapter I: State Board of Education, Subchapter b: Personnel, Part 24: Culturally Responsive Teaching and Learning Standards for all Illinois Educators," *https://www.isbe.net/Documents/23-24RG-P.pdf*.

5   Again, as quoted in Chapter 1, Kendi asked, "What if we measured intelligence by how knowledgeable individuals are about their own environments?" See Kendi, *How to Be an Antiracist*, p. 103.

DiAngelo and Gloria Ladson-Billings, along with those of other critical race theorists. This same presentation was delivered to Illinois teachers in 2017 and sponsored by the state board of education.[6]

In West Allis, a district that neighbors Elmwood and Mequon-Thiensville, district officials adopted a mission statement that says that educators must "acknowledge our own biases" in order for students to achieve and create a workforce of "racially conscious" employees (an earlier version of this mission statement's title included the word "non-negotiable," evidence of how critical race theorists consider their ideas to be above debate).[7] Perhaps in a different era, without the current critical focus on identities and discrimination according to skin color, the district's commitment could be applauded. But with the critical redefinition of equality under the law into "equity," which means the government enforcing the same outcomes for all, we must consider statements such as these as a direct affront not just to any reasonable understanding of equality, but to America's very creed.

Also nearby, in the small town of Oregon, Wisconsin, ninety miles west of Milwaukee, instructional materials for eighth-grade history include a set of readings to help students to become "antiracist citizen(s) in the future," making the lessons not history exercises, but activist training sessions. All parents should want their children to discuss complex topics in school, and slavery and America's racist past certainly deserve close study. But this lesson plan goes far beyond teaching historical

6   Illinois State Board of Education, "Special Education Programs: Annual Special Education Directors' Conference 2017," *https://www.isbe.net/Documents/cornerstone1_illinois_state_directors_17.pdf.*

7   West Allis-West Milwaukee School District, "Mission-Vision-Equity Beliefs," *https://www.wawmsd.org/discover/our-mission*; "Mission-Vision-Equity Non-Negotiables," https://web.archive.org/web/20210125165722/https://www.wawm.k12.wi.us/district/about_our_district/mission-vision-equity_non-negotiables.

events, and promotes (politicized and radical) student activism. Students are to read articles such as "Black Lives Matter May Be the Largest Movement in U.S. History" and connect this and other articles with public policy positions, such as ending cash bail and promoting reparations for the era of slavery in American history. Remember that we are talking about thirteen-year-olds.

Scarlett, who describes herself as Latina and is the mother of children with different skin tones, said,

> *I don't want my child who is brown to see themselves as a victim, and I don't want my child who is white to see my other child as an oppressor. This is completely wrong. They are individuals, and their character and their decisions make up who they are, not who their ancestors were.*

Scarlett adds, "It's exhausting and frustrating. I just hadn't realized how far things had come."[8]

OOO

Scarlett's experiences in Mequon-Thiensville, like those of Nancy Andersen in North Carolina (the introduction) and Megan from Los Alamitos, California, (Chapter 1) help to illustrate three of the most common myths about critical race theory in K–12 schools that parents and the general public must expose today. All Americans, but especially students, parents, teachers and policymakers should be prepared to identify these falsehoods and respond with relevant evidence to counter them.

Revealing myths for what they are will accomplish two important goals. First, educational institutions should foster the pursuit of truth. Schools can impart job skills, give students the

---

8   Author interview.

chance to make friends and learn to get along with others, and give children the basic tools they need to participate in life, such as reading and math. As Yale's Anthony Kronman and others have described in these pages, schools should help students to grapple with the big questions of life, such as "Why am I here and what should I do with my life?" The pursuit of truth is part of this exercise.

The second important objective that is accomplished by exposing myths is that once the truth is agreed upon, it allows you and your neighbors and family and friends and others in your community to have a habitus. We, as a society, can establish common ground about what is acceptable and authentic in our conversations with each other so that we can work together to solve the problems that societies inevitably face.

Exposing critical race theory as a Marxist philosophy that engages in racial prejudice would allow us to describe the theory for what it is—racially discriminatory—and then argue that application of the theory violates civil rights laws.

There are three myths, specifically, that concern how we discuss critical race theory in public life and in the media.

The first myth is that teachers do not teach critical race theory in schools today. American Federation for Teachers President Randi Weingarten stated this at a conference in July 2021. "Let's be clear: critical race theory is not taught in elementary schools or high schools," Weingarten said.[9] Loudoun County, Virginia, school superintendent Scott Ziegler said that critical race theory is "not something that we are teaching in Loudoun County."[10]

---

9   Brittany Bernstein, "Teachers'-Union Head Claims CRT Is Only Taught at Colleges," *National Review Online,* July 6, 2021, *https://www.nationalreview.com/news/teachers-union-head-claims-crt-is-only-taught-at-colleges/*.

10   John Battiston, "Ziegler Remains Firm LCPS Is 'Not Teaching Critical Race Theory,'" *Loudoun Times-Mirror,* July 2, 2021, *https://www.loudountimes.com/news/ziegler-remains-firm-lcps-is-not-teaching-critical-race-theory/article_146c1e8c-c3c9-11eb-9217-ebb5be4d3868.html*.

Kimberlé Crenshaw, the critical race theorist who conceived of the idea of "intersectionality" that holds a central place in California's ethnic studies curriculum and elsewhere in K–12 systems around the country, told ABC News that the theory is not being used in schools.[11] Others have made the same claims, including public school officials from states across the U.S.[12]

In fact, and as documented in these pages, K–12 school officials and educators are, indeed, teaching—and applying— critical race theory in the classroom, often without trying to hide the ideas or the very term "critical race theory." (At other times, teachers have attempted to hide the truth from parents, as described in Chapter 1.) In Oregon, the Portland Public School District makes videos of the district's "Critical Race Theory CRiT Coalition Summit," which met as recently as April 2021, available on YouTube.[13]

Despite the claims of its superintendent, district officials in Loudoun County contracted with a teacher training organization called the Equity Collaborative that used the words "critical race theory" in its presentations to teachers.[14] Hayward Unified School District officials, in a district located just across

11 Kiara Alfonseca, "Critical Race Theory in the Classroom: Understanding the Debate," ABC News, May 19, 2021, *https://abcnews.go.com/US/critical-race-theory-classroom-understanding-debate/story?id=77627465*.

12 John Aguilar, "Denver Metro Schools Don't Teach Critical Race Theory—But that Hasn't Stopped the Complaints," *Denver Post*, July 6, 2021, *https://www.denverpost.com/2021/07/06/critical-race-theory-colorado-schools/*, and Sophia Kalakailo, "Critical Race Theory: What You Need to Know in Michigan," *Bridge Michigan*, July 6, 2021, *https://www.bridgemi.com/talent-education/critical-race-theory-what-you-need-know-michigan*.

13 PPS Communications, "Portland Public Schools Critical Race Theory CRiT Coalition Summit," YouTube.com, April 22, 2021, *https://www.youtube.com/results?search_query=portland+public+school+critical+theory+working+group*.

14 Equity Collaborative, "Introduction to Critical Race Theory," On-Line Institute, May 7, 2020, *https://theequitycollaborative.com/wp-content/uploads/2020/05/Intro-To-Critical-Race-Theory.pdf*, news release, "How Critical Race Theory Infected Loudon County Public Schools," Fight for Schools, May 26, 2021, *https://fightforschools.com/how-critical-race-theory-infected-loudoun-county-public-schools/*, and "Loudon County Public Schools Service Agreement" with The Equity Collaborative, *https://documentcloud.adobe.com/link/track?uri=urn:aaid:scds:US:ae15f1d7-d4be-4153-9014-aef334b3c1b6#pageNum=1*.

the San Francisco Bay from San Mateo and South San Francisco, released a memo to the school community that said that the district's ethnic studies program is "informed by and will include critical race theory..."[15]

In case any doubts remain that K–12 educators are, in fact, teaching critical race theory from California to Virginia and many places in between, remember that the nation's largest teachers union committed its members to promoting the theory. As mentioned in Chapter 4, the NEA adopted a statement saying it would "share and publicize" information on critical race theory.[16]

But that's not all. As Heritage Foundation legal fellow Sarah Parshall Perry explained in the *Washington Examiner* in August 2021, an official for the Rhode Island chapter of the NEA admitted in court documents that union members do, in fact, teach critical race theory in schools.[17] This NEA chapter had the audacity to file suit against a parent for requesting more information about the books and lesson plans teachers were using in her daughter's school. According to the union's complaint, if school leaders turned this material over to the mother, Nicole Solas, it is "anticipated that teacher emails will be produced that may or will contain discussions about critical race theory curriculum."[18]

---

15 News release, "HUSD Board of Trustees Vote to Approve Ethnic Studies Policy," Hayward Unified School District,, June 25, 2021, *https://www.husd.us/pf4/cms2/news_themed_display?id=1624611250631.*

16 National Education Association, "New Business Item 39: Adopted as Modified," July 2021. This item is no longer active online, but screenshots are available here, for example: *https://twitter.com/realchrisrufo/status/1411473898491678720?lang=en.*

17 Sarah Perry, "Teacher Unions Go to Court to Deter Critical Race Theory Disclosure," *Washington Examiner,* August 15, 2021, *https://www.washingtonexaminer.com/opinion/teachers-unions-go-to-court-to-deter-critical-race-theory-disclosure.*

18 State of Rhode Island Superior Court, *National Education Association Rhode Island et al. vs. South Kingstown School Committee et al.,* *https://goldwaterinstitute.org/wp-content/uploads/2021/08/NEA-complaint.pdf.*

At the end of August 2021, the Goldwater Institute, which is defending Solas against the union, reported that the union had withdrawn its request for emergency relief. This means that Solas's public records request process will not be disrupted as the case moves toward final resolution. Goldwater Institute attorneys called the union's backtracking evidence of the special interest group's "flimsy legal standing."[19]

Such evidence puts the first myth to rest.

Second, some critical race theorists or educators who favor this worldview argue that it is only used to teach the subjects of history or social studies in schools.[20] As if that were not bad enough. In July 2021, Crenshaw, for example, wrote in *The Washington Post* that lawmakers who reject the theory, using the state legislative proposals outlined in Chapter 4, "[close] off room to explore the impact of America's racist history." She adds, "But the comfort of a ban on whatever conservatives imagine critical race theory to be will further deny students and scholars the chance to understand the past."

If critical race theory is a teaching tool needed for history and not a racially discriminatory perspective on all of life, why did the National Council of Teachers of Mathematics (NCTM) recommend *Critical Race Theory in Mathematics Education* to its members for summer reading?[21] And why was critical race the-

---

19 Goldwater Institute, "Union Withdraws Attempt to Obstruct Rhode Island Mom's Access to Public Records," In Defense of Liberty, August 23, 2021, *https://indefenseof-liberty.blog/2021/08/23/union-withdraws-attempt-to-obstruct-rhode-island-moms-access-to-public-records/.*

20 Kimberlé Crenshaw, "The Panic over Critical Race Theory Is an Attempt to Whitewash History," *The Washington Post,* July 2, 2021, *https://www.washingtonpost.com/outlook/critical-race-theory-history/2021/07/02/e90bc94a-da75-11eb-9bbb-37c30dcf9363_story.html.* See also, Anthony Hill, "In-Depth: What Is Critical Race Theory and How Might It Look in Classrooms," ABC Action News, June 10, 2021, *https://www.abcactionnews.com/news/in-depth/in-depth-what-is-critical-race-theory-and-how-would-it-theoretically-look-in-classrooms.*

21 National Council of Teachers of Mathematics, "What to Read? My Summer Reading List," February 16, 2021, *https://www.nctm.org/Search/?query=critical%20race%20theory#?wst=8d68e8aabd224087f95eead8b1570035.*

orist and teacher college professor Gloria Ladson-Billings the NCTM's keynote speaker at its 2019 conference?[22] (As noted in Chapter 1, an oft-cited article that Ladson-Billings wrote is titled "Just What Is Critical Race Theory and What's It Doing in a *Nice Field Like Education?*"[23])

Likewise, the National Science Teaching Association, a professional network of more than forty thousand science educators, wrote in May 2020 that its members now "work from the stance that scientific ways of knowing and science education are fundamentally cultural and inherently political."[24] The organization recently hosted a multiday online event that included a session titled "Critical Affinity Spaces for Science Educators," where teachers were taught to use a "critical lens that…exposes the hidden and master narratives" in science and affirms "that racial/social justice approaches to science teaching are needed." Just as with the 2019 NCTM conference, the organization featured a proponent of critical race theory as the keynote speaker.[25]

Critical race theory is not merely an intellectual vantage point that teachers can use when teaching history or civics or social studies. The theory is a radical, Marxist ideology that transforms every issue it touches into a fight for power in public and private life along racial lines. Again, we have clear evidence that the theory contains more than just accoutrements for history instruction.

---

22 National Council of Teachers of Mathematics, "2019 NCTM San Diego Annual Conference Program & Presentation," *https://www.nctm.org/Conferences-and-Professional-Development/Annual-Meeting-and-Exposition/Program-and-Presentation/*, and National Academy of Education, "Gloria Ladson-Billings," *https://naeducation.org/our-members/gloria-ladson-billings/*.

23 Ladson-Billings, "Just What Is Critical Race Theory and What's It Doing in a Nice Field Like Education?"

24 National Science Teaching Association, "Social Justice in the Science Classroom," May 26, 2020, *https://www.nsta.org/blog/social-justice-science-classroom*.

25 National Science Teaching Association, "Virtual Miniseries: What IS Social Justice Teaching in the Science Classroom?" *https://www.nsta.org/social-justice-series-2*.

Third, some have argued that critical race theory gives us a more thorough understanding of race relations in the U.S. Writing for MSNBC, columnist Kevin Kruse says that the worldview is one that talks "honestly about inequality."[26] The National Association of School Psychologists released a statement claiming that critical race theory instruction "affirms and validates the diversity of [students'] cultural and individual differences."[27] Critical race theory certainly affirms students' differences—and only their differences. Mandated affinity groupings by race and instruction about white privilege emphasize the "differences" with no plan of fostering a sense of belonging in a classroom community, neighborhood community, or national community.

That is where Americans find themselves today. For critical race theorists, such as Kendi, there are only tribes. Finding common ground is not the goal. "To be American is to be White. To be White is not to be a Negro."[28] He continues: "The White body no longer presents itself as the American body; the Black body no longer strives to be the American body, knowing there is no such thing as the American body, only American bodies, racialized by power."[29]

Race and power—not affirmation and belonging: critical race theory in two words.

26 Kevin M. Kruse, "Texas' Ban on Critical Race Theory in Schools Proves the GOP Still Doesn't Understand MLK's Message," MSNBC, June 17, 2021, *https://www.msnbc.com/opinion/texas-ban-critical-race-theory-schools-proves-gop-still-doesn-n1271101.*
27 National Association of School Psychologists, "The Importance of Addressing Equity, Diversity, and Inclusion in Schools: Dispelling Myths About Critical Race Theory," handout, 2021.
28 Kendi, *How to Be an Antiracist,* p. 28.
29 Ibid., p. 33.

OOO

"'Sometime,' concluded the old man, gathering his ragged toga about him, 'you must tell us some more stories of your country. We, who are elders, will instruct you in their true meaning, so that when you return to your own land your elders will see that you have not been sitting in the bush, but among those who know things and who have taught you wisdom,'" writes Laura Bohannan at the end of her essay about her visit with the Tiv people of Nigeria. As explained in the introduction, Bohannan was more confused about human nature at the end of her conversation with the Tiv than when she started.

Americans today are more confused about, well, everything, as critical race theory has entered the mainstream.

In an Associated Press-NORC Center for Public Affairs Research poll from February 2021, the "overwhelming majority believe the nation is deeply divided over its most important values, and, looking forward, 62% think the country will become even more divided or stay the same over the next five years."[30]

On average, 49 percent of respondents say that the country is "headed in the right direction," while 49 percent say the opposite. Not surprisingly, when responses are considered according to political party over time, the graph looks like a pair of scissors. In November 2020, 20 percent of Republicans said the country was headed in the right direction (after President Biden's election), compared with 76 percent of Democrats. Since 2017, responses among Democrats to this poll had hovered around 15 percent saying the country was

---

30   AP-NORC Center for Public Affairs Research, "Many Value
      Democratic Principles, But Few Think Democracy Is Working
      Well These Days," February 8, 2021, *http://apnorc.org/projects/*
      many-value-democratic-principles-but-few-think-democracy-is-working-well-these-days.

headed in the right direction, while Republicans hovered between 50 percent and 75 percent until the riots of summer 2020, at which point there was a steep drop off, plunging to 20 percent in November.

The poll also shows a divide over Americans' closely held beliefs. Between 2016 and 2021, the share of respondents who said that "Americans are united and in agreement about the most important values" fell from 19 percent to 11 percent. The remainder said that "Americans are greatly divided when it comes to the most important values."

Yet there is some hope. Despite the pessimistic answers to this broadly worded question, when asked about institutions and their role in civic life, 88 percent of respondents said that "a fair judicial system and the rule of law" are "important to the U.S. identity as a nation"; 85 percent said that "individual liberties and freedoms as defined by the Constitution" are important to our national identity; and 80 percent said that a democratically elected government is important.

The numbers started to fall, however, when the survey asked if people felt that sharing these values was important. Just 65 percent of respondents said that "a shared Americans [sic] culture and set of values" is important to our national identity. Perhaps they should read Laura Bohannan's "Shakespeare in the Bush." In order for a conversation—about virtually anything, and especially about values—to make sense to the participants of a conversation, a shared set of definitions for ideas and words, virtues and values, is essential.

Schools have an important role to play in the shaping of beliefs and shared ideas and experiences. E. D. Hirsch writes in *The Making of Americans*: "It is uncontroversial that schools in a democracy have a duty to help form competent citizens. Who is against educating young people so that they are able to judge the issue of the day, make a good living, raise a family, and help keep civic peace and order?"[31]

Hirsch also discusses a point that is especially important for conservatives. He says that conservatives have "tiptoed around the idea that the schools should form Americans" for the past half century. Progressives have been aggressive—and success-ful—in shaping this country's culture via K–12 schools and higher education. Those concerned about America's divide, and concerned that the scope of critical thinking will worsen this split, need to get involved. This is more than a call for con-servatives to start caring about school board elections (though that would be a good start).

More conservatives should be creating curricular materi-als, as 1776 Unites is doing, and parents must be ready to talk to their child's teachers and principal and school board when they find material that is objectionable in their child's class-es.[32] Likewise, policymakers should require that public school leaders allow taxpayers to see the materials that educators are using in schools.[33] Then, parents will not have to wait to read what an investigative journalist discovered to find out what their children are being taught. Remember the episode from Texas from this book's introduction, in which a teacher com-pared modern-day police to the KKK, and most did not know it had happened until the story hit the news. After the end of the 2019–2020 school year, and for much of the 2020–2021 school year, periods during which every teacher in the U.S. was deliv-ering content online, school officials have no excuses for saying

---

31 E. D. Hirsch, Jr., *The Making of Americans: Democracy and Our Schools* (New Haven: Yale University Press, 2010), p. 65.

32 1776 Unites, "Curriculum," *https://1776unites.com/our-work/curriculum/*.

33 Matt Beienburg, "De-Escalating the Curriculum Wars: A Proposal for Academic Transparency in Education," Goldwater Institute, January 14, 2020, *https://goldwater-institute.org/curriculum-wars/*.

that the task of making instructional material available online for taxpayers to review is too burdensome.

OOO

Today, critical theorists have stepped into a void created by a lack of shared knowledge, and are inserting ideas into K–12 schools that prior generations of Americans would have instantly recognized—and rejected—as discriminatory, if not downright racist. Schools are not preparing students to understand America's civic institutions and key historical concepts. More and more, schools are preparing American students to hate their country and each other.

There is no national report card for social studies. But because there is overlap among the materials taught in history, civics, and social studies, surveys of social studies teachers and other indicators of teaching and student performance are relevant to a discussion of history and civics. The National Council for the Social Studies even includes "civic" in its definition of social studies: "Social studies is the integrated study of the social sciences and humanities to promote civic competence," making the three subjects close relatives.[34] In a nationally representative survey conducted by RAND, "most social studies teachers reported not feeling well prepared to support students' civic development, and between about one-third and a little over one-half of both elementary and secondary teachers indicated that they had not received any training to do so."[35]

---

34   National Council for the Social Studies, "About National Council for the Social Studies," *https://www.socialstudies.org/about.*

35   Laura S. Hamilton, Julia H. Kaufman, and Lynn Hu, "Preparing Children and Youth for Civic Life in the Era of Truth Decay," Rand Corporation, 2020, *https://www.rand.org/pubs/research_reports/RRA112-6.html.*

Although other surveys have found that 50 percent or more of English and math teachers felt "well prepared to address academic standards for the subjects they taught," just 13 percent of elementary social studies teachers felt this way about civics, and 35 percent of secondary civics teachers reported feeling this way. Fifty-six percent of elementary teachers said that students' civic development was an "important but not essential priority." Sixty-three percent of high school educators said that civic development is an "absolutely essential priority."[36]

The low levels of student achievement in civics and history on national comparisons, and these reports of teachers feeling unprepared are frustrating because they mean that students are not learning to be contributing members of their communities. The survey results from social studies teachers indicate that schools have lost sight of their mission to equip students to make such contributions.

There is widespread agreement—on both sides of the ideological divide—that too many students struggle in civics and history, as well as math and reading, giving Americans looking for common solutions a place to start. In 2012, then Education Secretary Arne Duncan wrote that "unfortunately, civic learning and democratic engagement are add-ons rather than essential parts of the core academic mission in too many schools and on too many college campuses today."[37] The Trump administration's 1776 Commission Report, released in 2021, echoed Duncan's report: "Education in civics, history, and literature holds the central place in the well-being of both

---

36 Ibid., p. 48.
37 Arne Duncan et al., "Advancing Civic Learning and Engagement in Democracy: A Road Map and Call to Action," U.S. Department of Education, January 2012, *https:// www.ed.gov/sites/default/files/road-map-call-to-action.pdf.* See also Butcher, "Favorable Testimony before the Maryland General Assembly, Ways & Means Committee HB 1157," February 17, 2021, *https://mgaleg.maryland.gov/cmte_testimony/2021/wam/2234_ 02172021_9211-901.pdf.*

students and communities, [but in] most social studies and civics classes, serious study of the principles of equality and liberty has vanished."[38]

The progressive Center for American Progress also raises concerns about the content of civics instruction and says that civic knowledge today is "at an all-time low."[39] Even the NEA—again, a group that strongly supports critical race theory—said in 2017 that civics is the "forgotten purpose" of education.[40]

OOO

The Heritage Foundation survey cited in the introduction of this book asked parents if they wanted schools to "engage with character and virtue" in classroom instruction and other school activities. More than 80 percent of a nationally representative sample of parents said yes, and nearly 90 percent of school board members in the survey also answered in the affirmative.[41] Parents and school board members want schools to deal with issues concerning character and virtue, even as schools should also impart basic skills to students. The two responsibilities—representing character and teaching facts and skills—are interconnected.

The late Nathan Glazer, professor, editor at *Commentary*, and contributor to *The New Republic*, wrote in his contribution to the compendium titled *Making Good Citizens* that schools

38   The President's Advisory 1776 Commission, "1776 Report," The White House, January 2021, *https://trumpwhitehouse.archives.gov/wp-content/uploads/2021/01/The-Presidents-Advisory-1776-Commission-Final-Report.pdf,* and Butcher," Favorable Testimony before the Maryland General Assembly."

39   Sarah Shapiro and Catherine Brown, "The State of Civics Education," Center for American Progress, February 21, 2018, *https://www.americanprogress.org/issues/education-k-12/reports/2018/02/21/446857/state-civics-education/.*

40   Amanda Litvinov, "Forgotten Purpose: Civics Education in Public Schools," National Education Association NEAToday, March 16, 2017, *http://neatoday.org/2017/03/16/civics-education-public-schools/.*

41   Burke, Butcher, Gonzalez, and Kao, "The Culture of American K-12 Education: A National Survey of Parents and School Board Members."

serve an important function in the transmitting of character and facts from one generation to another. It is "inevitable" that divisions in society over moral issues, questions of character, "affect public education, and they affect it even when public education, as is commonly the case, is designed to be neutral on traditional morality. Neutrality on such issues will not satisfy large parts of our society."[42]

Glazer says that the "fragmentation" of civil society, which was already evident at the time of his essay in 2003, and the educational effects of this fragmentation, "must give us some pause." He writes,

> *I take it as a given that a major cause of the discontent with public schools among the minority population of the large cities is their [the schools'] ineffectiveness in bringing the children of these populations to a suitable level of academic competence, universally accepted as the necessary platform for economic and social mobility.*[43]

This is the point at which student achievement and values and beliefs meet—and when students are consistently low performing, adults should be skeptical of creative license with literature, math, and history. Glazer says that the American public might be willing to accept some level of revisionist history if students were excelling in math and reading and leading the world in international comparisons of academic achievement.[44] But U.S. students, on average, have scored lower than

---

42 Nathan Glazer, "Some Problems in Acknowledging Diversity," in Diane Ravitch and Joseph P. Viteritti, eds., *Making Good Citizens: Education and Civil Society* (New Haven: Yale University Press, 2003).

43 Ibid., p. 178.

44 Ibid. Glazer wrote, "We may be willing to accept the teaching of doubtful views of the history of the United States and the world if they are accompanied by a passion for reading and learning that improves basic skills. We are less likely to accept as a trade-off for the uncertain improvement of basic skills the teaching of views that challenge received biological and physical science."

students in many European countries in math and reading, with math scores trending down since 2003.[45] We have already covered the dismal student performance in history and civics in these pages.

In 1994, a very public debate had erupted over K–12 history instruction with the UCLA National Center for History in the Schools's release of its "National History Standards." As Natalie Wexler explains in *The Knowledge Gap*, Lynne Cheney, wife of former vice president Dick Cheney and former chair of the National Endowment for the Humanities, criticized the history standards for excluding discussions of prominent individuals from America's past. Wexler says that Cheney expressed disappointment that the standards downplayed America's significant role in the history of the world.[46] Cheney wrote in *The Wall Street Journal*, "I have abundant reason to be troubled by the way the history standards have turned out."[47]

Though the standards' primary authors disagreed with Cheney, arguing that the standards could not be taught without reference to the founding fathers and other notable historical figures, voices from the Left, such as historian Arthur Schlesinger, also criticized the material for "specific flaws" in the way the standards' authors discussed the Cold War.[48] As perhaps a precursor to President Biden's order rescinding the 1776 Commission, the National History Standards debate became a "media circus," says Wexler, and eventually reached Capitol Hill, where the U.S.

45   U.S. Department of Education, National Center for Education Statistics, "PISA 2018 U.S. Results," available at *https://nces.ed.gov/surveys/pisa/pisa2018/#/.*
46   Natalie Wexler, *The Knowledge Gap: The Hidden Cause of America's Broken Education System—and How to Fix It* (New York: Penguin Random House, 2019).
47   Lynne Cheney, "The End of History," *The Wall Street Journal*, October 20, 1994, *http://online.wsj.com/media/EndofHistory.pdf.*
48   Wilentz, "Don't Know Much About History," *The New York Times*, November 30, 1997, *https://archive.nytimes.com/www.nytimes.com/books/97/11/30/reviews/971130.30wilentt.html.*

Senate condemned the standards and asked federal agencies to "reject" the standards in January 1995.[49]

Here is where we find ourselves again today. We have debates over both the teaching of history and what it means to be an American, and perennially low scores in basic subjects, such as math and reading, especially among students from low-income families. Glazer forecast the 1776/1619 debate when he said, "In addition to concerns about basic skills, the values taught or not taught in the public schools constitute a major reason for the discontent and affect those with strong commitment to the traditional culture."[50]

It is worth noting here that Glazer was described as "the public intellectual who kept an open mind" and "never came to rest at a place of ideological certainty," so he hardly developed a reputation as a partisan with an axe to grind.[51]

NAME THAT SCHOOL

We can finish the discussion about the outrageous state of our schools and Americans' division over discrimination where we ended in the introduction, by considering why the names of schools matter.

Renaming schools is an issue that demonstrates the overlapping cultural tensions among civics studies, historical facts, and policymaking. Yes, a student can be successful in school and in life no matter the name of her elementary or high school, but the sharp debates over whom, or what, a school

---

49   Wexler, *The Knowledge Gap*, p. 161, and "Multicultural History Standards Rejected by Senate in 99-1 Vote," *Los Angeles Times*, January 19, 1995, *https://www.latimes.com/archives/la-xpm-1995-01-19-mn-21834-story.html*.

50   Glazer, "Some Problems in Acknowledging Diversity," p. 178.

51   David Greenberg, "Nathan Glazer: The Public Intellectual Who Kept an Open Mind," *Politico Magazine*, December 29, 2019, *https://www.politico.com/news/magazine/2019/12/29/nathan-glazer-the-public-intellectual-who-kept-an-open-mind-086482*.

building represents demonstrate the divide in America over what knowledge, civics, and character mean to individuals and communities.

In 2007, when I was a research associate in the Department of Education Reform at the University of Arkansas, two of my colleagues and I examined how school officials were changing school names around the country.[52] Turns out, the trend was to avoid history and notable individuals. We found that it was more common for schools to be named after trees or animals than after a founding father.

The findings made for clever headlines. In Florida, we found that twice as many schools were named for manatees than for George Washington, and in Arizona, schools were more likely to be named for a mesa or cactus than a U.S. president. At the time, the ideas from critical race theory and critical pedagogy were still mostly found in academic journals and some college syllabi and had not yet been splashed across the headlines for driving federal policy or K–12 curricula.

Our resulting report concluded that school board leaders were "shrinking" from debates over school names that had some sort of cultural or historical significance because officials were fearful of the debates that these conversations would engender. But we knew that the issue was important and symbolic of a cultural change taking place in school systems around the country. "To teach civics effectively," we wrote, "schools have to be willing to take a stand. To teach tolerance, they have to be intolerant of intolerance. To teach the virtues of democracy and liberty, schools have to argue that democracies are superior systems of government."[53]

---

52   Greene, Brian Kisida, and Butcher, "What's in a Name? The Decline in the Civic Mission of School Names," Manhattan Institute *Civic Report* No. 51, July 2007, *https://media4.manhattan-institute.org/pdf/cr_51.pdf.*
53   Ibid.

While we hypothesized that our findings had larger impli-cations for civil society, it would only take a little more than a decade for events to demonstrate that *values* are, indeed, the issue that those who are renaming schools are dealing with. The naming and renaming of schools is a civic responsibility deeply intertwined with the current conflicting understandings of the virtues and beliefs that are at the core of what it means to be an American.

For example, in 2018, the San Francisco Unified School District created the "School Names Advisory Committee."[54] Few outside the district would have had reason to care about the committee's existence until late 2020, when the committee announced it was considering changing the names of forty-four schools in the city, including a high school named for Abraham Lincoln, another school named for George Washington, and one for Senator Diane Feinstein.[55]

The committee had not yet made the decision to change the names before the topic attracted headlines. The mere announce-ment of the possibility that Abraham Lincoln and the founding fathers could be replaced was enough for conservative media to decry the move as an assault on history, while other media said the conservative backlash was "lacking context."[56]

This episode followed on the heels of President Trump's 1776 Commission, which itself was created to add to the debate over the (mis)interpretation of America's past that was mak-ing more and more headlines. Though the 1776 Commission's

---

54 San Francisco Unified School District, "School Names Advisory Committee," *https://www.sfusd.edu/connect/get-involved/advisory-councils-committees/school-renaming-advisory-committee.*

55 Butcher, "Don't Let Critical Theory Cancel History," *The Daily Caller*, February 1, 2021, *https://dailycaller.com/2021/02/01/butcher-welcome-to-2021-dont-cancel-history/.*

56 Camille Caldera, "Fact Check: San Francisco's Abraham Lincoln HS on Renaming List, But Decision Isn't Final," *USA Today*, December 20, 2020, *https://www.usatoday.com/story/news/factcheck/2020/12/20/fact-check-san-franciscos-abraham-lincoln-hs-name-change-isnt-final/3940580001/*, and Bethania Palma, "Is SF Changing the Name of a School Because Lincoln Didn't Show 'Black Lives Matter'?" Snopes, December 16, 2020, *https://www.snopes.com/fact-check/san-francisco-lincoln-blm/.*

report had not even been released in December 2020, when *USA Today* and others fact-checked claims that history was on the chopping block because of San Francisco's school renaming, commentary on the issue had reached a fever pitch. More context was needed in the midst of so much heated opinion, renaming sympathizers said.

Just four weeks after fact-checkers asked renaming opponents not to panic—it's not like Abraham Lincoln was under assault—the renaming committee announced that Abraham Lincoln was, indeed, on the chopping block. The U.S. president who freed the slaves was cancelled. Names also removed from local schools included George Washington, Paul Revere, Diane Feinstein, and dozens of other individuals of past and present national and local significance.

The renaming committee even listed the values that it wanted to honor, declaring that the names must be "grounded in social & economic justice; Honor individuals, living or deceased, who have made outstanding contributions to humanity or in defense of Mother Earth," and "Embody concepts and/or values that reflect the district's five core values: Student-Centered, Fearless, United, Social Justice, and Student-Driven."[57] Yet by "Fearless," the committee is not referring to courage, and by "social & economic justice" its members are not seeking equality of opportunity.

The committee also stated that it sought to change the names of schools named after anyone "directly involved in the colonization of people," slave owners, "perpetuators of genocide or slavery," and "those "connected to any human rights or environmental abuses." It did not matter that George Washington

---

57   San Francisco Unified School District, School Names Advisory Committee, "Guiding Principles for SFUSD School Names Advisory Committee," July 17, 2020, *https://www.sfusd.edu/school/mission-high-school/announcements/2021-02-10-ptsa-meeting-renaming-mission-high-school.*

freed most of his slaves after his death, and the rest after Martha's death. In fact, Washington directed his estate to support the elderly former slaves who could no longer work, along with those who were too sick to work.[58] Nor does it matter that a national forest is named for Washington or that he is considered the "Father of American Agriculture."[59] These are *not* excuses for slavery, these are factual statements that, to an open mind, put complex people in very different times into perspective. But when even Abraham Lincoln, who devoted the remaining years of his life not only to preserving the union, but to abolishing slavery, is canceled—are there any reasonable perspectives left?

Facts mattered little to the committee. The committee's justifications for canceling certain individuals included a litany of errors, and references to Wikipedia instead of official textbooks or historical documents. (Paul Revere's connection to the "colonization" of the Penobscot tribe, for example, is a secondary connection, at best.)[60] No historical role model is perfect (nor is any from present times), and if we can no longer honor imperfect people who brought about epic achievements, renaming committees have set a bar that is impossible for anyone to clear.

At the same time that the San Francisco Unified School District was scouring Wikipedia for reasons to cancel founding fathers, the Falls Church, Virginia, school board voted to remove Thomas Jefferson and George Mason, as mentioned in the intro-

---

58   George Washington's Mount Vernon, "A Decision to Free His Slaves," *https://www.mountvernon.org/george-washington/slavery/washingtons-1799-will/*.

59   Butcher, "Don't Let Critical Theory Cancel History."

60   Andrew Court, "Historians Slam Woke Teacher Responsible for Renaming 44 San Francisco Schools After It Emerges He Used WIKIPEDIA for Research to Denounce Paul Revere and Ridiculed Idea of Consulting Scholars," *Daily Mail* (U.K.), January 30, 2021, *https://www.dailymail.co.uk/news/article-9204835/Historians-slam-chairmans-decision-rename-44-San-Francisco-schools.html*.

duction, from two schools, citing Jefferson's and Mason's roles as slave owners.[61] The board made its decision despite the survey results from students, teachers, and community members demonstrating that survey respondents wanted to keep the names. More than half (56 percent) of respondents to surveys on both school names did not want to change the names.[62]

Not only did the Falls Church board deny educators and students the opportunity to grapple with George Mason's legacy as a slave owner, but also the chance to consider his decision not to sign the U.S. Constitution because he felt it did not do enough to end slavery.[63] Nor does the board's decision represent the values and ideas of the community it represents.

The debate over civics and history teaching comes full circle here, from the act of renaming a school to the values at the heart of the discussion and back to the importance of a representative process—one that failed to represent the community in this case. Ideas rooted in critical race theory are mixed throughout in both of these examples. Present-day interpretations of historic figures and their actions count more than facts and those figures' accomplishments, with a complete disregard for traditional liberal civic processes.

Any discussion of teaching and learning history and civics in school leads back to the purpose of teaching and learning anything at all. Such discussions should also serve as a stark reminder that Americans must be concerned with how the next generation plans to use the knowledge—or the misinformation and ideology—it is taught.

---

61 Falls Church City Public Schools, "School Board Finalizes School Renaming Process," October 6, 2020, *https://www.fccps.org/o/fccps/article/322150.*

62 Falls Church City Public Schools, "School Renaming Survey: Results and Analysis," 2021–2012, *https://go.boarddocs.com/vsba/fccpsva/Board.nsf/files/BVES73708CF1/$file/Falls_Church_City_Public_Schools_2020-2021_School_Renaming_Survey_Final.pdf.*

63 George Mason University Antonin Scalia Law School, "George Mason, the Man," *https://www.law.gmu.edu/about/mason_man.*

EPILOGUE

Scarlett Johnson, the Wisconsin mother introduced in the conclusion, is leading a recall effort against four members of the Mequon-Thiensville School District (MTSD) board in the Milwaukee, Wisconsin, suburbs.[1] Fed up with both the performance of the MTSD's schools as well as its penchant for promoting the divisive ideology of critical race theory, Johnson and other area parents, such as Amber Schroeder, gathered enough signatures in August 2021 for a special recall election.[2]

Johnson and Schroeder are living examples of what late sociologist Nathan Glazer referred to when he said that Americans may be willing to accept views of American history that are contrary to their own, if students have a "passion for reading and learning that improves basic skills."[3] But, as Glazer speculated, parents will not be willing to accept both revisionist history *and* poor academic performance.

Americans should not have to settle for either one.

The Mequon-Thiensville recall is not an isolated event. In April 2021, residents of Litchfield, Arizona, said that they were

---

1   Recall MTSD School Board, "Who We Are," *https://recallmtsd.com/who-we-are.*
2   Melissa Zygowicz, "Petition Reaches Enough Signatures to Recall Some Mequon-Thiensville School Board Members," CBS Channel 58, August 23, 2021, *https://www.cbs58.com/news/petition-reaches-enough-signatures-to-recall-some-mequon-thiensville-school-board-members.*
3   Nathan Glazer, "Some Problems in Acknowledging Diversity," in Diane Ravitch and Joseph P. Viteritti, eds., *Making Good Citizens: Education and Civil Society* (New Haven: Yale University Press, 2003), p. 178.

ready to attempt a recall of two school board members.[4] In May, two candidates for the Carroll Independent School District board near Dallas, Texas, won their elections after expressing firm opposition to the use of critical race theory in district schools.[5]

Loudoun County, Virginia, resident Ian Prior is leading the recall effort against board members in his district.[6] Loudoun County is the district where superintendent Scott Ziegler claimed that critical race theory was not being taught in district schools even after Prior obtained documents revealing that district officials had hired a teacher training service that specifically used the words "critical race theory" in its presentations.[7] In describing the debate over critical race theory and opposition to school board decisions, *The Washington Post* called Loudoun County the "face of the nation's culture wars."[8]

According to the online news site Axios, voters in fifty-one communities around the country had started or completed recall efforts between January and July 2021.[9] Axios reports

4   Carissa Planalp, "Second Litchfield Park School Board Member Under Fire Following Out-of-Control Meeting," AZFamily.com, April 15, 2021, *https://www.azfamily.com/news/arizona_schools/second-litchfield-park-school-board-member-under-fire-following-out-of-control-meeting/article_e574de2a-9e48-11eb-8cfe-97b1f50ec563.html*.

5   Sam Dorman, "Dallas-Area Critical Race Theory Opponents Win Big in School Board Election," FoxNews, May 3, 2021, *https://www.foxnews.com/politics/dallas-texas-school-district-critical-race-theory*.

6   See Fight for Schools, *https://fightforschools.com/*.

7   The Equity Collaborative, "Introduction to Critical Race Theory," On-Line Institute, May 7, 2020, *https://theequitycollaborative.com/wp-content/uploads/2020/05/Intro-To-Critical-Race-Theory.pdf*, news release, "How Critical Race Theory Infected Loudon County Public Schools," Fight for Schools, May 26, 2021, *https://fightfor-schools.com/how-critical-race-theory-infected-loudoun-county-public-schools/*; and "Loudon County Public Schools Service Agreement" with The Equity Collaborative, *https://documentcloud.adobe.com/link/track?uri=urn:aaid:scds:US:ae15f1d7-d4be-4153-9014-aef334b3c1b6#pageNum=1*.

8   Hannah Natanson, "How and Why Loudoun County Became the Face of the Nation's Culture Wars," *The Washington Post*, July 5, 2021, *https://www.washingtonpost.com/local/education/loudoun-critical-race-theory-transgender-rights/2021/07/05/3dab01b8-d4eb-11eb-ae54-515e2f63d37d_story.html*.

9   Russell Contreras, "Critical Race Theory Uproar Sparks a New Wave of School Board Recalls," Axios, July 6, 2021, *https://www.axios.com/school-board-recalls-soar-critical-race-theory-86823daf-a7e1-4a55-965c-32f79b64954f.html*

that, on average, only half as many school board recall elections occur annually in the U.S. Claims of corruption or poor management are what generally inspire school board recall efforts, and the sharp uptick in opposition to school board curricular decisions is unusual.

Some school boards have not waited for election season to reject the application of critical race theory. In Colorado Springs, the board for School District 49 adopted a resolution stating that schools in the district are not to use "principles of critical race theory...as a curriculum for classroom instruction."[10] Although taxpayers should be wary of federal or state lawmakers who ban content or ideas from classrooms, a traditional public school board's responsibility is, in fact, to oversee the curricula that schools in its district use. And even District 49's resolution is not limiting class discussions, but focuses on preventing individuals or groups of students from participating in or completing assignments *based on their racial identity* or engaging in "racial bias or stereotyping."[11] This resolution prevents educators from forcing students to participate in racially discriminatory activities.

In August 2021, Alabama's State Board of Education also adopted language expressing these ideas—that educators should teach all of American history to K–12 children while rejecting discrimination—in their statement rejecting critical race theory.[12] The board wrote that

10   Michael Ruiz, "Colorado School District Bans Critical Race Theory," Fox News, August 14, 2021, *https://www.foxnews.com/us/colorado-school-district-bans-critical-race-theory?cmpid=prn_newsstand.*

11   Ibid.

12   Alabama State Board of Education, "Resolution Declaring the Preservation of Intellectual Freedom and Non-Discrimination in Alabama's Public Schools," *https://www.alabamaachieves.org/wp-content/uploads/2021/08/ALSBOE-Resolution-Declaring-the-Preservation-of-Intellectual-Freedom-and-Non-Discrimination-in-AL-Public-Schools.pdf.*

the Alabama State Board of Education recognizes that slavery and racism are betrayals of the founding principles of the United States, including freedom, equality, justice, and humanity, and that individuals living today should not be punished or discriminated against because of past actions committed by members of the same race or sex, but that we should move forward to create a better future together.[13]

This statement captures two of the concepts described in Chapter 4 that are part of the proposal for a "civil theory" that answers critical race theory. The board acknowledges that slavery and racism are part of America's past and are inconsistent with our national identity. Now it is our responsibility to "create a better future *together*" (emphasis added), and what better way to do so than by showing kindness to those around us, even those with whom we disagree? Such behavior is the practical application of a civil theory.

Board members also resolved that, "students and educators should be encouraged to engage in the marketplace of ideas, subject to developmental appropriateness," allowing discussion of ideas with which some are sure to disagree. But the board rejected the teaching that one race or sex is superior to another, and rejected the use of federal grant money that would lead to the "implementation of the practices contrary to the sentiments expressed in this resolution."[14]

Since critical race theorists want even their most discriminatory ideas to be applied in the classroom, specific prohibitions against this ideology's prejudices are necessary. In May 2021, Montana Attorney General Austin Knudsen wrote an opinion recognizing that such applications are discriminatory and

---

13 Ibid.
14 Ibid.

likely violate federal law,[15] Knudsen wrote, "A school unlawfully discriminates on the basis of race if it has effectively caused, encouraged, accepted, tolerated or failed to correct a racially hostile environment."

"Notably, racial acts need not be targeted at any particular individual in order to create a racially hostile environment," he said.[16] Knudsen sees the racism in the so-called antiracist practices that Ibram Kendi and others advocate so fervently[17]: "Being a so-called 'antiracist' requires individuals to…advocate for specific policy proposals. Individuals who do not comply cannot truly be 'antiracist,' and are, therefore, considered racist." Knudsen concludes that, "Committing racial discrimination in the name of ending racial discrimination is both illogical and illegal."[18]

Just before the start of the 2021–2022 school year, two school district employees in Missouri filed a lawsuit in federal court claiming that school officials forced them to affirm discriminatory ideas.[19] According to the employees, the school district "forces teachers and staff to affirm views they do not support, to disclose personal details that they wish to keep private, and to self-censor on matters of public interest" as part of "equity" training sessions.[20]

Racial discrimination has no place in American life. Just ask the educators who are part of this lawsuit in Missouri. Or ask the Nevada mother who filed suit against critical race

---

15 Montana Attorney General Austin Knudsen, *Montana Attorney General's Opinion*, Vol. No. 58, No. 1, May 27, 2021, *https://dojmt.gov/agooffice/attorney-generals-opinions/opinions-2021-volume-58-opinions-1/*.

16 Ibid.

17 Kendi, *How to Be an Antiracist*.

18 Montana Attorney General Austin Knudsen, Opinion No. 1, Vol. No. 58.

19 *Brooke Henderson and Jennifer Lumley vs. School District of Springfield R-12 et al.*, *https://www.slfliberty.org/wp-content/uploads/sites/12/2021/08/20210818-Complaint-Doc.-1.pdf*, and Sam Dorman, "Missouri School District Employees Sue Over Allegedly Unconstitutional 'Equity' Training," FoxNews.com, August 19, 2021, *https://www.foxnews.com/us/missouri-school-district-critical-race-theory-lawsuit*.

20 *Brooke Henderson and Jennifer Lumley vs. School District of Springfield R-12 et al.*

theory's prejudicial applications in her son's school, or the Illinois teacher who cited mandatory affinity groups in her lawsuit, both described in Chapter 4. And ask members of the Alabama State School Board and Montana's attorney general. These statements and lawsuit filings are all evidence of a habitus, an understanding of the distinctions between good and bad that are necessary in order for members of a culture to communicate—and to live—with each other. This habitus is based on the rejection of racial bias.

These responses to prejudice use the basic principles of a civil theory. May this approach be our gift to current and future generations of Americans.

ACKNOWLEDGMENTS

I am deeply grateful for The Heritage Foundation's support on this project. Lindsey Burke, the Director of Heritage's Center for Education Policy and the Mark A. Kolokotrones Fellow in Education, provided the support and guidance that made this book possible. She is a tremendous scholar and leader, and I am honored to be her colleague. Mike Gonzalez, a senior fellow at Heritage and the Angeles T. Arredondo E Pluribus Unum Fellow, was and is a mentor and teacher before, during, and after the process of writing this. His research and writing in the areas of critical race theory, assimilation, and nationalism paved the way for me to discuss these issues as they relate to education. I would also like to thank Timothy and Christina Sandefur and Matt Beienburg from the Goldwater Institute for their comments on the text.

I cannot say enough about the help that Karina Rollins, editor par excellence, provided. She not only made the text better, but also made the writing and editing processes joyful ones throughout. I am excited for what the future holds, should she find the patience to guide me sometime again.

Thank you to my wife, Pearce, for believing in me. Thanks to Elijah, Ruth, and Jack—you give me hope for the future every day. Thanks to Mom and Dad—you laid the foundation that allowed me to follow my passion for the truth.

Any errors in the text are my own and will be corrected in future editions.